Serious Play
Modern Clown Performance

Louise Peacock

intellect Bristol, UK / Chicago, USA

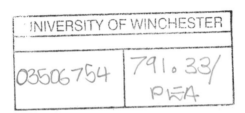
First published in the UK in 2009 by
Intellect Books, The Mill, Parnall Road, Fishponds, Bristol, BS16 3JG, UK

First published in the USA in 2009 by
Intellect Books, The University of Chicago Press, 1427 E. 60th Street, Chicago,
IL 60637, USA

A catalogue record for this book is available from the British Library.

Cover designer: Holly Rose
Copy-editor: Heather Owen
Typesetting: Mac Style, Beverley, E. Yorkshire

ISBN 978-1-84150-241-0

Printed and bound by Gutenberg Press, Malta.

Serious Play
Modern Clown Performance

Dedication

For my Mum
Who was always ready to watch clowns with me
In memory

CONTENTS

ACKNOWLEDGEMENTS

My interest in clowning was inspired by Slava and his Snowshow. I have watched it three times over the years and each time I have discovered something new about clowning. When I watched it for the first time I had no idea that the green clown 'Rough' would turn out to have such a strong impact on my understanding of clowning. The performer was Angela De Castro and since then I have been inspired and enlightened by her teaching and by her generous sharing of her thinking on clowns and clowning. I am grateful also to Bim Mason for talking to me about Clowning and Mummerandada.

Without the student clowns who worked with me and whose sense of play sustained me my understanding of clown training would be considerably poorer. Thank you: Arwen Prosser, Beth Lower, Clare Partridge, David McCaul, David Moss, Emily Stephenson, Eve Langford, Jackie Sanders, Jess Clark, Kate Mail, Leah Milner, Matthew Pereira, Phil McDonnell, Saffy Horrocks and, last but certainly not least, Steven Bell. Together we discovered new clowns and set them to play, with each other and with the audience, informing my thinking on play and complicité.

Thanks are also due to those who supported me through the completion of my PhD and through the drafting of this book; to Kate Adams, Channy Hall, Jessica Hartley, Ness Highet, and Amy Simpson, without whom my sanity would be in even greater doubt.

In the hunt for photographs the following people were particularly helpful Terry Lorant, Beatriz Paiva (of Gwenael Management), Andrea Lopez, Thierry Craeye (of Les Witloof) and Luc de Groeve (of Walrus Productions), Roly Bain and Jo Baxter, Claire Andrews (of TIN Arts) and Mark Dowd (at Topfoto).

My special thanks to my husband, Keith, for reading draft after draft and for offering such sound advice; to my father for listening to endless conversations about clowns; to my son, Toby who has watched so many clowns with me and who is always keen to watch more and, finally, a wish that my small son, Jonty, will grow up appreciating clowns too.

Introduction – Play: Serious and Frivolous

Serious play: the notion contains an internal tension, establishes a dichotomy. How can play be serious? How can something serious be play? Contemporary Western society undervalues play, assigning to it a frivolity, a time-wasting quality (or lack of quality). Children play; adults may play, but only in their spare or free time; the words spare and free indicating the extent to which play sits outside the main serious business of making one's way in the world. How then does modern clown performance bridge the two? That is what this book sets out to establish.

In *Homo Ludens* (1944) Huizinga presents a somewhat idealized view of the nature of play,

> First and foremost, then, all play is a voluntary activity. Play to order is no longer play: it could at best be a forcible imitation of it. By this quality of freedom alone, play marks itself off from the course of the natural process. It is something added thereto and spread out over it like a flowering, an ornament, a garment. (Huizinga 1944: 7)

Huizinga's views are contentious. Firstly he appears to imply that play is superfluous (unless, as he asserts elsewhere, you are an animal or a child). In relation to clown performance Huizinga's view that play to order is no longer play is problematic. Obviously, when the clown plays in front of an audience, he is playing to order. According to Huizinga, then, this is a 'forcible imitation' rather than what might be termed 'pure play'. However, this ignores the ability of the clown performer to ready himself for play. It also disregards the mutability of any clown performance in which, whilst an overall structure may exist for a performance, a clown will still respond to his audience. The nature of the interaction between the clown and the audience is spontaneous and here, genuine play occurs, creating an energy which also affects the planned sequences of the performance. In *Homo Ludens*, Huizinga presents the argument that play has no moral function and that, being voluntary, it stands outside 'ordinary' or 'real' life. In Huizinga's view play 'interpolates itself as a temporary activity satisfying in itself and ending there' (1944: 9).

Later chapters of Huizinga's work examine the connections between play and contest, play and law and play and war. These are of no relevance to clowning. Even when Huizinga comments on play forms in poetry, philosophy and art, he offers little of relevance to clowning. Huizinga does, however, offer the following direct comment on clowning: 'The mimic and laughter-provoking art of the clown is comic as well as ludicrous but it can scarcely be termed genuine play' (Huizinga 1944: 6). Given the time at which he was writing, Huizinga appears to have been referring to circus clowns. He may otherwise be evoking the activities of sacred clowns in primitive societies but gives no indication that this is the case. Huizinga connects clowning, not unreasonably, with laughter, but from there it is a short step for him to claim that it 'comes under the category of the non-serious' (1944: 6). This concept of play as serious or non-serious recurs in the work of other theorists. The subtitle of Turner's book, *From Ritual to Theatre,* is 'The Human Seriousness of Play' (1982).

Turner is an anthropologist but his focus on ritual as performance means that his theories are much more readily applicable to clown performance than those of Huizinga. In the first chapter of his book, Turner offers definitions of the liminal and liminoid, together with 'communitas' and flow. Whilst he notes that 'there are undoubtedly "ludic" aspects in "tribal" culture especially in the liminal periods of protracted initiation...such as holy fools, and clowning...' (Turner 1982: 32), his definition of the liminoid is more relevant for the modern societies in which both circus and theatre clowning occur. Initially clowning may have been located in ritual and, therefore, what Turner would identify as liminal space. However, as performances that are enjoyed as part of leisure time, clowning, in common with most theatre, is liminoid. 'Optation pervades the liminoid phenomenon' (Turner 1982: 43). An audience can choose whether to attend a performance; having arrived at the theatre, there remains an element of choice as to whether to stay. Turner makes the following key distinctions between the liminal and the liminoid. The liminal is 'collective, concerned with calendrical, biological, socio-structural rhythms', 'centrally integrated into the total social process', and tends to be 'eufunctional' (Turner 1982: 54). On the other hand, the liminoid is characteristically more individual, more experimental and marginal and more idiosyncratic. Most importantly, perhaps, 'liminoid phenomena...are often parts of social critiques' (Turner 1982: 54). Given the potential of clowning for parody and subversion one can see how it sits more readily within the liminoid than the liminal. Significantly, Turner identifies the *limen* as 'an instant of pure potentiality' (1982: 44). This potentiality is entirely applicable to clowning in which anything may happen as the performance occurs 'when the past is momentarily negated, suspended, or abrogated, and the future has not yet begun' (Turner 1982: 44). This notion of the limen is a perfect description of theatrical performance, occurring as it does in a dramatic time and place which is both within and outside real time.

Turner also identifies the concept of 'communitas' as existing in three separate forms the '*spontaneous, ideological,* and *normative*' (1982: 47). An audience in a theatre may experience spontaneous communitas, particularly in relation to clown performance when they may, as Turner puts it, 'become totally absorbed into a single synchronized, fluid event' (1982: 48). At this point the audience member exists in the limen between reality and theatrical illusion.

Closely related to 'communitas' is *flow*. Interestingly Turner suggests that 'there is no dualism in "flow"; while an actor may be aware of what he is doing, he cannot be aware that he is aware – if he does, there is a rhythmic behavioral or cognitive break' (1982: 56). This is a central and vital difference between the actor and the clown. Whilst Turner contends that the actor cannot be aware that he is aware, I would contend that the clown *has* to be aware that he is aware, as it is this awareness that facilitates a direct communication with the audience. Interestingly, whilst the clown performer, in common with any theatrical performer, exists in the limen, unusually the clown can step over the threshold into reality to acknowledge the audience and can then step back again. Turner (following Csikszentmihalyi in *Flow: The Psychology of Optimal Experience,* 1980) identifies six qualities of 'flow experience'. The notion of a lack of dualism is the first of these. Four of the other elements – *centring of attention; loss of ego; in control of his actions and of the environment; providing clear, unambiguous feedback* – are relevant to clown performance in much the same way as they are relevant to any performer. The final element of flow that it is *autotelic* connects directly with the concept found in the teaching of **Lecoq**[1], **Gaulier** and **De Castro** of *the pleasure to be in the moment.* In Turner's terms, 'to flow is to be as happy as a human can be' (1982: 58) and no one can be happier than a modern theatre clown in front of his audience. The clown in modern, post-industrial society operates, according to Turner's definitions, in the liminoid. One of the clown's functions is to help the audience reconnect with the luminal, as 'liminality is peculiarly conducive to play' (Turner 1982: 85).

More recently, in *Performance Theory,* Schechner (1988) has suggested that play occurs in symbolic time 'when the span of the activity represents another (longer or shorter) span of clock time' (1988: 7). In clown performance, the notion of time is often not directly addressed at all. In the theatrical presentation of drama the audience is often made aware of the passing of time; lines spoken by the actors, projections, lighting or set changes can all indicate both historical period and the passing of hours, days or months. Clown performance in many ways occurs in the crossover between Schechner's 'symbolic time' and 'event time' (when the activity itself has a set sequence and all the steps of that sequence must be completed no matter how long). This latter definition relates to the notion of the clown's exploit, which must be completed in time which is appropriate to the clown, but not necessarily appropriate for that action in reality. Thus it may take the clown fifteen minutes, for example, to complete the exploit of putting on one shoe. This time occupies both 'symbolic time' as part of the performance and 'event time' in that the exploit must be completed no matter how long it takes. Importantly, Schechner recognizes two key features of play. Firstly he identifies that in playing, 'a special world is created where people can make the rules, rearrange time, assign value to things' (1988: 11) and he also recognizes that 'play is "free activity" where one makes one's own rules' (1988: 13). Clown performance and the play inherent in that performance relies entirely on the clown performer's ability to make his own rules and to convince the audience of the validity of those rules for the duration of the performance. Later still, in *The Future of Ritual* (1993), Schechner asserts that '[i]n the West, play is a rotten category, an activity tainted by unreality, inauthenticity, duplicity, make believe, looseness, fooling around, and inconsequentiality' (Schechner 1993: 27). Schechner suggests that play is viewed as rotten because of society's preoccupation with and prioritizing of reality. He posits a 'pyramidical hierarchy of increasing reality' (1988: 27).

This societally held view that play is rotten or, more commonly, suitable for children, lies at the heart of the devaluing of the contribution that clowning can make to our society. Rather than accepting the view that play is 'rotten', what needs to be asserted is the importance of play in allowing us to connect with and interpret symbols and metaphors in a way which may allow us to connect with deeper truths about human existence.

The value of the metaphorical and symbolic nature of play is most commonly identified in theorists whose backgrounds are in psychology, such as Winnicott (1991). For them play is important as an element of normal development and as a way of re-establishing that development after, for example, a trauma. In common with the sociologists and anthropologists considered above, these theorists recognize the centrality of play to human existence. Winnicott's focus is on play as part of a natural development in childhood and he also considers the use that can be made of play in Freudian psychoanalysis: '...in playing, and perhaps only in playing, the child or adult is free to be creative' (1991: 53). This view chimes perfectly with Lecoq's view that the performer can only be truly responsive when he is able to play. Winnicott's views also overlap with those of Turner. Turner's concept of the existence of liminal and liminoid space has already been established. Winnicott suggests that 'playing and cultural experience can be given a location if one uses the concept of the potential space between the mother and the baby' (1991: 53). He also suggests that the area of play contrasts with the inner psychic reality and the actual world, creating a third indeterminate space. These spaces, the liminal/liminoid and Winnicott's potential space, have an affinity with what occurs in clown performance, which takes place neither in reality or fantasy but in another liminoid or potential place where reality and fantasy meet in the play of the clown.

More recent play theorists, like Sutton-Smith (1997), rightly recognize the centrality of play in human life. In his 1997 book, *The Ambiguity of Play*, Sutton-Smith seeks to draw together the different forms of play theory. He offers seven 'rhetorics of play', describing these as discourses about play. They are play as progress; play as fate; play as power; play as identity; play as imaginary; play of the self; and play as frivolous (1997: 9–11). The most relevant of these to clowning are 'play as imaginary' and 'play as frivolous', which relate to circus and theatre clowning; 'play as progress', which is often most relevant to work with children and aids the consideration of clown doctoring; and 'play as identity', will be explored in relation to Clown Ministry and the Clandestine Insurgent Rebel Clown Army. Finally 'play of the self' is initially identified by Sutton-Smith as play which is usually individual and which involves risk to the self. In this sense it connects to Geertz's notion of 'deep play', as described in *The Interpretation of Culture: Selected Essays* (1975), which involves excessive risk. There is rarely an element of significant physical risk in clowning (in comparison say to *corde lisse* work where one slip can result in death). However, it will be necessary to touch on this concept in relation to the brief consideration offered of Archaos' chainsaw-wielding metal clowns. Later in the same work, Sutton-Smith expands his definition of the 'rhetoric of self', to include such elements as individualism, freedom, metaphor and subjectivity. In this expanded form, the 'rhetoric of self' has a relevance to all clowning.

In addition to the various ways of theorizing the significance of play, Bateson (1973) suggests the concept of 'play frames'. Bateson contends that how individuals receive communication depends on the frame in which they receive it. We are, therefore, more able to enjoy play in performance if we understand that it is play. According to Bateson, a frame can be consciously identified, for example through words or actions. In clown performance a number of elements and techniques help to establish the play frame. The red nose, comments addressed to the audience and the clown's rhythm of looks out to the audience all reinforce the playful nature of the performance. John Wright (2006) identifies that separations (the looks and comments directed by the clown to the audience) are another technique which can aid in the establishment of a play frame. The play frame is also established by costume, makeup and performance styles and, through this, clowns become conduits for play. Schechner claims that 'serious issues are always involved in play; just as in humans, play is inextricably involved in all "serious" work' (1988: 101) and the following chapters seek to examine the serious work of clown play in all its guises.

In this book, the term clown is primarily taken to refer to the consistent clown character that may be established and developed by a performer and which is theirs for life. It can also refer to a range of characters or personas created by a performer who defines himself as a clown rather than as an actor. As with circus clowns, these clown characters are unlikely to be taken over by anyone else. This points towards the intensely personal nature of clowning which generates play from within the performer. It is also interesting to explore the ways in which a variety of writers have made use of the iconicity of clowns in scripted dramas, where their potential for a playful relationship with the audience or for demonstrating play is exploited. Whilst such clown performance is marginal rather than central to the argument of this book, the fact that clown roles have demonstrably existed in scripted dramas since the plays of Aristophanes, through the works of Plautus (*The Brothers Menaechmi*), Shakespeare (the clown in *Titus Andronicus*, Stefano and Trinculo in *The Tempest*, Bottom in *A Midsummer Night's Dream*, Feste in *Twelfth Night* and the Fool in *King Lear*) and, more recently, Brecht (Galy Gay in *Man Equals Man*) and Beckett (Didi and Gogo in *Waiting for Godot* and the players in *Act Without Words 1 and 2*) means that they cannot be ignored. The basis of the clown performance in scripted drama is different from devised work. These characters are only rarely created by the actor who has been cast in the role (one exception is **Dario Fo**). They are sometimes written with a particular performer in mind, as was usually the case for Shakespeare. More often, as is true for both Brecht and Beckett, the playwright recognizes something in the iconic status of the clown and in the connotations of a recognizable clown figure that will serve the thematic function of his work. These clown characters are not the creations of individual performers who are unlikely ever to play any other role.

Establishing an answer to the question 'what is a clown?' is vexatious and commentators on clowning (Swortzell), clown teachers (Lecoq), directors (John Wright) and clown performers (**Oleg Popov**) have repeatedly made the attempt. Swortzell contends that a number of elements combine to create a performer who can be identified as a clown. He distinguishes as important 'a way of looking at the world that is different, unexpected, and perhaps even disturbing', adding that 'to be a clown is to create and express a total personality' (Swortzell

1978: 2–3). Both of these elements are key to clowning. The clown clowns not simply to amuse his audience but because he has observations about the world, about life, to communicate to them, and play becomes a conduit to aid that communication. Unlike the actor, the clown performer does not convey the feelings and ideas of one entity created by another. When an actor performs, what the audience normally sees are the ideas of one individual (the playwright) encapsulated in a fictional creation (the character) which is then conveyed through the efforts of another individual (the actor) who seeks to erase his own individuality in the act of performing. When a clown performs, the audience sees the ideas and attitude of that individual conveyed by an adopted persona that has developed out of the individual's personality and which could never be adopted and lived in the same way by anyone else. The clown is not an interpreter. In his or her performance the view of and reaction to the world is the same for the creation (the clown persona) as for the performer. It is for this reason that actors who clown (when performing in the plays identified above or other similar works) must be treated rather differently from clowns.

Oleg Popov, a Russian clown performing from the 1950s to the present day, argued that clowns should emphasize the best in the human spirit, criticizing the more negative creations of his contemporaries, which appeared to him to rely overly on silliness, ineptitude and absent-mindedness. 'I went ahead and created a positive character' (Popov 1970: 94). Clowning for Popov expressed the triumph of optimism and idealism over adversity. More recent clowns such as **Slava Polunin** have created characters who comment on the absurdity of life with a particular emphasis on an existentialist viewpoint, making their message accessible by playing for and with his audience.

In order to facilitate the discussion of clowning in this book, I offer the following definition of clowning. The clown is distinguished from the actor by his or her ability to play with the audience and to create a sense of complicité with them by using play to connect with them. There is always something of the 'other' about clowns. This may be expressed in the way that they look different from ordinary everyday people (through make-up, costume, the use of a red nose), but the most striking feature of the clowns' 'otherness' is their attitude to life as expressed through their performance. Whilst the clown often fails to achieve what they set out to achieve, their failure is framed by their optimism and by the simplicity of their approach to life. Clowns can also be distinguished by their physical skill. That is not to say that acting does not require physical skill, which of course it does. Rather, the fact is that clowns make use a wider range of skills, which may include circus skills such as juggling or balance, mime and great physical control and comic timing.

As indicated above, it can be possible to recognize the clown by his (clowns are predominantly male) appearance. Whilst there are a number of variations of clown dress which can be observed in different countries or in different periods, there is some commonality to the clown's costume. Most significantly, the clown is always readily identifiable as separate from the society in which he moves. The style of clown costume usually works with the mask or make-up to reinforce the sense of otherness. Often the elements of a clown's costume will be recognizable items of everyday dress, but the way in which these items are combined will separate the clown from the world of everyday fashion. Commonly, the clown, particularly in Western theatre and circus, will wear clothing that does not fit him properly. One example of this is the outfit adopted by **Charlie Chaplin,** which combines trousers that are too baggy, a jacket that is too tight and a hat that is too small. Although Chaplin's clown is often referred to as the little tramp, he is not so much a tramp as a parody of the city dandy who places great importance on the way he looks. It is the swinging of his cane, a vital part of his costume, that indicates his insouciance and his belief that he looks like a gentleman. The traditional costume of the circus Auguste relies on outsize clothes together with the traditional clown's shoes that extend well beyond the length of the clown's feet. The modern Auguste's clothes are often brightly coloured and some elements of clothing have a function beyond the traditions of dress. For example, the flower in the Auguste's jacket can squirt water. In *Slava's Snowshow,* Slava's hat becomes the funnel of a train, spouting smoke as he departs on a journey.

The use of mask or make-up has a long-established history in both sacred ritual and theatrical performance. The wearing of a mask, red nose or make-up has a number of effects on the individual or performer. For a performer, the use of a full or half mask shifts the spectator's focus away from facial expression as a clue to what he intends to communicate. This means that the performer has to develop greater levels of physical skill, often in mime, to allow for communication of emotional nuance. Masks depersonalize the wearer; the individual's identity is abnegated, replaced instead by a new and different individual. The mask separates the performer from the spectator and reinforces the spectator's role as observer of a world different from their everyday reality. The mask also frees the performer psychologically, for the behaviour is the behaviour of the mask and not of the individual behind it. In contrast, the red nose focuses the audience's attention on facial expression rather than bodily movement. It also signals the clown's difference from ordinary people and the brightness of the colour draws the audience's eyes to the clown's face, thus highlighting nuance, which is particularly important in a silent performance. Make-up has a similar impact in that it creates a sense of otherness and the positioning of colour on the face, particularly in combination with a red nose, makes the clown's face fascinating for the audience.

The clown's make-up and costume are open to semiotic interpretation: they signal to the spectator of ritual or theatre that the clown is a clown and they act as cues to the nature of the performance that is likely to follow. The costume symbolizes the clown's relationship to the society in which he operates. The clothing will be similar enough to everyday dress to indicate that the clown is aware of society's dress code but the transgressions from the norm will be obvious enough to mark him out as different; to indicate that he stands beyond the normal limitations of society. According to the contemporary Brazilian clown, Angela De Castro, when we see the clown in costume it should be possible for us to believe that this person might exist in the real world and, if we should see them on the street, would draw no more than a second glance. ('How to be a Stupid', course held in London, November 2005). Clearly, this more subtle approach is more suitable for theatre clowns than circus clowns. The level of costume transgression from society's norms is, therefore, affected by the clown's performance style and the frame in which the performance occurs.

The clown Oleg Popov in the movie *Allez Parade*.

The Russian realist clowns, of whom Oleg Popov is a good example, eschew the use of grotesque make-up preferring a more realistic style. Even so the hair is usually a wig, altering the colour or style of the performer's own hair.

Popov also builds up his nose to emphasize its naturally turned-up appearance. Similarly, the size of the outfit, whilst not so extreme as that of the European Auguste, will incorporate some element of mis-sizing. This more subtle use of costume and make-up relates to the clown's more realistic and parodic approach to life whilst still signalling clearly to the audience to expect playfulness and humour.

The use of make-up and costume in such a clearly defined way allows for instant identification of the clown. The clown has only to walk into the ring wearing his outsize shoes and red nose; we need no introduction. Immediately a set of expectations, related to our knowledge of clowning and previous experiences of clowns, is established that enables us to recognize the clown's play frame. This artifice is carried further in what appears to be the instantaneous communication of emotions to the audience. The clown does not hesitate to laugh, to cry, to show us fear, and his display of his feelings provokes a public sharing of emotion, most often through laughter. It is easiest to identify the clown when he appears in the circus ring, as that is the frame with the strongest performance conventions. That is to say that a circus audience has the clearest expectations of what a clown performance is likely to involve. In the theatre when the clown enters, the costume will be more subtle. Indeed such a range of clown costumes exists in modern theatre clowning that it is difficult to claim that there is a general convention, except to say that the clown will look different in some way from societal norms. In modern society, conventions governing dress are more relaxed than they were, for example, in the nineteenth century. For clowns today, moving in a society where a busy street may include gentlemen in suits, men and women in shorts, goths and punks (to identify a small range of accepted and recognized dress codes), it is much harder to be different. Therefore, in defining the clown in the theatre, we must rely on a combination of elements such as costume, makeup and behaviour. One clear indicator of the clown today is his willingness to play, and his eagerness to connect with the audience from his performance space to encourage them to play.

A further indicator of the clown today is his creation of laughter and humour through physical comedy. Whilst some of the shows discussed later in this book have a wider purpose than simply to make the audience laugh, all of the shows *do* make the audience laugh. Even in scripted dramas the verbal humour is supported by physical comedy. The term physical comedy can encompass a range of performance styles, from the broad slapstick most often found in the circus to the more subtle techniques of double takes, clocks and separations found in all the performance venues considered in this book. For the clown, mime skills and a sense of playful *complicité* with the audience allow for the audience to be drawn into the humour of the performance without the need for any or many words. The laughter provoked by physical comedy is immediate. Its emphasis on the physical rather than the cerebral emphasizes the importance of play in the clown's creation of humour.

The easily recognised clown accesses play, that 'rotten category', and revitalizes it, makes it shine as a means of communicating, readily and viscerally, serious messages about the nature of human existence. In the hands of the clown, play stops being rotten and becomes serious. Exactly how clown play functions is the focus of the next chapter.

Note
1. Bold indicates that brief biographical details are to be found in the clown index.

1

CLOWNS AND CLOWN PLAY

Definitions of the clown types found in the circus and in the theatre are derived from a number of sources. The Auguste, Whiteface and Tramp have long been familiar in the world of circus, and these types and their variants, therefore, provide a good starting point for exploring clowning. Sometimes the long established circus labels can be applied to theatre clowns but, more often, these more modern clowns demand a different taxonomy. Much of this chapter will focus on establishing a taxonomy of clown types and the nature of their play which will provide a reference point for the analyses of clown performance that follow. Some of the definitions offered (*Clown Show, Clown Theatre,* and *Clown Actor*) are original definitions created by the author to fix some landmarks in a relatively uncharted territory. Reference will be made to the terms *clown* and *bouffon* as used by Lecoq and also to Wright's definitions of *simple, pathetic* and *tragic* clowns. The term *clownesque* is also considered later in this chapter as a way of discussing the overlap between clown theatre and physical theatre.

Traditional Clown Types
Between the late eighteenth and mid-nineteenth centuries there was very little development or change in the nature of the clown. Clown types developed around the basic dichotomy of talking and non-talking. Famous clowns before the end of the nineteenth century include the talking clowns **Billy Hayden** (whose acts revolved around internal illogicality) and **Whimsical Walker** and **Ducrow, Gontard, Durang, Rice, Auriol** (skill or acrobat clowns). By the end of the nineteenth century, two key clown types had been established: the Whiteface and the Auguste. A third, the Counter-Auguste was created by **Albert Fratellini** in the 1920s, and a fourth, The Tramp or Hobo clown, was popularized in the United States, again in the 1920's, by clowns such as **Otto Griebling, Emmett Kelly** and, on film, Charlie Chaplin. It is these types that will be defined and traced through to their continued existence in clown performance in modern society. As clowning has developed, these later types have absorbed the activities carried out by clown parleurs (talking clowns) and acrobat clowns, so that now we may see, for example, an acrobatic Auguste such as Oleg Popov who includes slack-rope work in his act.

The three brothers, Albert (grotesque Auguste), François (Whiteface) and Paul (Auguste) Fratellini, French clowns of Italian origin. *Photo taken by Roger Viollet.*

The Whiteface
The Whiteface clown was a development from the clown parleur (as exemplified by Billy Hayden). The Whiteface had a sense of importance that was reflected in his make-up and costume. Face make-up consisted of a plain white base on to which elegant lips and delicate eyebrows could be painted. **François Fratellini** (one of the three Fratellini brothers who became famous in France in the 1920s) can be taken as an example. The illustration above clearly shows the elegance of François's make-up in comparison with that of his brothers **Paul** (the Auguste) and Albert (the more grotesque counter-Auguste).

Onto his white base were painted gracefully curving eyebrows, his nostrils and eyes were highlighted and his lips were darkened. The Whiteface clown's costume was very smart. It was often a tight-fitting outfit with trousers that stopped at the knee. On the lower leg, the clown wore stockings. The fabric was richly covered and sparkly. The outfit would be completed by a neat conical hat. The costume signified to the audience apparent status, wealth and control, and this semiotic message was reinforced when the Whiteface was seen in combination with the Auguste.

The Auguste
The Auguste clown made its first appearance in 1877 although there are conflicting stories, as Hugill (1980) and Towsen (1976) suggest, as to how the name originated. In contrast to the

Coco the Clown (in private life Mr Nikolai Poliakoff) leaves in his full Auguste clown's regalia for Cologne, where he will entertain orphan children.

Whiteface, the Auguste was clumsy, incompetent, and eager to do well, but, ultimately, incapable and provided a butt for the tricks and jokes of the Whiteface. The role of the Auguste has been adopted and developed by a number of clowns over the years. Such clowns include **Tom Belling**, **Chocolat**, **Grock**, Paul Fratellini and **Coco the Clown**. The Auguste's costume is typified by clothing that does not fit, including trousers which are too long or too short, too tight or too baggy; a jacket which is too big or too small; shoes or boots which are often overly long; and a hat. In the early days of the Auguste, the costume tended to be comprised of an ill-fitting dinner suit. The Auguste tries to be smart but fails. His costume has all the elements of clothing required by a smart gentleman but the mis-sizing of each article of that clothing creates a haphazard effect. More recently, the Auguste often, but not always, has wild hair, often red in colour. Early Augustes wore very subdued make-up but after Albert Fratellini created the counter-Auguste, the original Auguste tradition has faded as it has been replaced by the conventions of the counter-Auguste. The term Auguste, following the widespread influence of Albert Fratellini, can now be taken to mean a clown whose clothes are an unusual mix of colours, patterns and sizes. Augustes now tend to adopt the face pattern of a white base onto which exaggerated features are painted, such as an oversize mouth and huge eyebrows. Typically the Auguste wears a red nose.

The costume can be viewed as a parody of the ringmaster's costume. The counter-Auguste now tends to be more subdued both in costume and make-up, often without a red nose. In this way, the traditions of the Auguste and counter-Auguste have been reversed with the once subdued Auguste becoming more garish and extrovert. The subdued style associated with the original Auguste has become much more established in Europe than in the United States and it is sometimes referred to as the European Auguste.

The Tramp

There is one further important clown type: the Tramp. The tramp or hobo originated in America in the 1920s and can be seen as a variation of the Auguste. The main characteristic of the Tramp clown is that he looks uncared for. The elements of costume are similar to those of the Auguste but in addition to being wrongly sized they are also very shabby. The Tramp's make-up usually includes painted-on stubble and a down-turned mouth, often highlighted in white. Typically the Tramp looks mournful and connects with his audience by appealing for pity. Famous Tramp clowns included **Joe Jackson**, Emmett Kelly, Otto Griebling and, of course, on film, Charlie Chaplin.

Double Acts/Group Play

As soon as the Whiteface and Auguste came into existence, they tended to be paired. This pairing increases the varieties of play which become possible. One early pairing was **Footit** and Chocolat who began working together in France in 1894. Their partnership can be taken as indicative of the way such acts work. Footit was the Whiteface and Chocolat was the Auguste. According to Towsen, Footit 'reunited the great twin traditions of the talking and acrobatic clowns' (1976: 218). Whilst Footit had a circus background (his father ran the Great Footit Allied Circus), Chocolat (a Cuban whose real name was Raphael Padilla) was unskilled. Chocolat developed an Auguste character who was 'a would-be man of the world, a fool attempting to appear dignified but rarely getting away with it' (Towsen 1976: 219). Together the pair began to establish the conventions by which the Whiteface is always in control while the Auguste tries desperately to match up to his higher status partner. Later pairings continued this notion of status imbalance because it provides a good source of play. The clowns' irritation with each other can be played out to the audience and the audience can be encouraged to take sides. In this way they are drawn more firmly into the play frame established by the clowns. Remy (1997) provides us with records of some of the entrées performed by a number of clown acts. An entrée is a rehearsed clown sequence, involving one or more clowns. Entrées are usually structured to have a beginning, a middle and an end; and are used when the clowns have the audience's full attention, rather than being used to cover the entrance and exit of other acts. One of these was performed by **LuLu** (the Whiteface) and **Tonio** (the Auguste) in 1950 (Remy 1997: 196–203). In this entrée the Whiteface is a barber in need of an assistant. The Auguste is hired as the assistant and promptly gets tangled up in the barber's smock. He annoys LuLu by interfering when they have a customer. He keeps knocking the customer down and each time he does something wrong, LuLu gets more cross with him. At each point the reaction of the clown can be played to the audience. As well as each clown being able to interact with the props of the entrée, there is the added element of interacting with each other as a source of play. As can clearly be seen at this point, the Whiteface is still the dominant partner on stage and this was usually the case offstage too. The Whiteface, **Antonet**, always retained the upper hand over his working partner by being the one who approached other clowns each time he needed a new collaborator. However, one of his partners, Grock, was the Auguste who began to change this situation by creating entrées and routines in which the Whiteface became the foil of the Auguste. This is true to such an extent that, later in Grock's career, the Whiteface is not even identified, with Grock being billed as 'Grock and partner'. This dominance of Grock over his partner made the transition into theatre, working almost as a solo clown, much easier for him.

In the first decade of the twentieth century, a further development in clowning occurred when the Fratellini brothers began working as a group of three clowns (a Whiteface, an Auguste and a second more grotesque Counter-Auguste). This expansion in numbers allowed for the development of more complex entrées with a greater range of dramatic contrast. The performance style of the Fratellini exemplified ensemble performance and this ensemble was a significant development in moving entrée performance towards theatre performance despite the fact that the Fratellini were committed circus performers. Other trios and groups followed in their wake, such as **Los Rivels** and the Pickles Family clowns, and their influence can be traced to the ensemble clown companies of today such as **Mimirichi** and **Tricicle**.

Whilst these early clown types are helpful in identifying and discussing clowns, it is also important to consider how far a clown can be defined by what he actually does: the type of play in which he engages. Clowning routines and actions can be classified into types. These types are 'interruption of ceremony', 'subversion and parody', 'physical skill' (acrobatics, juggling, contortion, high wire), 'incompetence', 'interaction with objects', 'interaction with other clowns', 'status', 'food' and, more recently, 'the exploration of the human condition'.

The 'interruption of and commenting on a ceremony' exists in many types of clowning and is in itself a form of subversion, incorporating elements of parody. The main function of clowns in the Pueblo (New Mexico and Arizona), Mayo-Yaqui (Sonora, Mexico) and Maidu (North East California) peoples is to interrupt religious ceremonies and to comment on them. These clowns disrupt the ceremony in a display of transgression, but the clowning is, in fact, an integral part of the ceremony and the use of make-up or mask clearly indicates the role and nature of the clown. Interruptions on a less socially-significant level occur when the clown interrupts the ringmaster in a circus. In both of these examples the clowns model playful behaviour as a way of responding to authority figures or potentially dull situations.

The Maidu clown's interruption of ceremony is closely linked to the clown's frequent recourse to subversionary tactics and the use of parody. The sacred clowns' treatment of the priests can be seen as parodic, as they often mock the priest's style of chanting, moving and dancing. More recently, parody for the circus clown operates in two ways. The first is self-referential within the circus; the clown parodies the act which has gone before. In Cirque du Soleil's *Alegría*, one clown enters with a candle, which symbolizes a minimalist parody of the fire act that went before and which used flames in a much more dramatic way than the clown is able to. Secondly, clown acts may parody or satirize events that are happening in wider society. For example, Popov constructed a routine that centred around a washing machine which initially was able to wash hens, turning them from black to white but which ultimately fell apart. Popov developed this sketch in reaction to common problems with Soviet washing machines at the time. Greater use of parody and subversion has been made towards the later part of the twentieth and early twenty-first centuries, in the work of Dario Fo and the political demonstrations of CIRCA (Clandestine Insurgent Rebel Clown Army).

In many areas of clowning, clowns display considerable physical skill. For example, some Native American clowns leap from rooftops. Circus clowns, as well as clowning, are able to demonstrate a range of other circus skills. Popov, the Russian clown, is able to perform on the slack wire. Grock (a Swiss clown whose career began in 1903 and ended in 1954) was a musical clown able to play many instruments. Coco, another Russian clown performing earlier than Popov beginning in the 1920s, trained in several areas of the circus such as juggling and slack-rope before focusing on clowning. Another significant physical element in clowning is the clown's ability to mime

Circus, and by extension clowning, is not, and never has been, a primarily verbal form. It has also long been a nomadic form, with circuses touring the world in search of new audiences. For the juggler, the acrobat, the equilibrist, the language spoken by the audience is not significant, as the impact of their acts relies on physical skill, not verbal communication. For the clown, where verbal exchanges might form an important part of the act, the matter of language had to be addressed. A range of techniques was developed in order to allow clowns to communicate fully with their audiences. Some clowns chose not to speak, often using whistles or squeakers instead. Other clowns reduced the language in their act to a minimum and compensated for lack of verbal communication by improving their physical and mime skills, ensuring that their act could be understood wherever they went.

Failure or 'incompetence' is a staple ingredient of clown performance. Clowns demonstrate their inability to complete whatever *exploit* they have begun. In doing so, they speak to the inner vulnerability of the audience whose members are often bound by societal conventions which value success over failure. When the clown provokes laughter by failing, he provides a release valve and allows his audience to enjoy a feeling of superiority that relates to the Hobbesian theory of superiority in relation to laughter. Clown sketches that focus on specific examples of incompetence, such as tripping and/or falling, as part of the laughter provocation, are relying on the laughter release mechanism which occurs psychologically when we believe someone may have been hurt, but then realize they have not. According to Bergson, the 'laughable element...consists of a certain mechanical elasticity' (1911: 10). We might expect the person to avoid the trip or fall by checking the impulse to fall, but we laugh when they do not. In this way the clown who slips on the age-old banana skin is funny as long as he gets up with only a pretence of being hurt. If he turns out to be really hurt, the audience stops laughing. Clowns in the theatre are able to create much longer sequences involving failure or incompetence, due to the longer time frame of their performance.

The remaining elements of clown routines – 'interaction with objects', 'interaction with others', 'status' and 'food' – are most readily exemplified in the work of both circus clowns and theatre clowns and have been developed in response to the clown's limited use of language-based sketches. Remove language and the remaining sketch must communicate clearly and immediately through physical action. In many ways these elements are interconnected because clown interaction, whether with objects or other clowns, tends to be governed by status. For example, the clown who performs the simple 'walk-around' act (a circus clown act where the clown fills in between other acts by working around the circus ring, entertaining the audience) of trying to pick up a ball or balloon, is engaged in a status interaction. Every time he goes to pick up the balloon, he kicks it. The balloon floats into the air and the clown cannot reach it. As soon as the balloon falls to earth the sequence is repeated. Each time, through look and gesture, the clown signals to the audience that this time he will succeed and then time and time again he fails. In this routine the clown has lower status than the balloon because it always defeats him. Of course, in a way, the balloon does not defeat him; he defeats himself because he remains unaware throughout that it is his own fault that the balloon keeps heading skywards. In this way, the whole act is a demonstration of performed incompetence in which the clown cannot establish a higher status than the object he seeks to control.

A particular kind of interaction with objects is found in what can be defined as 'mechanical play'. Rather than playing with an everyday object, such as the balloon, 'mechanical play' involves a clown interacting with a mechanical gadget that has usually been specially constructed. Interaction of this nature is particularly popular in the circus and clowns who created these mechanical gadgets were often known as 'producing clowns'. One of the most important 'producing clowns' was **Lou Jacobs,** who performed with Ringling Bros. and Barnum and Bailey between 1925 and 1985. Jacobs constructed mechanical and gadget-based entrées where the clown's body in combination with a machine gadget becomes the source of humour. A new range of games opens up when the potentially vulnerable body of the clown is pitted against the potentially dangerous gadget. The audience's laughter is provoked either by relief when the clown finally emerges from the entrée physically intact or by incongruity, as in the following example. One of Jacob's most famous production gags is the tiny car entrée, described by Hugill as follows,

> Behind the scenes he will cram his six-foot-one-inch frame and enormous clown shoes into the car; then he will speed around the ring accompanied by numerous backfirings and midget policemen and finally emerge from the tiny vehicle to roars of laughter and disbelief. Jacobs' early career as a contortionist is obviously a great help to him, for the car is a mere yard long and a foot-and-a-half high. (Hugill 1980: 215)

In such an act the humour lies not in the relationship between the clown and the audience but rather in the surprise at Jacobs' size when he extricates himself from the car. The presence of what Hugill describes as 'midget policemen' suggests that the driver of the car will prove to be equally small. Jacobs' extrication of himself limb by limb is funny because it is unexpected and the entirely visual humour is reinforced by the contrast between his extreme height and the lack of height of his fellow performers. It is entirely incongruous that such a tall clown should extricate himself from such a small vehicle. The audience gains additional pleasure from recognizing the levels of skill required by the act.

Circus routines involving one or more clowns tend to work according to a clearly defined status order, with the Whiteface usually having higher status than the bumbling Auguste. In brief, the Whiteface is usually competent, neat and high status whilst the Auguste is bumbling, untidy and low status. Occasionally the Auguste's status becomes so low that it crosses back into high status. In this way, the Auguste can take control of the routine because his continually bungled attempts at whatever task he has been set prevent the routine from moving on or prevent the Whiteface from achieving what he wishes to achieve.

Food plays a significant part in clowning in many cultures. The Maidu clown uses his acorn bread (which plays an important part in the religious ceremony) as a symbol of his transgression by eating it before the ceremony has finished. Circus clowns also develop routines which focus on food. For example, one common entrée involves the clown adopting the role of waiter. In circus scenes such as this it is inevitable that the food will not actually be eaten. It is much more likely to be thrown at other clowns or at the audience, or both (as seen in Billy's Smarts Circus, Hull, 2003). Clowning with food is both transgressive and regressive (a common time for playing with or throwing food is when we are young children).

More recently clowns in the theatre deal with what it means to be human. Through a number of the actions listed above, but particularly though incompetence, clowns develop performance pieces which deal with themes such as what it means to be a success (usually by repeatedly failing), and what is important in life (often the relationships we form with those around us and how we cope when we are left alone). The clown's traditional role as both an outsider and a truth-teller render him perfectly placed to comment on the interaction between individuals and the societies in which they live.

With the exception of performances focused on the human condition, all of the above clown actions demonstrate transgression of, or deviance from, socially accepted norms. In clowning there are a number of common transgressions or deviations from the societally defined norm: clowns fail and are stupid; they misbehave socially, for example by throwing water and food. They are violent. Clown acts often involve scatological jokes about urinating, defecating and breaking wind. Clown actions can also involve sexual antics which involve a level of obscenity that would not be acceptable in everyday society. All of these contravene the conventions established by society for morally and socially acceptable behaviour. Lapses from the behavioural norm also involve interacting with objects in ways that are not common in everyday life. Common deviations can be identified as behavioural, disruption of performance conventions, and linguistic. These deviations can occur within any of the types of clown routine identified earlier.

Behavioural Deviance
One form of 'behavioural deviance' involves interacting with objects in ways which are not common in everyday life. In each of these cases the audience members can feel superior as

they recognize what the clown *should* be doing with the object. At the same time, the audience members may experience a vicarious pleasure in witnessing the clown behaving in ways in which they may wish to behave but which the constraints of society forbid. Misusing objects is often an example of the topsy-turvy way in which the clown views the world. Such performances are entertaining but do not offer any form of societal catharsis or relief. On the other hand, performed violence and performed sexual activity within clown acts, which also come within this category of deviance, may well have a cathartic function. According to Cheesmond, 'The figure of the clown/jester fulfilled, or was conceived to fulfill, a therapeutic/ antagonistic purpose in the regulation and moderation of individual or establishment aspirations' (In Robb 2007: 9).

There are examples of sexually obscene clowning to be found in the Hatambura clown figure of Sri Lanka who, in one ritual, indulges in mimed imitations of intercourse together with imagery connected to masturbation, ejaculation and orgasm. There are similarities in performance style between these ritual performance and the less transgressive performances of western circus clowns (in the use of props, costume and mask or make-up) but Cheesmond suggests that here 'the comedy functions also as a therapy and an exorcism for key collective and individual problems and anxieties' (in Robb 2007: 11). Examples of transgressively violent clowning can be found in the clowns of Archaos circus who threaten the audience with chainsaws. In one sequence drawn from *Metal Clown I*, the clowns combine sexual performance and violence by performing an execution by cutting off a clown's head, which is then used by a female clown to simulate oral sex. Whilst the execution and the oral sex are simulated, both actions are highly charged transgressive acts which are likely to shock an audience rather than offering any kind of catharsis. The clowns know that they are only playing and that no harm will come to the audience, but the anarchic performance still minimizes the communication of play, or makes it so aggressive that the audience struggles to remain within the play frame.

Disruption of Performance Conventions
The circus clown sometimes interrupts other acts and thus transgresses performative conventions, except that, ironically, this transgression is so well-established in the circus that it has almost become an expected mode of behaviour for clowns. In this case it would be more transgressive not to transgress.

From an analysis of practice, these conventions of transgression can be seen as cathartic. They create a release valve for society where behaviour which is tempting to the individual but criticized by society can be enacted and, as a result of the clown's creation of audience empathy, can be shared vicariously without fear of retribution. In the structure of traditional circuses, the clown acts often allowed for the release of tension by being placed immediately after a 'fear' act, such as lion taming – now largely a thing of the past.

Circus clowns perpetrate another form of performative disruption in their interactive destruction of the usual spectator/performer boundaries by moving out of the circus ring and into the audience. In the circus this has come to be expected but transgression is still possible when the clown, in his interaction with an audience member, goes further than the audience expects. An example of this is a common clown entrée which involves spraying the audience with water. Such spraying is likely to be accepted as part of the fun as long as no one member of the audience is unfairly targeted and left soaking wet. The moment a member of the audience is singled out and soaked, the clown has found a way of extending the disruption beyond the limits of expectation and acceptability towards transgression. This is a transgression, literally in physical terms, of the boundary between actor and spectator and of accepted social interaction.

In a circus, the 'run-in' clowns fill the gaps between the other acts whilst equipment is cleared from, or brought into, the ring. The act which they perform at this point may take place around the ring edge or occupy the centre of the ring. The routine may contain a simple narrative, such as preparing for a music recital, or the act may parody the previous act, with an acrobat act being followed by a clown tumbling act. Rarely, if ever, is there a narrative line which runs through the totality of clown routines in the circus performance. Kelly and Otto Griebling's ice gag, performed in 1933 as part of the Hagenbeck-Wallace Circus, is an exception to this rule. This routine was comprised of a series of entrances made by Kelly and Griebling throughout a performance. When they first appear, Kelly has a 25lb block of ice on his back and Griebling is calling for 'Missus Jones'. They return several times as the performance progresses. Finally Kelly appears licking an ice-cube with Griebling still calling hopefully for 'Missus Jones' (Kelly 1956: 101). A series of clown entrances which build a narrative (in this case around the delivery of a rapidly melting block of ice) in this way is, ironically, more transgressive of the usual circus structure than the clowns who simply provide a variety of distractions between the other acts.

A final kind of disruption of performance clowning arises when the internal logic of the routine is destroyed for comic effect. Commonly, clowns use mime and physical skill to establish a situation in which the audience can follow the internal logic of the scene, even if the sequence of events would be unlikely in normal life. This logic is then destroyed, often by the arrival or intrusion of another clown who appears to be unaware of the established logic. For example, in *Slava's Snowshow* (seen Hackney Empire, January 2004 and The Lowry, October 2006), Slava and a green clown are on a bed which is being used as a boat. This is indicated to the audience by use of a sail, by another clown lying horizontally on a skateboard with a shark's fin on his back, and by sound effects. An internal logic for the routine appears to have been set. Then the green clown gets off the bed and walks away. There is no sound of water. Slava then steps off the bed and his foot makes a splash as it makes contact with the 'water'. Slava pauses and looks out to the audience and in this way the internal illogicality is highlighted. Nothing can be taken for granted in a clown-presented reality, no matter how carefully it appears to have been established.

Linguistic Variation
Clowns employ a variety of techniques for disturbing the usual linguistic modes of communication current in any society. The most obvious disturbance of societal conventions is to abstain from speaking completely. Many clown routines are mimed, with the only noises coming either from props or sound effects. In this last instance, it may be that each time the clown opens his mouth

to speak, another clown's horn or drum makes such a noise that he cannot be heard. This strikes the audience as humorous for a number of reasons. Firstly, the horn noise seemingly issuing from the clown's mouth is incongruous. Secondly, the audience is witnessing a status battle and the clown who tries, unsuccessfully, to speak, is being beaten in the status battle by the clown who drowns him out.

Other clowns replace the spoken word with a series of whistles, accompanied by gestures which make the narrative content of their whistling clear. This occurs in a common 'walk-around' in which the clown pits different sections of the audience against each other in a cheering competition. The whistle attracts the audience's attention and can be used expressively to indicate the clown's pleasure or displeasure with their efforts (Billy Smart's Circus, Hull, 2003). Traditionally the absence of language in circus clowning (as mentioned earlier) may have arisen from the clown's need to be understood in whichever country he was performing. Acts and routines that relied heavily on language and wordplay were at a disadvantage for international touring. When clowns did perform spoken routines in countries other than their own, their strong accents could make them difficult to understand. To compensate for any loss of comprehension, the clowns turned the accent into a virtue, creating laughter out of pronouncing the words appallingly, saying the wrong word or wilfully misunderstanding what the ringmaster or any other performer is saying to them. For example, Billy Hayden when performing in Paris would entertain the French audience by deliberately mangling the French language (Towsen 1976).

What has become evident is that it is not simply what the clown does that makes him funny (although action and interaction are vital), it is who he is. The audience must be able to empathize with the character who struggles to get things right, but he must not descend to such depths that our attitude towards him becomes mocking or satirical. Whilst we may not have experienced the clown's social status for ourselves, there has to be a commonality, a meeting point between what the clown shows and what we have felt. Out of such a meeting point comes the prompting to take the clown and his vulnerability to our hearts. Then when he manages to triumph, we cheer whole-heartedly at his success because it is what we would wish for ourselves.

To these definitions of clown types and clown routines I have added the terms *Clown Theatre*, *Clown Shows,* and *Clown Actors* which facilitate analysis of the ways in which clown types may combine, and which help in clarifying the positioning of the performance along a spectrum with circus at one end and theatre at the other. Both Wright and Lecoq focus on the individual performer without seeking to define the theatrical genre within which the performer appears. The definitions below seek to identify the different settings within which clowns can be found in the theatre. How the audience responds to the clown performer will be governed as much by setting and expectation as by individual performance techniques.

Clown Shows are those which are closest to classic circus clowning. The acts performed could readily form part of a circus but take on a different resonance through being performed in a theatre space and through the sustained nature of the show, uninterrupted by other acts. In publicity for the show, the word clown is likely to be prominent in communicating the style of performance to the potential audience. The work of a number of clowns and clown companies including **Les Witloof**, Mimirichi, and Tricicle will, later, be analysed as examples of *Clown Shows*.

Clown Theatre is theatre where all the performers are clowns and where the visual aesthetic is surreal or has elements of fantasy about it. The performance is not based on a script but will have been devised by the company in keeping with the skills and strengths of the performers. It may or may not involve the spoken word but there is likely to be close interaction between the performers and music or sound effects. *Clown Theatre* also tends to establish an interactive relationship between the performers and the audience that may involve the performers leaving the stage. Examples of *Clown Theatre*, including Slava Polunin, **Nani** and **Ingimarrson**, **Nola Rae** and **Teatr Licedei,** will be analysed later. These shows tend to have a narrative thrust in which plot or character motivation or both are explored and, in this way, they are closer to the linear impetus of conventional theatre than the performances defined as *Clown Shows*. When the clown performer creates fixed characters (like Polunin's early clown character, Asisyai), the shows then created are more likely to reveal the performer's personal philosophy and the show becomes an expression of that. In terms of publicity, the word clown may appear in the description of the show but it will not be as prominent as it was in the *clown show* publicity. It may also appear in combination with the definition mime, or the whole show may be described as physical comedy. In this area, then, distinctions between areas and styles of performance become blurred and a potential audience may not have such clear expectations of the performance.

Shows featuring *clown actors* tend to have a thematic or abstract content which may originate within something that the performer wishes to communicate, as is the case with *Only Fools (No Horses)* (Woods 2005), which was commissioned by Angela De Castro. The significant difference between this and *Clown Theatre* is the dominance of text and the interaction of the clown actor with non-clown actors. Some performers, like De Castro, move between these categories, so that for a show like *Only Fools* she can be defined as a *clown actor*, whereas for earlier shows like *The Gift* or whilst she was playing 'Rough' in *Slava's Snowshow,* she might more readily be defined as a *clown theatre performer*. This highlights the flexibility of these labels and demonstrates the need to evaluate each production according to its performance style.

Clown actors can be found operating in a range of relationships to their text. In the case of De Castro, the text was commissioned by the clown. Earlier examples of collaboration between clown and writer are to be found in the works of Shakespeare, whose clown characters were often written for specific performers with talents well-known to the writer. What remains in the text gives an indication of the possibilities for clowning, and where the clowning was primarily verbal: relying on puns and quips, the text gives a clear idea of the content of the performance. The nature of the performance in terms of delivery and physical or sight gags is lost to us in its original form but the text allows for the clown character to be brought to life again by subsequent performers. Further relationships between clown and text are to be found in the work of Beckett, where there are indications within the text (as is the case in *Waiting for Godot, Act Without Words 1* and *Act Without Words 2*) that a clown style of performance may be appropriate, and in the work of Dario Fo, who performs his own plays in the style of a clown jester but whose texts are also available for interpretation by other performers. For the clown performer working in *Clown Theatre* or as a *Clown Actor,* there are three levels in creating a performance (unlike the more common acting duality of the actor and the role). For the clown performer, the three elements can be identified as follows: the performer, the persona (the clown found within the performer) and the personage (the part played by the performer whilst in the clown state).

The term *clownesque* is here taken to mean theatre that is influenced by clowning both in its process of creation and in the act of performance. The outcome is often a playful theatrical performance. Thus clown and clown techniques may, in the case of devised or collaborative theatre, have influenced the development of the piece. Subsequently, the use of clown techniques (connection to the audience, play, the flop, separations, the clock, the drop,) or clown semiotics (make-up and costume) in performance may provoke a different response in the audience from that produced by other genres of theatre. It is also likely that theatre companies working in this way may acknowledge the influence of clowning on their work[1] (Kneehigh Theatre) but are unlikely to define themselves as creating clown theatre. The work of theatre companies such as Complicite provides examples of the clownesque.

However, helpful as these suggested definitions of clowning are, it is unlikely that they would exist in the ways that they do, or indeed that theatre clowning would exist in the way it does, without the underlying principles established by Jacques Lecoq (1921 – 1999). One difficulty in researching Lecoq's influence on clowning in particular, and British Theatre in general, is the paucity of material on his working methods. Necessarily, much of what follows is drawn from *The Moving Body* (Lecoq 2002) and *Theatre of Movement and Gesture* (Lecoq et al. 2006) with additional material from the only other two full-length books which focus on Lecoq; *Lecoq and the British Theatre* (ed. Chamberlain and Yarrow 2002) and Simon Murray's *Jacques Lecoq* (2003). To further supplement this, some personal responses to Lecoq's teaching of clowning have been sought from graduates of Lecoq's school.

Lecoq introduced clown into the training programme of The International Theatre School in Paris in the 1960s expecting it to be a temporary element of the training. In line with Lecoq's notion of 'Tout Bouge', clowning might have been expected to disappear at some point between the 1960s and the present. However, as Lecoq himself observed in *The Moving Body,* '[t]oday I notice that the students are always asking to work on clowns and consider it one of the high points of the school's educational journey' (Lecoq 2002: 158). Lecoq's teaching covered two distinct forms of clowning, Clown and Bouffons, at his school from the mid 1960s. Whilst bouffon clowning is less common in contemporary theatre, the form is still worthy of consideration. Initiated in its modern form (the original form dates back to medieval times) by Lecoq, bouffon is now also taught by Philippe Gaulier whose courses echo those which he studied formerly with Lecoq. **Bim Mason**, another Lecoq graduate, sometimes performs as a bouffon and John Wright (British Theatre Director and founder of Trestle Theatre Company) offers a range of exercises for working with bouffon in *Why is That so Funny?* (2006). Bouffon has influenced the work of British theatre companies such as Peepolykus, Right Size and Trestle Theatre.

Vicious Play

For Lecoq, bouffons were 'people who believe in nothing and make fun of everything' (Lecoq 2002: 124). The play in which they engage, and in which they encourage the audience to engage, is not the naive fun of the simple clown. Instead it has a vicious, potentially risky element. Also, importantly, whilst clowns may appear alone, bouffons always appear as part of a gang, making them potentially more dangerous. A key difference for Lecoq between clown and bouffon is that 'while we make fun of the clown, the bouffon makes fun of us. At the heart of the bouffon is a mockery pushed to the point of parody' (2006: 118). Lecoq identifies two levels of parody offered by bouffons. The first parodies through mimicry and can be identified as the friendly stage of bouffon performance. Beyond this level comes a second, potentially more spiteful, level in which the bouffon parodies deeply held convictions. It was this level of parody which prompted Lecoq to experiment with creating strange body shapes for bouffons (effectively whole body masks). This corporeal transformation has its roots in the tradition of the medieval King's fool and prevents the parody from becoming too spiteful. In transforming themselves physically, actors playing bouffons were able to make the unacceptable acceptable. Bim Mason suggests that bouffons were taken up by street performers and performers in new circus because 'they may have experienced prejudice towards the world of beggars, travellers and the disadvantaged and are excited by the use of comedy as a weapon rather than the naive, sexless comedy of clowns' (Mason 2002: 52). Mason here identifies the distinction between bouffons and clowns: bouffons are potentially nastier and more knowing than their naive clown counterparts. This perhaps arises from the ability of bouffons to 'confront [the] public with their own limitations' (Mason 2002: 53). By presenting an image of the physically malformed, bouffons place themselves beyond critical comment in our politically correct world. They also free themselves to comment more sharply on society. 'If you look "worse than life" from the outset, you tend to feel less inhibited about making comments about somebody else, especially if they look socially more acceptable than you' (Wright 2006: 304). Bouffons are one step further removed from everyday reality than clowns and they can, therefore, go one step further in their comments on the world around them. Wright, therefore, acknowledges that bouffons are confrontational in a way which clowns are not.

Lecoq's other, more far-reaching, definition is that of 'clown'. Put simply, for Lecoq the 'clown', unlike other theatrical performers, has an immediate contact with his audience: 'he comes to life by playing with the people who are looking at him' (2002: 157). Central to this is the concept of *jeu* – play. The underlying principles of *jeu* and *complicité* are both central to the way in which Lecoq teaches clowns to reach out to their audience. For Lecoq, following in the theatrical footsteps of Copeau and Meyerhold, *jeu* or play is vital. Whilst Gaulier teaches *Le Jeu* as a discrete course at his training school, for Lecoq, the concept of *jeu* runs through all his teaching. This distinction is recognized by Murray (2002: 33) and Alan Fairbairn (in Murray) further emphasizes the importance of play 'The whole notion of *play* is essential to Lecoq's School' (2002: 33). Fairbairn goes on to suggest that for Lecoq, play is closely connected to the idea of making the most of the theatrical material available to the performer. The importance of play to Lecoq is demonstrated by the fact that, when the time comes to select which students will continue from the first year of the course to the second, 'the main criterion for selection is the actor's capacity for play' (Lecoq 2002: 103). Play, therefore, is not a technique but a state of being, a readiness to perform. It is '...the motor of performance. The driving force is not *what* to play but *how* it should be played' (Lecoq 2002: 118). For Lecoq, play exists in the space between the actor's ego and the character he is playing. This raises the notion, as Turner (1982) and Winnicott (1991) suggest, that play exists in a space between the real and the imagined, containing elements of both but belonging to neither. Murray offers a convincing summary of the significance of play in Lecoq's way of working,

> Play is a dynamic principle which informs the quality of interaction between performers and their audience, but also opens up possibilities for action which can...liberate the actor (Murray 2002: 34).

Play, then, operates on a number of levels; it can be the motor of the performance, driving the actor forward; it can exist between actors in a scene and it can and, according to Lecoq, should exist between the actors and the audience. Lecoq makes this final element of play clear in his analysis of the interaction between a clown and his audience: '[i]t is not possible to be a clown for an audience; you play *with* an audience' (2002: 157).

Closely related to *jeu* is the concept of *complicité*. Lecoq offers the following example of *complicité* in action: 'Two characters pass, each one meets the other's eye and comes to a stop' (2002: 34). *Complicité*, at one level, is a silent communication, an unspoken understanding. Like *jeu*, *complicité* can occur between the actors on the stage and between the actors and the audience. Out of *complicité*, play may arise. Murray suggests the reverse, that 'complicité is an outcome of successful play' (2002: 72). It is likely, however, that the relationship between the two is symbiotic: *complicité* leads to play and play leads to *complicité*. *Complicité* is closely connected to the concept of ensemble, representing, as it does, what might be described as collective imagining. When two performers' imaginations work in the same way instinctively in the moment of performance or rehearsal, they are experiencing *complicité*. In playful performance – that which creates an open relation between the performer and the spectator where communication transcends the stage/audience division – *complicité* occurs when the actor and the audience experience instinctive communication. The concepts of *jeu* and *complicité* lie at the heart of Lecoq's approach to clowning.

Lecoq's clowning is quite distinct from common conceptions of circus clowning. Clowns in training at the Lecoq School *do* use the traditional red nose (which Lecoq came to see as the smallest mask) but this was introduced by **Pierre Byland** when he returned to teach at the school and was not part of Lecoq's original conception of clowning. 'The reference to circus, which is bound to surface as soon as clowns are mentioned, remains marginal, in my view... Apart from the comic register, we took no external models, either formal or stylistic...' (Lecoq 2002: 154). Initially, for Lecoq, clowning was about encouraging the student performer to reveal 'the person underneath, stripped bare for all to see' as 'the clown doesn't exist aside from the actor performing him' (2002: 154). Students were encouraged to reveal their own vulnerabilities and weaknesses on stage and in rehearsal. Lecoq believed that this personal vulnerability could be a source of great dramatic strength. From this came the notion of the 'search for "one's own clown"' (Lecoq 2002: 154). The idea that each individual has one or more clowns within him or herself is situated at the heart of Lecoq's approach to clowning and, subsequently, to the approaches of Byland and Gaulier. Indeed the notion of the 'inner clown' is also to be found in the work of Angela De Castro and is referred to in the training publicity of other organizations such as 'NosetoNose' (www.nosetonose.info/) and 'Bataclown' (www.bataclown.com). For Lecoq, the concept of *jeu* is connected with the idea of clown because the clown's success depends on his ability to *play* with his audience.

It can be argued that clown is a natural conclusion – a drawing together of all Lecoq's teaching from the starting point of *Jeu* and *Neutral Mask*. After years of offering clown training as part of his two year programme, Lecoq came to the conclusion that

> [t]hey [clowns] have become as important as the neutral mask, but working in reverse. While the neutral mask is all-inclusive, a common denominator which can be shared by all, the clown brings out the individual in his singularity. (Lecoq 2002: 158/159)

It is clear, therefore, that the creation and performance of a clown is a particularly personal process in which the student or performer is encouraged to reveal his or her personal insecurities that are offered to the audience members to give them a sense of being drawn into the performer's world. This sharing of vulnerability encourages the audience to empathize with the clown. Another important feature of creating a clown is, as Lecoq identifies, to 'discover the audience'. The clown does not simply perform in front of the audience, he or she plays with the audience, connects with them. 'Unlike theatre characters, the contact the clown has with his audience is immediate, he comes to life by playing with the people who are looking at him' (Lecoq 2002: 157).

Another important feature of clown for Lecoq is that 'clowning also demands a feat, one that defies logic; overturning a certain order it thus allows one to denounce the recognized order' (Lecoq 2006: 115). This notion of clown logic is central to many clown performances in that it allows the clown to look at the world anew, with the eyes of an unknowing innocence and, out of this, comes an increased potential for play. In Lecoq's work can be found the beginning of principles of clown techniques for theatre performance which have been taken up and extended by John Wright, Philippe Gaulier and Angela De Castro.

As Wright suggests, '[c]lowning turns idiocy into an art form' (Wright 2006: 180). This concept of clown has been developed in a variety of ways in contemporary theatre. John Wright offers four definitions which are an aid to analysing and discussing clown performance. These definitions are *simple clown*, *boss clown*, *pathetic clown* and *tragic clown*. Wright's definitions do not describe different kinds of clown in the way the terms Whiteface and Auguste do. Instead, Wright's terms describe different levels of clowning which draw different emotional responses from the audience. So whilst it is unlikely that a circus clown will switch from Whiteface to

Auguste in the course of a single performance, it is quite possible that a *simple* clown may become a *pathetic* clown or a *pathetic* clown a *tragic* one, depending on the way in which the clown responds to provocation within the scene.

Wright describes the *simple clown* as 'fun-loving, childlike, amoral, irresponsible, mercurial, bizarre, destructive, chaotic and anarchic' (2006: 203–4). The *simple clown* plays in front of and with his audience. This accords with Lecoq's view of the centrality of play to clowning. Like Lecoq, Wright identifies the personal aspect of clowning: 'A Clown is a credibly stupid version of *you*' (2006: 193). He also recognizes the importance of what he identifies as bafflement. Just as we each have our own clown, we each have our own state of bafflement which Wright suggests is vital for the *simple clown*. Potentially, a state of bafflement is a rescue strategy that comes into play when the clown is caught out or confused. By revealing his bafflement, he can make time for himself and signal his difficulty to the audience. Wright offers a number of examples from clown performance.

> Grock would punctuate his work with the constant question 'Pour quoi?' That was his point of bafflement. **Simon McBurney**, of Complicité, would use his usual slight stutter: 'I- I- I – er...' Angela De Castro will look at us as if to say 'Oh dear' and then adjust her trousers. (2006: 195)

It is important that bafflement is a state rather than a technique. If, as a performer, your point of bafflement becomes too fixed, it is unlikely to produce effective communication with the audience. Wright also emphasizes the importance of self in clowning. For Wright, clowns are 'fun-loving, childlike, amoral, irresponsible, mercurial, bizarre, destructive, chaotic and anarchic' (2006: 204). In order to discover his or her clown, a performer must be able to access all these aspects of his or her personality. When clowning, these aspects of the self are not performed but *revealed*.

Within the frame of *simple clown* a *boss clown* may emerge. The *boss clown* is what Wright defines as a provocateur, in that the *boss clown* provokes developments in the scene. He may, for example, give the *simple* clowns a job to do which they are not capable of completing successfully. There is a direct parallel here to the status interactions in circus performance between Augustes and Whiteface clowns. The emergence of a *boss clown* allows for the creation of conflict which, in turn, creates the opportunity for introducing or extending narrative within the scene. *Simple clowns* may work alone by establishing a relationship with the audience, attempting *exploits* and communicating bafflement. The introduction of a *boss clown* allows for greater complexity. According to Wright (2006), the *boss clown* is not a role because in the anarchic world of clowning any clown could become the boss at any time. By facilitating the introduction of dramatic conflict, the *boss clown* also helps move towards the creation of a narrative which, in turn, aids in the creation of longer and more developed clown sequences.

Pathetic clown, as defined by Wright, is unlikely to perform alone because he needs to find games in which he reacts to the other people in the scene and puts their feelings before his own. In contrast, the *simple clown* responds spontaneously and playfully to the world. In addition to this, the *pathetic clown* has to establish a 'credible emotional engagement with the dramatic situation in hand' (2006: 226). In this way he plays comedy without debunking it. The nature of the performance is more subtle and thus the *pathetic clown* increases his own and the audience's emotional engagement with the scene. If the principles of *simple clown* are to use the point of bafflement, find games to play, develop complicity and avoid acting, then the principles of *pathetic clown* are to 'find games where you react to other people in the scene and put their feelings before your own' (Wright 2006: 226), to avoid the obvious, to go for clashes and to do the things which the audience members would not do in the situation. It is clear here that there is a development of the level of engagement on the part of the clown between *simple* and *pathetic*:

> The fascination of simple clown lies in us seeing the separation between the pretence of the game and the naked reality of the person behind the game...In pathetic clown, the drop, the moment of separation, becomes an emotional transition and this change of feeling relaunches your clowning, so you start another game to rescue yourself from the flop of the first...in tragic clown there is no rescue. (Wright 2006: 237)

For Wright, *tragic clown* connects not with the notion of making us laugh but with the idea of extending play as far as it will go. Clowning in this way pulls the clown in a number of directions at the same time. The desire to make the audience laugh is likely to be present, just as it was in *simple clown*, but that impetus is over-ridden by whatever preoccupation lies at the heart of the clown's tragedy. The *simple clown* gives away his dignity when he debunks the comedy of his situation. The *tragic clown* retains his dignity and the audience is encouraged to respect him as he transcends the idiocy of the *simple clown*. The bafflement of the *simple clown* becomes the trauma of the *tragic clown*. In this kind of clown performance the audience's attention is held by the clown's determination and perseverance. In *tragic clown* there is a potential for the clown to develop: 'there's the potential of a huge transcendent arc – from the hapless idiot, deserving little but our ridicule, to the focused, dignified and determined protagonist, whom we've grown to admire and respect' (Wright 2006: 238). There is a strong connection between what Wright and Lecoq believe can be achieved through clowning. Wright's *pathetic* and *tragic* clowns are extensions of clown as taught by Lecoq. At the heart of all of them is the notion of play and the importance of establishing complicity with the other performers and with the audience.

The idea of the clown *flop* is found in Lecoq, Gaulier and De Castro's teaching of clown. In *The Moving Body*, Lecoq identifies two kinds of *flop*; these are the *pretentious flop* and the *accidental flop* (2002: 160). By this, Lecoq indicates that whilst all clowns working in the way he suggests share a central action of trying to complete an *exploit* and failing, there are different ways in which the failure may be shared with the audience. In the *pretentious flop*, the clown performs a simple *exploit* that he believes to be a fitting example of his own brilliance. The humour, therefore, arises from the audience's superior recognition of the fact that what the clown is doing is really nothing special. The more the clown communicates his pride in his achievement, the funnier the audience will find him. On the other hand, with the *accidental flop* where the clown fails to complete his *exploit*, the humour arises from the clown's incompetence. This kind of flop is particularly funny when the *exploit* is relatively simple. The audience members recognize that they could easily complete the task with which the clown is struggling. At the opening of *Slava's Snowshow*, De Castro as the green clown, 'Rough', repeatedly fails to cross her arms. This is an example of the *accidental flop*. Crossing one's arms is a simple manoeuvre which the clown should be able to complete but again and again, she fails. The audience members, adults and children alike, feel superior because they are able to complete the *exploit*. The idea of an *exploit* is central to the way Lecoq's clowns operate. Whilst they enjoy being in front of an audience and playing with them through establishing a sense of *complicité*, their presence alone has a limited potential for creating humour.

The *flop*, whether *pretentious* or *accidental*, has to be deliberate. As Gaulier identifies, in clown training many clowns flop unintentionally and the results are not amusing; they are painful to watch. Therefore Gaulier suggests that the *flop* helps the clown to play but

> [i]n my school, we call him Mr Flop, because we treat him with a hell of a lot of respect. It is funny that playing with Mr Flop happens as the end after many, many other flops that weren't at all deliberate, that weren't playmates then. (www.ecolephilippegaulier.com)

This echoes Lecoq's experience when he first introduced the teaching of clowning by drawing his students into a circle and asking them to enter the circle and be funny. He reports how student after student failed until 'they stopped improvising and went back to their seats feeling frustrated, confused and embarrassed. It was at that point, when they saw their weaknesses, that everyone burst out laughing' (Lecoq 2002: 154).

For Gaulier, the *flop* is also linked to the idea of pleasure. If Mr Flop is a playmate, then the clown 'lets the audience see the great delight of a child who wants to stay on the stage...if the pleasure in staying is great, then the clown is forgiven. He's allowed to be no good over and over' (www. ecolephilippegaulier.com). De Castro's clown training (she trained with Gaulier) also has this emphasis on what she describes as the clown's 'pleasure to be in the moment' ('How to be a Stupid', course, London, November 2005). Beyond *flop* and *exploit,* John Wright also identifies the importance of *separations* which can be established through use of *drop* and *clock*. Wright offers the following definition: '[a] drop is an abrupt and clear separation, a clock is the smallest of all' (2006: 201). *Separations* are also closely connected to the idea that a clown can debunk what he has been doing. In order to debunk a sequence of play, the clown needs to be able to distance himself from the play and comment on it to the audience from a distance. 'Separations enable you to keep a comfortable distance from what you are playing' (Wright 2006: 202). All of these techniques can be used in clown performance, regardless of its setting. They can also be used in performances which are not purely clown performances but which use clown techniques to establish a playful theatrical performance.

In identifying the similarity in conceptualization of clown between Lecoq and his one-time student, Gaulier, it is also important to highlight the differences in their approaches to delivering training. Clown training, in common perhaps with other areas of actor training, is a field where the attitude and teaching style of the tutor significantly affect the experience of the student and their likely success in finding their clown. Lecoq opened doors for his students; he 'never pretended to "teach the territories" ...one doesn't come out having done a clown training' (Laura Eades, personal correspondence 2006). For Lecoq, clowning was another territory that could create possibilities for a performer. Gaulier's approach to teaching can, according to some former students, be a painful experience (particularly in an area which requires the performer to reveal vulnerabilities and insecurities). 'If anything [Gaulier's] style inhibited the discovery of my clown' (Daniel Bye, personal correspondence 2006). According to another former student, Mark Evans, 'Gaulier also used to like to produce a certain amount of panic – he would declare a three knocks and you're out policy...You learn to live on the edge of failure and recognize the importance of this to clowning' (Mark Evans, personal correspondence 2006). In Lecoq's approach, clown is a natural progression for the students. For Gaulier, the clown comes at the end of his training course, but he is much more concerned with the notion of failure. Andy Crook (who trained with both Lecoq and Gaulier) describes how Gaulier 'pushed us very hard with that being quite cruel at times (I got hit and slapped several times)' (Andy Crook, personal correspondence 2006). Crook identifies the difference between the two practitioners as 'with Lecoq clown was a fantastic thing with Gaulier clown was a disaster. But for Gaulier disaster is the clown' (2006). This contrast lies at the heart of the two differing approaches. Another significant difference is that Lecoq's teaching, as already identified, revolves around the students finding their inner clown while those who have studied with Gaulier report how he often gave people clowns in such a way that the student was encouraged to transgress type.

As mentioned above, little is recorded concerning clown training beyond Lecoq. However, from personal experience, I am able to describe one approach developed by Angela De Castro. Her training course 'How to be a Stupid' (offered by the Why Not Institute) is influenced by both Lecoq and Gaulier and her emphasis is on using play to open participants up to reveal elements of their inner selves in their clowns. Recently, De Castro has offered both one- and two-week courses introducing her approach to clowning. The two-week course offers participants the opportunity to establish their clowns more securely and to experiment with a wider range of clown improvisations. For De Castro, clowning is a state rather than a character, which coincides with Wright's view. Students are encouraged to find their inner clown in a positive and supportive atmosphere through exercises which focus participants on increasing their self-awareness and ability to accept the notion of failure. Once a supportive and playful group dynamic has been established, participants work through exercises that are intended to improve their ability to connect with the audience (complicité), to give and take focus, to find games on stage and to show their pleasure to be in the moment. De Castro also introduces specific clown techniques, such as the double take, and participants spend time discovering costumes for their clowns that are 'not to do with a show, but to live with. It is for life. It is like a skin' ('How to be a Stupid' course material). At the end of the first day, in order to help individuals find appropriate costumes, De Castro guides the participants through a meditation and visualization exercise which takes them to their 'Land of Why Not'. In this land they are asked to visualize their perfect selves, in whatever form that may take. After the visualization, participants draw an image of their 'Land of Why Not' and put themselves into the image. This is a metaphorical exercise and they may appear in the land as anything. They may be a person, an animal, an imagined creature or even one of the elements. Anything is possible. From this image they then draw inspiration to help them find a costume for their clown. The costume may relate to the colours, shapes and textures of the image. Many participants find this exercise challenging because it requires a letting-go of everyday agendas and judgements. Some participants find costumes that are too ridiculous; others, costumes that are too ordinary or which restrict them. As participants strive to discover their costumes, De Castro sometimes offers help; sometimes leaves individuals to work through their own difficulties. The discovery of a good costume helps the clown to create a link between 'the contemporary world of the day by day where we live most of the time and the non-verbal "land of the imagination where we sometimes visit"' (De Castro, teaching comments). De Castro begins each day of her courses with a meeting, which enables her to introduce the focus of that day and to prepare the participants for the exercises that lie ahead. Whilst the meetings are not intended to be therapeutic, the emotional challenge of Dec Castro's highly personal approach to clowning means that participants can make use of the chance to check in order to explain how they are responding to the work they are doing. These sessions reinforce the supportive nature of the group, and increase the likelihood that participants will take risks in the exercises that follow. The one-week course ends with a particularly challenging exercise. Pairs of clowns come onto the stage charged with being funny. If you stop being funny (or don't start being funny), De Castro starts to countdown from five. The clowns have to change tack, trying new strategies to avoid failure. This balance of support and an awareness of the closeness of failure lies at the heart of finding one's inner clown. During the two-week course, De Castro encourages the participants to establish a stronger connection between them and their clown by making them write to their clown, and then by making them write a response while they are in the clown state. As clowning for De Castro is a state not a technique, she provides participants with a list of commandments to help them access the qualities necessary to reach and sustain the clown state. These include notions like truth, curiosity, pleasure, commitment, imagination, surrender, spontaneity, compassion, naivety, freedom and serenity. De Castro's clown work represents an example of an approach to clowning which relies on participants making use of their inner self to discover their inner clown. Doing this enables them to introduce a greater level of play and playfulness into their clowns, into their everyday lives and into their performance.

Note

1. One example of this can be found in the teachers' resource pack on the website of Kneehigh Theatre.

2

THE DEVELOPMENT OF THE CIRCUS CLOWN: FRAME AND CONTENT

The dominant form of clowning in western society since the eighteenth century has been in the circus. The only other significant venue for clowning (largely from the twentieth century) is the theatre. A consideration of the frame in which the clown performer appears is fundamental to this study. One of the most significant features of modern clowning is its transference from the frame of Traditional Circus to other apparently incongruous locations. This re-framing has inevitably affected the nature and aim of clown play and its reception by its audiences. However this re-framing cannot be explored without a thorough understanding of the original framing of the clown in the circus.

Constructing the Frame

In 1756, Phillip Astley (1742–1814) opened the first circus, creating the circular performance area to suit equestrian acts. This 'circus ring' was to remain the norm for circuses through to the present day, influencing the creation of acts and the performance style in which they were and are delivered. However, there is no clear indication of the presence of a clown in the circus until an advertisement appeared in 1775 (Croft-Cooke 1948). Here, the clown, whilst unidentified as an individual performer, may be seen to be clearly in existence. The nature of the clown acts described indicates the element of parody of the other serious circus acts, which is still common in the circus today.

By the early 1800s, the circus had been established as a popular form of entertainment across Europe and in America. At the beginning of the nineteenth century, tenting circuses began to appear and the popularity and survival of the circus seemed secure, whilst the role of the clown within the circus began a period of development and consolidation. In these early days, clowns established two kinds of acts beyond the pantomime sketches that formed a consistent part of the circus programme in its early years. Clowns used other circus acts as a basis for theirs, hence the existence of terms such as 'clown to the horse' or 'clown to the wire', two examples of the many opportunities for parodying of other acts. In these acts, the clowns mocked and parodied the highly skilled performers. At this stage in the development of circus, a second clown type began to emerge, drawn from the word-playing clowns of the stage (such as **Kempe**, **Armin** and **Tarlton**). These clowns engaged in repartee with the ringmaster, entertaining the audience with their wit rather than with physical skill. Thus there came to exist two broadly definable clown types: those who speak and those who do not. Over the years, some clowns such as Coco (**Nikolai Poliakoff**) performed both as a speaking clown and as a non-speaking clown, according to the demands placed upon them by the circus they were performing in.

From this point through to the 1960s, clown performance in circuses continued in much the same vein, with some developments in costume (including the increased popularity of the use of face make-up). There were occasional innovations: for example the Fratellini brothers worked as a clown trio rather than as the traditional Auguste/Whiteface double act, and in the 1960s **Annie Fratellini** (the granddaughter of Paul Fratellini) became one of the very few female circus clowns by developing her own Auguste character.

These clown performers developed carpet-clowning, where they welcomed the audience and ventured into their space during the show. They also introduced clown entrées, which were longer acts focusing on the clown's particular talents. The nature of the entrées varied from circus to circus because in each case the entrée would be developed by the resident clown.

In defining his 'rhetoric of the imaginary', Sutton-Smith suggests that 'the key is that the playful is disruptive of settled expectations' (1997: 147). The clown, by his very nature, is disruptive of expectation, as is demonstrated by Emmett Kelly's development of the progressive gag (for example the ice gag described earlier). He behaves within his act in unexpected ways in relation to society, and even the very structure of his performance can be disruptive. In *Clown: My Life in Tatters and Smiles*, Kelly describes another of his entrées, developed after the Second World War, in which he brought out a plank which he 'would slant...into the seats and practically stick it under people's noses and start sawing as though what I had to do was so terribly important that I didn't even notice they were there' (1956: 108–9). In terms of clown behaviour, this act demonstrates social incompetence. Kelly's actions accord with Sutton-Smith's notion of the Self in play 'play is a state of mind, a way of seeing and being, a special mental "set" towards the world' (Sutton-Smith 1997: 174). This perfectly describes the clown state. Both clowning and playing are states of mind and in both states the clown or player views the world in a highly individual way, which then governs his interaction with the world. In his writing on child phantasmagoria (which he links to the rhetoric of the imaginary), Sutton-Smith asserts that 'children's play fantasies are not meant only to replicate the world...they are meant to fabricate another kind of world that lives alongside the first one' (1997: 158). Kelly's carpentry act, in common with many clown acts, creates a world in which there are elements of the real world (in this case the plank and the saw) but in which those elements are framed in such a way as to remove them from the real world and place them in a parallel world governed by clown logic. These brief examples indicate the way in which such techniques of clowning can be usefully analysed by employing Sutton-Smith's theories of play.

The clown types established in Europe and America and the combinations used have already been established and little in the way of innovation occurred until the 1970s. Since the mid 1970s a number of key developments have taken place alongside the continued inclusion of clown entrées in Traditional Circuses, such as the development of clowning in 'New' or 'Contemporary' Circus; the performance of female clowns (limited in number but significant in the ways in which they help to re-define what is meant by the term clown in contemporary society); and the renaissance of theatre clowning. It was, however, the impact of the duality of framing created by the division between Traditional and Contemporary circuses that had a significant impact of the way clowning developed.

The Frames of Traditional and Contemporary Circus

The nature of the clown entertainer varies according to the venue and structure within which he performs. Some definition is therefore necessary of the various performance and production elements of Traditional Circus and Contemporary Circus of the last thirty years, as these elements inevitably affect the audience's response to the clown performer. In Bateson's (1973) terms, the physical setting of the performance establishes the frame. Thus an audience in a theatre or concert hall has a set of expectations associated with that venue. It has another set of expectations of a circus. When a circus performs in a theatre, those two frames of reference collide, creating an ambiguity in how the performance should be read.

This recent development in circus creation and programming was originally referred to by the term 'New Circus' (a literal translation of the French – nouveau cirque) but by 2001, in the Arts Council of England Strategy and Report on Circus, Felicity Hall chooses to define new circus as that which 'distinguishes itself as not belonging to the traditional circuit'. She goes on to suggest that 'the binary oppositional definitions of "traditional" and "new" are no longer helpful' (Hall 2001: n. pag). Whilst it may suit the Arts Council's agenda to be able to view Traditional and Contemporary Circus as part of the same circus 'ecology', it is clear that there are differences in terms of programming, act inclusion, production values, design concept and thematic content. The most rudimentary comparison of the Moscow State Circus and Cirque du Soleil makes it evident that they are certainly not part of the same ecology.

Traditional Circuses have a number of defining features. They tend to be family run and to use performers who are either drawn from that family or from members of other circus families from around the world. In this way, acts are passed on from generation to generation, and many performers, including the clowns, are skilled in more than one area of circus performance. Traditional Circus programmes include a range of acts, which can be divided into three categories: clown, physical skill and strength. Until the mid-1960s, a common fourth category was the animal act. Programmes are designed in such a way that the setting and removal of equipment is often covered by the clowns, who distract the audience from the technical and logistical requirements of the circus. There is no narrative connection between the acts. Performers in these circuses tend to have been trained within the circus by family members. These circuses tour the country, usually performing for no longer than a week in any one location so as to maximize their audience. Originally, Traditional Circuses announced their presence in a town by means of a circus parade in which all the members of the circus and its animals paraded through the town to create a stir of publicity. Such parades became popular from 1840 onwards but the trend towards removing animals from circuses diminished the impact of such parades and they have now fallen out of popularity.

The Traditional Circus Frame

Traditional Circuses perform in Big Tops (single rings in Europe and three rings, most commonly until recently, in the USA). The audience experience of the circus begins outside the Big Top. The creation of a number of distinct areas, which must be passed through before reaching the interior of the Big Top, increases the impact of the venue by drawing the audience gradually into the world of the circus. Often there is a fenced area around the Big Top which is accessible only to ticket holders. The next part of the experience is usually an outer tent where refreshments can be bought. Even the nature of these refreshments is dictated by tradition: pop corn, candy floss and ice creams. All of these signs contribute to the creation of a *play frame* (Bateson 1973) which readies the audience for what is to follow. At this point the audience has left the outside, real, world and entered the world under canvas. This world is situated between the real world and the world of fantasy and, as such, is akin to Turner's *liminoid* space. Sometimes, one or more clowns may be in evidence in this area prior to the show. This raises the audience's expectations still further by giving it a taste of the show to come. It is increasingly popular amongst circuses to offer for sale at this point not only the traditional programme but also flashing lights on sticks or headdresses. When the audience member buys one of these, he or she takes another step further away from the everyday self into a world of spectacle and fantasy, adopting a costume element which is a channel for play and which, particularly for adults, signifies their transition away from their normal selves. The final stage before approaching the ringside is often a tunnel that draws the audience into the inner world of the circus. The people selling programmes and refreshments are usually performers who will be seen later on the high wire or performing feats of great skill. Whilst the impetus for this doubling of roles may be financial, it can also have an impact on the audience. For the audience member, there is a moment of stunned recognition when he or she realizes that the highly skilled trapeze artist is the same person who was selling programmes. This forced realization of the ordinary humanity of the circus performer prevents the audience from viewing them as super-human and underlines the everyday ordinariness which is equally a part of the performers' lives. This combination of ordinariness and skill accentuates the high level of that skill. Finally the audience member reaches the Big Top proper. Traditionally, the seating is arranged in almost a full circle, with the performers entering through a curtained off passage, also known as a vomitory. Usually the musicians are seated on a platform above this entrance. There is a waist-high barrier around the ring with boxes of floor-level seats. Outside these seats will be a pathway used by the audience to reach their seats, and by the clowns when performing 'run-ons'. From this point on, the seating will be tiered, with the most expensive seats being those directly opposite the performers' entrance. The emphasis is on functionality rather than comfort. Tiered seating usually takes the form of wooden benches or fixed plastic seating. The potentially complex rigging for the circus acts and the lighting is all in full view of the audience. This contributes to the audience's awareness of the spectacular nature of the performance that they are anticipating. At this point, the audience members may well experience a clash between the often slightly shabby reality of the Big Top and their own expectations of that spectacle.

Two elements combine to reassure the audience that the world of circus is indeed a wonderful one. As the start time of the show approaches, clowns appear and begin to work the crowd. At this point it is necessary only to consider the function of this element of performance. The clowns perform simple acts, which pull the audience's attention away from their surroundings and onto the performers. During this 'carpet' clowning, the clowns leave the ring and venture around the pathway behind the boxes and into the audience. This quickly establishes the nature of the performer/spectator relationship in the circus, particularly that between the clowns and the audience. The second element that offers the promise of the spectacular nature of the circus is the opening parade in which all the acts that will perform appear, each giving a small taster of the nature of their act. This will be accompanied by enthusiastic introductions from the Ringmaster, loud music and swirling, flashing lights.

Performers are usually responsible for their own costumes and, consequently, there is no coherent design concept for the whole circus. Those circuses which come closest to a design concept are those constructed around the notion of a theme. Uncle Sam's Circus which toured Yorkshire in 2004 is an example of such a themed circus. All the acts, regardless of their country of origin, are presented as being connected to the United States of America, with performers dressed as either cowboys/girls or Native Americans. This adoption of a theme is a marketing ploy which connects this otherwise little-known circus to the age-old tradition of circus names reflecting the geographic origin of the circus. Thus Uncle Sam's American Circus associates it with the spectacular American circuses, like Barnum and Bailey's, and also through the patriotic label implies that it is on a level with such circuses as the Moscow State or the Chinese State Circuses.

The loss of animal acts for so many circuses necessitated a change in the way circus programmes were designed. One of the traditional functions of the circus clown (tension relief) had been lost. Increasingly, clown entrées developed that depended either on the demonstration of the clown's skill or on parodying other circus acts. These areas of skill or parody are also to be found in clowns in Contemporary Circus. As mentioned above, performance of this kind existed before the disappearance of animals but, in as far as circus clowning advanced in Traditional Circuses during the 1980s and 1990s, it is in this area that development can be traced. The removal of animals from the structure of the circus show created the opportunity for longer clown entrées. Years before, clowns such as Grock had moved out of the circus because the circus structure could not accommodate his longer entrées and now the opposite is occurring. Unfortunately, this demand for longer entrées in Traditional Circus is taking place at a point when Traditional Circus clowning appears to be in decline. The dynasties of circus clowns which existed in the first half of the twentieth century (the Fratellini, the Rivels, and the Cairoli) have died out and the younger clowns performing today have not had the training from childhood in absorbing both content and skill.

Traditional Circus Clown Play

Billy Smart's Circus ceased touring in 1971 and from then until 2003 its only performances were static Big Top shows or television specials. **Henri** was the Circus's lead clown between 2003 and 2005. It is not possible to identify Henri as either a traditional Auguste or Whiteface and this seems to be a common element of clowning in late twentieth century traditional circus clowning. Young clowns working in the circus now are seeking to redefine the role of the clown, both as a character in the show and as a part of the structure of the show. It is arguable how successful this redefinition has been. Henri wears the red nose of the traditional Auguste but the swirls of black on his whiteface are more indicative of Pierrot than Circus clowning. His costume is soldier-like (reminiscent perhaps of a ring-master) and his hair is styled just as it might be in everyday life. This mixed semiotic code is difficult to read in relation to Traditional Circus conventions.

Whilst Henri's appearance indicates a departure from a conventionally defined clown types, both his entrées are derivative; reminiscent of old-school clowning. One of these, the Spaghetti entrée (described and analysed below), is very similar to an entrée called 'The Waiter' performed by **Fabri** and **Mimile** (Remy, trans Shalins 1997: 34) decades earlier.

Spaghetti Entrée

For this entrée Henri changed costume, appearing in an ill-fitting dinner suit (under which he was padded) with a wig of hair that looked like a mop. He performed with a partner who was not another clown but a woman who fulfilled the role of straight person as the customer. The simple plot of the entrée is that Henri is a waiter who tries incompetently to serve a meal to a customer. In order to get the items for the meal Henri goes behind a panel and mimes going up and down stairs. He tries to open a bottle of wine and for a long time cannot succeed. When it does open he spills some of the contents. Then he gets his finger stuck in the neck of the bottle. Once he extracts his finger he moves on to cleaning a glass. He blows his nose and then uses the cloth to 'clean' the glass. He drinks some of the wine and then sprays it onto the customer and the audience. He brings a meal of spaghetti to the customer and ties a bib round her. She extracts a sock from the meal. Henri puts the sock on. He takes a drink of her wine and walks away, spraying the wine on her. He takes the plate of spaghetti and spills it. In the chaos that follows his wig comes off and he ends up with it on backwards. He throws spaghetti at the audience and encourages them to throw it back. He puts what is left of the spaghetti on the customer's head. Finally he brings a custard pie for dessert. He trips and it looks as if the pie will land on a member of the audience. The customer takes the pie off him and pies him. He chases her off stage.

Despite the substitution of a woman as the customer, rather than the ringmaster or a Whiteface clown, this remains an example of traditional clowning. It contains a number of the elements of clowning identified earlier. Henri repeatedly engages in status interactions with objects where the objects come off best, as happens with the wine bottle and the spaghetti. The instigation of a food fight is an example of clowning overstepping social conventions, and the moment when Henri blows his nose on the cloth he is using to wipe the wine glass is an example of clowning demonstrating the socially unacceptable. The occasions when Henri mimes going up and down stairs are examples of clown skill. As in traditional clown entrées, there is no connection between this entrée and the acts which precede or follow it. The whole entrée sits comfortably within Sutton-Smith's 'Rhetoric of the Imaginary', containing as it does elements of the ridiculous, signalled by the clown's over-padded costume and his mop-like wig. This visual signal combines with the action. Once again (as with Kelly earlier) we see a clown creating an alternative reality in which he can play without any real consequence. Much of the clown activity in Billy Smart's Circus was devoted to covering the get-in or get-out of equipment for other acts. One run-in involved a clown who engaged the audience in a shouting competition. He divided the audience and signalled with a whistle when each group should be shouting, pitting one group against another. In this way, the attention of the whole audience was engaged whilst the ring was readied for the next act. Neither the entrées nor the run-ins demonstrated true vitality in their play with the audience. The clowns appeared to be trapped within their frame.

Whilst most Traditional Circuses still tour in the Big Top tradition, some circuses are also beginning to perform in more conventional theatre venues. For example, the Moscow State Circus, which usually tours as a tented circus, performed in some conventional theatres such as the New Theatre in Hull during the 2005/06 season. This moves the Traditional Circus closer to the performance space of Contemporary Circuses, although not enough attention is always paid to the demands of the theatrical space in relation to this re-framing. Tumbling and somersaulting acts lose their impact when the performer disappears behind the proscenium arch at the somersaulting climax of their routine.

The Contemporary Circus Frame

As the world of circus moves into the twenty-first century, the Contemporary Circuses that have emerged since the 1980s have a number of production elements in common: high performance skills (often merging circus, gymnastics, dance and theatre); a coherent design concept for the show including costuming and lighting; and technical change-overs being effected by the artistes in such a way that they become part of the artistry of the show. It also appears to be the case that in many Contemporary Circuses the clowns have become less important to the structure of the show and, perhaps as a result of this, the standard of clowning there and in Traditional Circuses has generally declined.

A number of sub-categories can be suggested within the 'Nouveau Cirque' or 'New Circus'. These are 'Updated Traditional Circuses' in which a conventional circus structure is followed; conventional circus acts are included but there are more modern influences in terms of design, lighting and music choice. Most importantly, these circuses tend to perform in non-conventional settings. Circus Oz (Australia) is one of a number of circuses of this kind (other examples include Swamp Circus (UK) and Circus Eloise (France)). There are also 'Theatrical Circuses', like Cirque du Soleil (Canada). Here, the show attempts to communicate a message, often socio-political, through a coherent thematic line. There are also one or two circuses whose work is inspired either by danger or horror. One of the earliest of these circuses was the French circus Archaos which was founded by Pierrot Bidon in 1984. Jenkins explains that 'in the postmodern times of Archaos, the clowns seem to have been fully ingested by and cross-bred with the mechanical devices that threaten to devour them' (1994: 5). The clowns perform violent and aggressive entrées in which they beat themselves and set fire to props with blow-torches. These clown performances unusually stray towards what Geertz (1993) defines as 'deep play', which is play that involves the player in personal risk, often physical. Once again, the audience is aware of an ambiguity in the framing of the performance. They feel that as the clowning is part of a performance they must be safe, but the performance style is anarchic enough to unsettle that belief. In A Circus Spectacular shown on Channel 4 in 1991, Archaos clowns move into the audience wielding chainsaws. Some members of the audience laugh but others move out of the way. Despite the performance frame, when confronted with a buzzing chainsaw they are not prepared to rely on that frame to keep them safe. Here, the subversive nature of clowning is brought to the fore. The violence of hitting someone in the face with a custard pie pales into insignificance in comparison with flinging a wheelchair-bound midget clown out of his wheelchair and into a garbage can. Chipperfield's Circus of Horrors follows in the Archaos tradition. It was founded in 1995 and had the purpose of 'bringing the circus and theatre crowds kicking and screaming into the 21st Century with a mix of horror and humor' (www. circusofhorrors.co.uk/home.html). The show has established a cult following, making a virtue out of challenging notions of political correctness by, for example, including a topless nun in the 2007 Edinburgh Festival show.

Contemporary Circuses are more varied in their performance style and production values than Traditional Circuses. It is, therefore, harder to generalize. However, taking three circuses as examples, it is possible to highlight the different ways in which audience expectations are generated and realized by different styles of Contemporary Circus. The three circuses discussed here are the Pickles Family Circus (open-air and tenting), Circus Oz (who use touring tents and non-circus static venues), and Cirque du Soleil (who use touring tents, purpose-built static venues and non-circus static venues). There are, of course, many other Contemporary Circuses (for example the fantasy horror circuses mentioned above) but for the purposes of this exploration, these three will suffice to convey something of the variety of emerging styles.

The work of the Pickles Family Circus (founded 1975 and closed in 1993) can be analysed in tandem with the work of the closely related New Pickle Circus (1993–present). The Pickles Family Circus was not tented and its performance area was defined by striped canvas walls, which functioned as a screen in front of which the acts were performed and which curved around the audience to contain them within the performance space. This structure was not roofed and the circus made use of natural rather than theatrical light. The audience sat on wooden bleachers behind a low horseshoe-shaped arrangement of blocks. In this way, the audience space was demarcated from the performance space, but the divider was so low that its clowns could and did move amongst the audience. The nature of the framing, with its light and proximity, also meant that 'in a sense, spectators became performers, too as they watched one another' (Schechter 2001: 13). The stage area was further reinforced by the use of a floor cloth to indicate the ring. The intimacy of this spatial relationship made it possible for the clowns to be heard by the audience (which was far from the case in the American three-ring circuses, where the vastness of the three-ring performance space has always rendered clowns necessarily silent). So from the very start the Pickles clowns (with one or two exceptions) were verbal clowns. In The Pickle Clowns, Schechter comments on the difference between Pickles clowns and those in traditional three-ring circuses:

The Pickles Family Circus performing outside in 1979. *Photo taken by Terry Lorant.*

> They speak audibly from the center ring – their only ring – and they address the audience as well as one another. They are not there to cover the scene changes but to run the circus, more or less, as they replace the traditional ringmaster and introduce and perform the featured acts. (2001: 4)

There are, therefore, a number of key points about the clowns in a Pickles Family Circus show: they are verbal, they are in control, and their acts are featured. All of this was a significant move away from American circus clowning as it had hitherto existed. In many ways the Pickles clowns were closer to European clowns. The original clown trio of **Pisoni**, **Hoyle** and **Irwin** can be likened to the Fratellini. However, the content of Pickles' shows is quite different from Traditional Circuses. The most significant variant factors are the prominence of clown acts and the total avoidance of animal acts. For this is a circus founded and generated by clowns rather than being a circus that hires clowns as one of a number of acts. It is also important to address the social (and to a lesser extent political) imperative driving the performers who founded the Pickles Family Circus. In the San Francisco Bay Area in the mid-1970s, many performers and companies performed in the open-air, in part at least, as a way of searching for new audiences and as a way of distancing themselves from the 'establishment'. Many of the Pickles Family performers had worked with the San Francisco Mime Troupe – a company that was known for creating topical political satires based on the theatre of Brecht and drawing on the performance style of Commedia dell'Arte (Orenstein 1998). The circus, founded by Larry Pisoni, had the notion of co-operation at its heart. This notion of co-operation would be mocked and parodied by the clowns (Schechter 2001: 18) but nonetheless the circus, in the 'alternative' fashion of the time, was founded on the concept of co-operative collaboration and all company members worked together to erect and dismantle the performance space and seating. Pisoni also had the idea of 'staging performances of his new circus for the benefit of socially relevant agencies which he would involve in the entire process of presentation' (Albrecht 1995: 129). In this way, the circus developed with an emphasis on social responsibility rather on financial profitability and its open-air framing and the easy interaction between performers and audience enhanced its accessibility. In fact, the circus established itself as a not-for-profit organization, a route followed, more successfully, by other American circuses like the Big Apple Circus and Circus Flora.

Contemporary Clown Play in the Pickles Family Circus

The Pickles Family Circus show's dedication to the twin notions of collaboration and co-operation was presented to the audience in the form of action rather than as an extraneous message. Their shows traditionally ended with an act called 'the big juggle'. In this, all the performers who could juggle came onto the stage for an Indian-club juggling act. Here, play is used in what Sutton-Smith defines as 'play as identity' because the game with the clubs is used to reinforce 'the identity of the community of players' (1997: 10). It also expresses to its audience the company's central ideology. Co-founder of the Pickles Family Circus, **Peggy Snider,** described it as

> saying to the audience: 'We're really just like you, and we've chosen this path to entertain you...Working together we can help work out this juggling act and a few other things'. (Schechter 2001: 18)

The principles behind the founding and running of the Pickles Family Circus were, therefore, performed as an integral part of the show rather than needing to be added verbally at the end. As was suggested earlier, the Pickles Family Circus show structure developed differently from those of the Traditional Circus, being more co-operative and clown-driven. This difference became more marked as the Circus progressed. Over a period of time the shows took on a more clearly defined theatrical narrative (without ever becoming like Cirque du Soleil). This can illustrated through analysis of two entrées from the early years and examination of one of the longer, more narrative, shows from the 1990's. Given that it has not been possible for the author to see either the original or the new company, this analysis is based on the entrées included in Schechter's book The Pickles Family Clowns (2001).

From the beginning Pickles clown entrées were very different from the clowning seen in other American Circuses. There are many reasons for these differences. Bill Irwin and Larry Pisoni, who originally performed the 'Spaghetti entrée' (not the same as Henri's Spaghetti entrée for Billy Smart's, analysed earlier) did not come from circus families. Pisoni was a juggler and an actor before becoming a clown whilst Irwin completed the clowning programme at the Ringling Bros. Clown College. Neither had worked in traditional circuses and when Pisoni founded the Pickles Family Circus in May 1975, he did so around the notion that clowns were to be central to the structure and content of the show. For the Pickles, clown acts were developed as features of the show rather than as covers for scene changes. This meant that the entrées could develop with clear beginnings, middles and ends rather than having to be adapted in accordance with the time taken to do a set change. Importantly, many of those performing in the early company had been involved with the San Francisco Mime Troupe and so for many of them, performing was also about communicating a political or social message. 'Spaghetti' included references to being wage slaves and to working on commission as well as the more usual clowning fare of being unable to control the props. In Sutton-Smith's terms, the Pickles Clowns are engaging in a 'rhetoric of power', where play is used to encourage the audience to see the flaws in the dominant social and political system which oppresses the subordinate classes through low wages and poor working conditions.

In late 1975, Pisoni and Irwin were joined by Geoff Hoyle and, together, the three of them 'revitalized the art of the entrée...which clowns like the trio of Albert, Paul and François Fratellini popularized at Cirque Medrano in Paris half a century earlier' (Schechter 2001: 3). Together, the three Pickles clowns developed an entrée known as 'The Three Musicians', which demonstrates the importance of physical control in clowning. The earlier comparison between the Pisoni, Hoyle, Irwin trio and the Fratellini brothers was initially made in terms of the number of clowns in each act but, more significantly, the style of playing developed by the three Pickles clowns was also much closer to the playing style of the European circuses than to the American three-ring extravaganza. This was probably as a result of the performance frame within which the Pickles clowns performed. Their ring was much closer to the European single ring circus convention, although they played to much smaller and more intimate audiences. Geoff Hoyle articulates the similarity to the Fratellini by describing Bill Irwin as 'the contre-auguste, like Albert Fratellini, completely incompetent, unable to do anything, but extremely anxious' (Schechter 2001: 74). In the Pickles entrée, the three clowns enter together in a carefully choreographed manner. The body of the act is taken up with traditional clown ineptitude as the three clowns attempt to sit on three chairs in order to play their instruments. Two of the chairs get broken, the clowns somersault off the third chair and finally manage to play three or four bars of music, thus successfully completing their exploit. This is closer to the European tradition of clowning in that there is no social or political message underlying the act. It relies instead on a demonstration of skill and timing as the clowns tumble over each other and the furniture as they attempt to set up to play. True to the usual Pickles Family Circus clown style, the three clowns talked to the audience (in Italian accents – an echo of earlier clown acts in which clowns adopted or emphasized foreign accents for comic effect) as they carried out the physical routine of the act.

Another important feature of The Pickles Family Circus was the inclusion of female clowns. In the 1989/1990 season **Joan Mankin (Queenie)** and **Diane Wasnak (Pino)** clowned together. According to Schechter, they were 'the only female clown duo featured in the world of circus at that time' (2001: 100). Certainly there had been occasional female clowns in the Traditional Circus (such as Annie Fratellini) but Queenie and Pino appear to have been the first significant female duo, clowning together in clown entrées in 1989, and as part of the longer more narrative show, *La La Luna Sea,* in 1990. One entrée involved Queenie being left in charge of a baby carriage containing the baby from hell (Pino). As part of the entrée, Queenie tries to balance the conflicting demands of attempting to introduce the show with trying to take care of the baby.

Given the social and political content of other Pickles entrées, this can be seen as a feminist comment on the need for women to balance the demands of home and work. Eventually the carriage tips over and the baby escapes and has to be chased through the audience. This entrée relies on what Sutton-Smith identifies as 'frivolous play'. Here, the seeming spontaneity of the play could be regarded as an example of pointless play but, in typical Pickles style, the entrée both highlights play and a social message about the role of women. The nature of the play, then, is finely balanced between 'frivolous play' and 'play as power'. However, not all the Pino and Queenie routines were so gynocentric. Schechter's The Pickles Clowns contains an entrée called 'Saxophones', which is a very traditional clown act with jazz music. Queenie comes on with a saxophone and wants to play with the band. After an exchange with the bandmaster (full of malapropisms on Queenie's part), she plays. Pino enters a number of times (first with an accordion, then a violin and then a sousaphone) and each time she is sent packing by Queenie. Finally Pino enters with a saxophone and is allowed to play but her saxophone has to be jump-started from Queenie's (a gag relying on the age-old concepts of object status interaction and incongruity). Pino and Queenie play a duet until they are joined by Larry Pisoni in a gorilla suit, also playing a saxophone, and so the duet becomes a trio. The core material of the act is not original. Many clown acts over the years have revolved around the clown's seeming inability to play a musical instrument before revealing a high level of skill as part of the pay-off. The audience of a Traditional Circus would be used to seeing such an entrée performed by men, whereas here it is performed by two women. Queenie appears to aspire to the high status of a whiteface clown in her put-downs of Pino, although Queenie herself is repeatedly corrected by the bandleader for the words she muddles. Interestingly, in the hands of women the act becomes more about collaboration than about status, as is demonstrated by the resolution of the act where Pino's saxophone is jump-started from Queenie's. The arrival of Larry Pisoni in the gorilla suit confirms the idea of tolerance and inclusivity. In the Pickles Family Circus, skill is what counts, not gender or even species. Once again play is used to communicate their view of how society should be.

In 1990 Wasnak and Mankin were central to the longer show La La Luna Sea. This was not the Pickles first attempt at a narrative show (Café des Artistes came earlier in 1988) but it was the first which truly integrated the clowns and made their actions central to the scenario. In trying to integrate clowns into a longer narrative, the Pickles Family Circus struggled to retain the anarchism and energy of the clowns once they became an element of a much greater whole. Mankin herself suggested that 'the best clowning comes when you don't have to follow a line. You can go where you want to go...and not have to be faithful to a narrative' (Schechter 2001: 28). It is in the nature of clowns to be anarchic. In Traditional Circus the content of an entrée may well be carefully plotted but it rarely has to connect narratively with anything beyond itself. As Contemporary Circus began to theatricalize circus and develop longer shows bound by a single artistic vision, addressing a narrative or thematic line, the clowns found themselves marginalized. Even circuses like the Pickles Family Circus, which was described by Mankin as 'clown sensitive circus...a "clown-love zone"' (2001: 106), struggled with integrating the longer, narrative clown entrées.

The motivation of the founders of the Australian Circus Oz was performative rather than social. They focused on creating a new kind of circus in which clowns appeared but in which they were not as central as the clowns in the Pickles Family Circus. The Circus Oz website credits them with being the 'first contemporary circus in a now significant international industry' (www.circusoz. com). However, their founding date of 1977 (when two previously successful circuses, Soapbox Circus and the New Circus merged) means that the Pickles Family Circus was two years ahead of them. The two companies' aims in contemporizing circus were, however, very different. As has already been seen, the Pickles Family Circus was founded around the twin notions of co-operation and clowning. For Circus Oz the impetus was 'to make a new sort of show that a contemporary audience could relate to, adding elements of rock'n'roll, popular theatre, social comment and satire' (www.circusoz.com). It is for this reason that Circus Oz is best defined as an 'Updated Circus' as many of its performance ideals are very close to those of Traditional Circus but the style of presentation is more overtly theatrical. The Circus Oz website identifies the original Circus Oz philosophy as having the following principles: 'collective ownership and creation, gender equity, a uniquely Australian signature and team-work' (www.circusoz.com). While there is an echo of the collaborative approach of the Pickles Circus, Circus Oz has had a much greater degree of commercial success, performing in twenty six different countries to over two million people. Circus Oz also claims an interest in what it identifies as 'social justice' but its approach to social issues varies from the community-based approach taken by the Pickles Family Circus. Nevertheless, Circus Oz performs benefits, gives away tickets and collects donations for charity at the end of its performances, raising $225,000 since June 2002 in donations to support refugees and asylum seekers (www.circusoz.com).

Circus Oz do own and perform in a Big Top but they also visit static venues – for example, in the United Kingdom they have performed in the Royal Festival Hall (better known for classical music concerts) and in the United States they have performed on 42nd Street. For the audience a conflict of expectations is immediately induced by this collision of frames. The venue suggests one set of expectations and the notion of circus sets up another. Part of the interest for the audience lies in seeing how this space can be adapted for circus performance. There is nothing in the way of theatrical set design. Instead the stage contains functional rigging, which allows the various acts to take place in the way that they might in a Big Top. The potential for lighting and sound is, however, extensively exploited. Some elements of Traditional Circus performance take on a new resonance when performed in this setting. The show, as performed in London in 2004, opened with a display of fire. In a Big Top this would be impressive but in a theatre building or concert hall it takes on an anarchic and more threatening quality as the audience members are likely to feel, however erroneously, that the level of risk is higher.

Contemporary Clown Play in Circus Oz
During the time that the audience was arriving for the Circus Oz performance at the Royal Festival Hall (September 2004), two clowns performed the equivalent of Traditional Circus clown run-ins. These established to the audience that, while the performance was taking place in a theatre building, the usual circus rules of the clowns crossing the audience/performer boundary would be observed. The first clown, dressed in white three-quarter-length baggy trousers, white oversize boots and a small hat, dusted the drum-kit which stood on stage. The costume of the clown was a contemporary version of the badly fitting clothes of the Auguste but without the traditional face make-up or wild hair. This reference to Traditional Circus, but

up-dated or adapted, is typical of the Circus Oz approach to the creation of circus performance. Their clowns are used in the ways clowns are used in Traditional Circuses but look slightly different. The clown acts are incorporated into the Circus Oz structure in much the same way as in Traditional Circus. As a result of the jarring of frames, the use of fire in the theatre, as with the clowns mingling with the audience, seems much more threatening in a theatre building than it would have been in a circus ring. The implication is that Circus Oz is indeed innovatory and daring. However, consideration of the structure of the show reveals how close it is to that of the Traditional Circus structure of clown run-ins, opening parade, discrete acts, and grand finale. The content of the acts is very traditional (juggling, clowns, contortion, pole acts); the most innovatory inclusion is a cycle act but such acts have featured in Traditional Circuses for years (the Amsterdam State Circus used a cycle act in 1999 and Uncle Sam's American Circus used a motorcycle act in 2004). Where Circus Oz attempts to be contemporary, for example by including a social message in a clown act, the didacticism overweighs the entertainment value of the act, as will be seen in the analysis of the 'World Scout Entrée'.

World Scout Entrée

This entrée revolves around a character introduced as Matthew who is trying to get his Scout's achievement badge for world peace. The clowns come on to help him and encourage the whole of the third row of the stalls to go up onto the stage to help Matthew too. One small boy is taken to one side by one of the performers and is given a world peace badge to hold. The clowns then help arrange the audience members to create lines on stage which are described as 'the border guards of brutality' and the 'razor wire fence of repression'. The clowns then help load Matthew into the 'humanitarian cannon'. The small boy is asked if he will be able to catch the boy scout when he is fired from the cannon. The clowns then organize what they call the 'crash mat of human kindness'. The small boy helps to hold it. One of the clowns mimes what will happen when the cannon is fired. It is clear the crash mat is too small. (At this point the small boy looked scared). The clowns bring on a bigger crash mat and other audience members help to hold it. There is a very long drum roll. At this point the MC began to adlib about the United Nations having been brought in. [It appeared at this point that something had gone wrong with the cannon mechanism]. Eventually the scout is fired out and somersaults onto the crash mat. The scout is awarded his world peace badge and the MC offers a commentary about how only the co-operation of those individuals on stage made it possible.

This entrée is a clear example of a more contemporary, social message driven act. Such humour as is created is overwhelmed by the MC (Circus Oz's version of a ringmaster) offering a running commentary on what the clowns are doing. The description of the evils of the world which can be overcome by a humanitarian cannon and a crash mat of human kindness seems to offer the potential for a satirical poke at political correctness and woolly-minded liberalism, but the sketch is offered in all seriousness. This act is a potentially interesting combination of the human cannon and the clowns. The clowns feature because of their already-established freedom to move off the stage and into the audience. Additionally, their ability to mime and to interact with the audience and the objects being used increases the potential for humour. Whilst the message of the need for humanity and co-operation is a worthy one, the overt didacticism of the act makes the whole thing feel laboured. The intellectualism of this sketch is a prime example of Circus Oz's uneasy mix of the traditional (superficially modernized) and the sanctimoniously message-laden, with Circus Oz not trusting its audience to understand the message without explanation. It is an indication of how play as means of establishing a sense of community identity has to be handled with care. When adults or children play together, they quickly establish a sense of community; play becomes a means of bonding. However in this instance, the playfulness of the clowns is not enough to draw the audience into a sense of play. The worthiness of the message outweighs the potential fun of play. There are, indeed, instances in which profound meaning can be communicated through play without the need for pseudo-intellectual commentary, examples of which will be explored later.

Elsewhere in the show the clowns are used exactly as they would have been in Traditional Circus to cover the change-overs between acts requiring different kinds of rigging or stage apparatus. They also interact entertainingly with a cockatoo-themed trapeze act in the second half of the show which involves more traditional clown humour when the fat cockatoo relieves himself on the little one below him. Despite the superficially contemporary feel of Circus Oz, the structure of the show remains essentially that of Traditional Circus. However Circus Oz cannot resist the urge to append a social message to the whole show, which ends with an announcement dedicating the show to diversity, tolerance and human kindness.

Whilst Circus Oz has established a reputation for anarchic, Contemporary Circus, Cirque du Soleil has established a reputation of a rather different character. Cirque du Soleil was founded in 1984, significantly later than the other circuses considered here. Its founder, the Canadian Guy Laliberté, had been interested in circus performance since his teenage years, spending a year in Europe when he was eighteen, earning a living as a street performer. In 1982 Laliberté secured funding for a festival of street performance under the name *La Fête Foraine*. In order to find performers for the festivals, which ran in 1982, 1983 and 1984, Laliberté turned to Guy Caron (the two had been friends for years) who was actively involved with the National Circus School based in Montreal. Babinski (2004) gives a relatively prosaic account of Laliberté's journey towards Cirque du Soleil in *Cirque du Soleil: 20 years under the sun*. The Cirque du Soleil website puts a more mythical gloss on the same series of events, describing the connection between La Fête Foraine and Cirque du Soleil as follows:

> This talented group of young Quebec street entertainers had come together under a lucky star. Although a full two years pass before Cirque du Soleil as we know it today is created, its founders say that it was at that mystic moment in Baie Saint-Paul in 1982 that Cirque du Soleil was conceived. (www.cirquedusoleil.com)

Cirque du Soleil markets a myth of the creation of circus, neatly avoiding any reference to Laliberté's equally strong intention to make the Circus commercially successful.

> Guy Laliberté...felt that business and art should work together as equal partners. His vision prevailed then and continues today. That collaboration between what are often antagonistic forces distinguishes Cirque du Soleil from other creations in the New American Circus. And it is that difference that accounts for the organization's amazingly robust financial health. (Albrecht 1995: 144)

Replication of shows lies at the heart of Cirque du Soleil's financial success and allows the company to maximize its investment in the creation of any single show. For example, in August 2008 Cirque du Soleil had seventeen shows in performance (giving them coverage in Europe, North America, South America and South East Asia). Of all the circuses analysed in this chapter, Cirque du Soleil has the strongest theatrically influenced performance style. Laliberté's vision for the kind of circus Cirque du Soleil was to become was significantly different from that pursued by either Pisoni or the founders of Circus Oz. What Laliberté wanted to create was circus fused with the spectacle of theatre. He wanted to create 'the circus of tomorrow, the circus of the future' (Albrecht 1995: 96). The Cirque du Soleil website claims that Cirque 'creates a new theatricality and adopts a vision whereby rules exist only to be broken' (www.cirquedusoleil.com).

This vision begins with the concept of the show and is fostered and strengthened as it is shaped by the design team (set, costume, and lighting) and by the choreographer and artistic director. Many of these creative roles have been held by the same individuals over the years, reinforcing the notion of a Cirque du Soleil style. The negative impact of Cirque du Soleil's vision of itself as creating a new kind of theatricality is that the shows become pretentious, imbued with a meaning which Cirque du Soleil claims in its marketing of the show but which is rarely discernible to the audience. In over-theatricalizing, Cirque du Soleil seems to have lost sight of one of the potential purposes of *theatrical* performance; to communicate meaning.

Cirque du Soleil performs both in its own *Grand Chapiteau* (Big Top) and in pre-existing static venues (some of which have been built to their specifications, for example the performance space at Disneyworld, Florida). The audience's initial reaction to a tenting show by Cirque du Soleil is likely to have many similarities with those generated by a Traditional Circus. The brightly coloured Big Top can be seen from some distance. However, once inside the tent, it is clear that the production values and attention to customer comfort are of a very different order.

When Cirque du Soleil toured *Quidam* in 2001, the outer tent took the form of a modern bar area. The parallel is to theatre bars rather than to Traditional Circus refreshment areas. There are variations in the seating arrangements with the Grand Chapiteau. The audience is not seated in a circle but around a number of intersecting circus rings. The performance area is much larger than that available in Traditional Circuses and the level of technical support in terms of lighting and sound is more advanced. Design is an important element of the performance for Cirque du Soleil. Costumes, including make-up and head-dresses, are designed to reflect the thematic content of the show in much the same way as designers work in the theatre. Lighting effects are very important and attention is also paid to the design of the set, but many of these elements are governed by necessity in order for sequences of acts to be performed quickly and with maximum impact. For example, the fast track (an X-shaped arrangement of trampe just below floor level) must be built into the set in order to allow for the impressive rou. acrobats criss-crossing the stage at speed. In keeping with the heightened theatricality, i. also became part of the Cirque du Soleil way of working that changes to the set are effected by the performers as an integral part of the performance.

Cirque du Soleil began developing narrative circus in Canada at around the same time as the Pickles Family Circus in America similarly struggled. Some might argue, however, that Cirque du Soleil has never fully integrated clowning into its shows, but entrées worthy of analysis are to be found in their show *Alegría*.

Contemporary Clown Play in Cirque du Soleil

Given Cirque's ethos of creating a theatrically unified show, the clown entrées in *Alegría* must be interpreted as part of an ongoing narrative. This involvement with the narrative reduces the opportunity for play. The clown cannot make his own rules but must fit within the structure dictated by the company. According to Cirque du Soleil's website, *Alegría* is a show about

> ...a mood, a state of mind. The themes of the show, whose name means 'jubilation' in Spanish, are many. Power and the handing down of power over time, the evolution of ancient monarchies to modern democracies, old age, youth – it is against this backdrop that the characters of *Alegría* play out their lives. (www.cirquedusoleil.com/Alegría)

Interestingly, the clowns appear to sit outside the mainframe of the narrative, such as it is. According to the website, the different acts have a different signification as representatives of elements of society. However, the clowns reflect not a social group but 'the eternal spirit of mankind, the clowns are witnesses to the passing of centuries, the social commentators of the world of *Alegría*.' (www.cirquedusoleil.com). In this way the clowns represent the universal element of human existence. Thus in the entrée 'Storm' (analysed below), the clown on his journey epitomizes the sorrow humans feel on parting; the journey represents the journey of life and the battle against the elements signifies the battle each of us experiences during that journey. In terms of the costuming of *Alegría*, the clowns' difference is highlighted. Other groupings within the show have their unity reinforced by the similarity of their masks and costumes. The main groups are the Old Birds, the Bronx and the Angels.

Whilst the Old Birds wear different colours, the similarity of mask shape (reminiscent of Pantalone in Commedia dell'Arte) and the lines of the costumes signal a coherent grouping with the gaudy colouring being indicative of their wealthy aristocratic origins. The Bronx costumes are identical, their unity conveying power while the combination of leather and metal signifies strength. The Angels also wear identical costumes, the colours and textures of which work against conventional expectations of angels. In line with the usual cultural codes of western society, theatrical and artistic depictions of angels portray them in white, symbolizing purity. Angelic costumes are often diaphanous and may be accompanied by wings or haloes.

The White Angels are the graceful guardians of *Alegría*. Agile, confident, and daring, the Angels are the youth of tomorrow who have alighted in the palace from the heavens. (www.cirquedusoleil.com)

The *Alegría* designs, created by Dominique Lemieux, put the Angels in grey (not white) costumes with cobweb motifs. The use of curly-haired wigs and red make-up on the noses appears to align the Angels with the clown tradition. As a result, it is difficult to read the semiotic of these costumes. Lemieux claims that *Alegría* is 'the force inside every individual that allows them to resist corruption. *Alegría*'s a path, like a scream that gives us the strength to keep living no matter what happens to us' (cited in Babinski 2004: 172). The mystical, philosophical quality of Lemieux's comments is in line with the Cirque du Soleil company style. It appears to present us with the essence of what it means to be human, but the true meaning of the piece disappears under the weight of such pronouncements about its intended message. For example, the whole show is described as being 'a show about both the abuse of power and the weight of powerlessness, and their opposite – the possibility of liberation.' (Babinski 2004: 170). It is difficult to see how such a message can be conveyed by non-narrative acts such as contortion, the aerial high bar and the Russian bars. It is possible to see that such a message might, however, be conveyed by clown entrées and by the interaction between the clowns and the Fool character who acts as a ringmaster.

Indeed, the individualized costumes of each of the clowns lend themselves more readily to semiotic interpretation, linked more closely as they are to recognizable conventions. In this way each of them is clearly established as a clown but their individuality is not compromised, which seems significant in the light of the website's assertion that the clowns are able to resist social transformation. Two of the clowns wear red noses but the modern convention means that the appearance of the nose indicates clown rather than specifically an Auguste. On the DVD and in the live show, all three clowns wear some form of make-up: one wears almost complete whiteface, a second highlights the eyelids in white and the cheeks in red whilst the third highlights the eyes and mouth. The image below shows two of the clowns. The clown on the left closely follows the traditional August costuming. His orange dungarees and his shoes are both over-sized. Similarly his make-up is traditional Auguste combined with a red nose and a wig of shaggy red hair. The only difference is that the lower half of his face is blackened (emulating the traditional tramp make-up) but the black is much more solid than would have been seen on clowns like Emmett Kelly and Otto Griebling. This is an example of Cirque du Soleil nodding towards circus traditions but not entirely absorbing them. The clown on the right is harder to define. The long purple coat and red nose suggest Auguste but the highly stylized make-up on a solid white base suggests Whiteface.

These clowns, therefore, can be seen to base their make-up on the old traditions but with contemporary variations. The same is true of their costumes, all of which are wrongly sized in some way. Although there is a suggestion of Auguste in this mis-sizing, the interaction of the clowns does not suggest the Whiteface, Auguste and Counter-Auguste of other clown trios such as the Fratellini (or the Pickles clowns mentioned earlier). Even when, on the DVD,

Alegría – Cirque du Soleil Clowns: Yuri Medvedev and Marcos De Oliveira Casuo Royal Albert Hall – London. *Photo taken by Nigel Norrington.*

all three Cirque du Soleil clowns are on stage together in the entrée entitled 'Clown with Rope', it is not possible to distinguish traditional roles very easily. The clown entrées represent an uneasy mix of Traditional Circus entrées and mime-clowning within the recent tradition of theatre clowning.

The reasons for this lie in the genesis of the clown acts in *Alegría*. One entrée which can be analysed is 'Storm' which was developed and performed by Slava Polunin.

Clown Entrée – Storm

The lighting and music changes from the previous act. A blue backdrop flies in with a circular hole which could represent the moon. A clown enters, unrolls a miniature train track in a curve around the stage and exits. A second clown enters wearing a very baggy grey suit and a tie which reaches to the ground. He has a shock of white-blond hair and a small red nose. His face make up is largely white except for a section of his right cheek and jaw, which is left flesh-coloured. He carries a large suitcase, and follows the train track. He puts the suitcase down and opens it. Two small balloons escape. He takes out a coat and drags it across the stage. As he hangs the coat on a hanger on a ladder near the backdrop, a small furry object emerges from the coat and trembles on the stage. He retrieves it and puts it in the case. He takes out a hat, brushes dust off it and takes it to the coat. Together with the coat this gives the appearance of a person. The clown puts one of his arms into the sleeve of the coat as he begins to brush the dust off the coat. The coat comes to life. The clown is scared but is drawn into being stroked by the 'coat person'. They embrace as in parting. The 'coat person' slips a letter into the clown's pocket. The train blows its whistle. The clown is torn between staying and leaving but picks up the case and walks off. Steam has been coming through the hole in the backdrop. The clown rushes back on stage carrying a case which emits steam like a train and he is wearing a tall hat which also emits steam. He stops and puts the case down in front of the backdrop. Then using the case as a seat, he sits. He pulls his hanky out of his pocket. The letter falls out. He reads it then tears it into small pieces. He holds his hand above his head and drops the pieces like snowflakes. More snow falls from the above. The music changes. He sits alone as the snow falls harder and harder. He exits and the backdrop swings round and is white. Another clown enters, pulling behind him a string of little houses which he places against the snowy backdrop. The lead clown re-enters and stands in the snow. Wind sound effects begin. Wind blows the backdrop and the clown. He fights the elements. The music changes again and is much more agitated in mood. A bright white light shines out at the audience. Suddenly it goes black.

'Storm' has a discrete narrative which appears to be about the loneliness of man as he journeys through life. The very distinctiveness of the clown's costume marks him out as an individual rather than as part of a social group. Within the entrée he enacts a parting that implies the heartbreak of leaving someone whom you love. The entrée has at its centre an illogicality which the audience accepts. We realize that the coat person is in fact only an extension of the clown but the spectacle of the parting is so convincing that we accept the existence of two people where we know there is only one. The game of the clown playing two parts is an example of Sutton-Smith's 'play as imaginary'. The 'rhetoric of the imaginary' identifies a connection between art (represented here by the clown's performance) and play (the game of animating the coat). Play here is applied as a metaphor for the pain of parting. The notion of heartbreak (a universal human experience) is heightened by the tearing of the letter into tiny flakes. At this point the spectacle takes over. As further snow falls from above, the image of the clown alone against the elements is a powerful one. His vulnerability is highlighted by the sound effects of wind, by the bright light and by the power of the wind against which he struggles.

The impact of a mimed entrée designed, as it was, for performance in a theatre is lessened when performed in venues the size of those favoured by Cirque du Soleil. Its Grand Chapiteau for Alegría seats 2,500 and when Cirque du Soleil performed at the Royal Albert Hall the audience capacity was, according to the Royal Albert Hall Box Office, between 5,000 and 5,500. In a performance venue of this size the nuance of mimed gesture is lost and it is on such nuances that modern clown-mime relies in order to connect with the audience. Watching the show from the upper dress circle is a little like watching something through the wrong end of a telescope; audience members this high up are aware of the broad shape of the entrée but remain untouched by it. When Slava's Snowshow, which ends with a climactic version of 'Storm', was performed at the Piccadilly Theatre (one of the largest in the West End), it was seen by a maximum audience of 1,400. Audience members sitting in the dress circle stared straight into the white light from back-stage and could feel the disturbance created by the wind machine. As the entrée is about man's struggle to survive, it is undoubtedly more effective when the audience experiences its physical impact rather than just observing it. In observing the clown, rather than engaging with him, the central element of clowning, complicité, is lost.

The very isolation of the clown acts in Alegría – they connect only tangentially with the rest of the show (in a candle's echo of fire and in a clown's tangling with the flying man's ropes) – diminishes their connection with the thematic content of the show. According to the contemporary female clown, De Castro, this separation arises as a result of Cirque du Soleil's attitude to clowns, whom they believe cannot be understudied. In terms of ensuring that the show can continue when a clown is ill, they therefore prefer that the clown's act is a detachable element which can simply be dropped (interview with the author October 2006). As a result, it is impossible for the clowns to fulfil the role claimed for them on the Cirque du Soleil website. They do not appear to be witnesses to the passing centuries and they cannot be 'Alegría's social commentators'. That role could more easily be filled by any of the characters who are on stage while other acts are performed. The Old Birds are witness to far more of Alegría than the clowns are. Cirque du Soleil seems to have encountered the same difficulty as the Pickles Family Circus in integrating the clowns into the narrative line of the show. In order for the clowns to fit, their entrées have to take on a pseudo-philosophical rather than anarchic or transgressive tone as they attempt to suit the narrative and thematic thrust of the show. However, the entrées new in 2006 do not contribute to that thematic content. If anything, they are further removed from the show and demonstrate a similarity to traditional clown entrées, suggesting that Cirque du Soleil is no closer to resolving its difficulties with integrating clown entrées. This lack of clown integration is not peculiar to Alegría. In Cirque du Soleil's La Nouba, the 'Cowboy Clowns' entrée, featuring a shoot-out between a cowboy and a Native American, has little connection with what precedes or succeeds it.

The 2006 version of Alegría demonstrates how Cirque du Soleil's shows develop after their initial creation and reinforces the notion that the company has decided that clowns should not be integrated into the narrative. In 2006 there are three new clown entrées to consider: one which involves clowns pretending to be on a motorbike, another which involves a game of paper airplanes and one which involves parodying an earlier Russian bars[1] act. The entrée based around the motorbike is extremely simple, relying mainly on the interaction of the clown who is pretending to be riding a motorbike and the timing of the motorbike sound effect. The entrée does not appear to have any thematic connection to the content of the show. The other clown, who does not have a motorbike, begins a new game of playing with paper planes, leading into a new entrée. This was the most successful sequence of clowning in the show because its much larger performance style allowed it to communicate more effectively with the huge audience. Although clearly heavily influenced by traditional clown entrées, it also appears to be influenced by what John Wright defines as 'finding the game'. This game involves making larger and larger planes, with some of them being flown out into the audience. The strongest sense both of play and of connection between the clowns and their audience occurred when an audience member managed to launch a plane back onto the stage. The Russian bar parody works in a similar way to an earlier parody of the fire act. In the Russian bar parody, the clowns have bars like the real gymnasts. They use these bars to perform a version of the act which sees them jumping over the bars whilst they are on the floor. They do not take any of the risks take in the acrobatic act. Similarly in the older fire parody, the clown enters as the preceding fire-knife dance act exits. The clown is carrying a candle. He waves the candle around, looking to the audience to elicit a response. The murmurs on the DVD indicate an audience response of sympathy and pity which was mirrored in the live performance. He mimes attempting to put the candle flame in his mouth but he is too scared. He licks his fingers and puts out the flame. He winces dramatically in pain and is shooed off the stage by the Fool character. This brief performance is interestingly fraught with contradictions. Its element of parody of the previous act harks back to Traditional Circus (despite its theatricality and spectacle, Cirque du Soleil does not deviate from the Traditional Circus structure) but the silent mime style is closely connected with modern theatre clowning, as was demonstrated earlier in the analysis of the 'Storm' entrée, which was performed by the same clown.

The different styles of Contemporary Circus handle clowns and their place in the structure of the show in different ways. Clearly the Pickles Family Circus has made clowns a central feature but they have struggled to develop longer shows that are useful vehicles for the clowns (as was demonstrated in the analysis of *La La Luna Sea*). Circus Oz's response to clowning demonstrates divisions even within one show. The clown entrée that opens the show is a traditional clowning entrée but the 'World Scout' entrée that appears later in the show is a prime example of how humour and anarchy can be crushed by good intentions and political correctness. The clown entrée with a message does not work unless the entrée grows out of the message, or offers an exploration of a concept. In Cirque du Soleil, more than in any other Contemporary Circus, clowns have been marginalized. They have been deprived of their run-ins and carpet clowning, as the change-overs between acts have become more technically slick. Clown entrée slots appear in the structure of a Cirque du Soleil show as they might have done in a Traditional Circus show but they no longer have to dispel the audience's tension after a terrifying act – in part because all Cirque's performers are wired. Cirque du Soleil may have made circus an international money-spinner but in doing so they have lost the humorous heart of circus, the link with the audience created by the clowns' playing and parody, in favour of meaningless spectacle which purports to have meaning.

Unfortunately, therefore, circus clowning appears to be in decline. Many of the taboos and codes of behaviour which clowns transgressed, to the great pleasure of the audience in pre-second world war society, are not as funny today because the taboos are less relevant to late twentieth and early twenty first century society. For example, a society that has watched *The Young Ones* and *Bottom* is unlikely to be very amused by the relatively innocent scatological and violent transgression found in circus acts. The transgression of clowns beating each other up or hitting each other over the head with frying pans is simply less funny in a society which is exposed daily to images of violence, courtesy of the television news. Equally, clown entrées no longer relieve the tension created by the presence of potentially dangerous wild animals. It appears that the future of clowning lies not in the circus (whether it is performing in a Big Top or a theatre building) but in the greater subtlety to be found by clown performers working as discrete acts who are able to entertain an audience for a full evening.

Note

1. Flexible poles, supported on the shoulder, on which acrobatic acts are performed.

3

Clowns on Stage

This together with the following chapter explores the nature of clown performance in theatrical settings. In order to do this, some consideration of the frame in which theatrical clowning takes place is necessary. In *Clown Shows* and *Clown Theatre*, as defined earlier, the nature of clown performance and the audience's reception of such performance are heavily influenced by the structure of the performance space and the prior conventions attached to its use.

The Frame

Performance in a conventional Big Top in Europe demands that the clown performs in a space almost equivalent to that of Theatre in the Round. The only point at which the audience does not surround the clown(s) is the opening from which they make their entrance. Such an audience configuration makes significant demands on the clown(s) to engage the audience either by working close to the entrance so that the whole audience can see the act in a manner akin to end-stage performance or, alternatively (and more commonly), moving to the centre of the ring but establishing contact with all elements of the audience by moving around the ring and using looks and comments to draw it into the action. It has been shown that circus clowns are heavily reliant on their ability to draw the audience into a relationship with them. The freedom experienced by the clown in the Big Top ring allows for a range of possible contacts with the audience, as described earlier. In the theatre it is likely that this spatial relationship will be different, creating both new opportunities and new challenges for the clown. Whilst there are theatres where in-the-round performance can be staged, many of the clown performances that have occurred in the United Kingdom since the early 1990s have taken place in theatres where the clown performs end on to his/her audience. In order to analyse these challenges and opportunities, a number of performances will be considered, including *Slava's Snowshow* at The Piccadilly Theatre (1999), The Hackney Empire (2004) and The Lowry (2006), Les Witloof (2004), Nola Rae (2005) and Nani & Ingimarsson (2004) at the Purcell Room in the South Bank Centre, Mimirichi (2005) at the Riverside Studios, Tricicle (from DVD), and Teatr Licedei at the Edinburgh Fringe Festival (2006).

Such performance venues allow for the possibility of a set (permanent or changing) and elaborate lighting that highlights the clown(s) against the backdrop. In terms of framing, the relationship between the clown and the audience is also altered, inevitably, by the shift in audience expectation. In the circus, the audience expects the clowns to invade the audience space. This is, in effect, part of the contract you enter into as a member of a circus audience. However, audience expectations in the theatre are different. The range of theatrical genres and styles current in the twenty-first century means that it is no longer possible to claim that the audience expects the actors to remain on the stage whilst they themselves remain safe in the auditorium. Many contemporary companies work in site-specific or reality-challenging ways (Station House Opera, for example). It is true, though, that some venues, particularly mainstream West End theatres, do not have a reputation for presenting shows which are likely to involve the performers having direct physical contact with their audience.

As Skidmore (2002) following De Toro (1995) identifies when writing about Cirque du Soleil, particular codes exist which indicate to the audience what they may be about to witness. Thus the Big Top delineates a space in which a particular kind of performance occurs; a space where red noses and trapezes might be expected. De Toro identifies this as a *general convention*. There exists a parallel convention for theatre – when attending a show in a building which describes itself as a theatre, the spectator realizes that he or she is 'watching an artifice, which is distinct from the outside or real world' (Skidmore 2002: n. pag.) and will have certain expectations about how such a show might proceed. In modern theatre clowning these two general conventions collide, creating a conflicting expectation as to which performance convention will dominate: that of the circus or that of the theatre. In many instances it does not seem that the theatre buildings with their high stages and proscenium arches make it easy for the clown to leave the stage (The Piccadilly and The Hackney Empire). However, this does not mean that the clowns will not find a way. Thus a tension is set up in which the audience can never be sure exactly what to expect. Some clowns performing in the theatre leave the stage (Slava, Nola Rae, Mimirichi) whilst others (Nani and Ingimarrson and Les Witloof) remain on the stage. Equally, in the circus there is a tradition of bringing audience members into the ring to be part of the act. This can also occur in theatre clowning; Mimirichi's show *Paperworld* breaks down the conventions of actor space and audience space to the extent that it is difficult to tell where each begins and ends as the stage is invaded by children during a paper snowball fight and the clowns invade the audience's territory on a number of occasions. In Teatr Licedei's *Semianyki,* one audience member is victimized throughout the performance and is brought onto the stage; at another point in the show the clowns engage the audience in a pillow fight by coming off the stage with their pillows to attack people and be attacked by them. In *Exit Napoleon Pursued by Rabbits,* Nola Rae enters through the auditorium and, later, brings a member of the audience onto the stage. In this way, the general conventions of circus and theatre are brought into conflict.

There are also *particular codes* (De Toro 1995). For example, a circus audience has some prior knowledge of a how a clown might behave. The red nose, mis-fitting costume and anarchic performance style are expected. One of the difficulties of approaching modern theatre clowning is that it is not sufficiently widely known to have established its own *particular code*. Audience members watching modern theatre clown performances, therefore, have to rely on *unique conventions* (De Toro 1995) which arise out of what occurs during a specific performance. This encourages a more active form of spectatorship in which the audience member relies on what Skidmore identifies as 'cultural baggage or amassed knowledge' (2002: n. pag.) to help in the interpretation of the *particular* codes of a performance.

One early clown who made the transition from circus to theatre, blurring conventions as he went, was Adrien Wettach, later famous as Grock. His two autobiographies *Life's a Lark* (1931) and *Grock, King of Clowns* (1957) detail his early life in Switzerland. Travelling circuses came to the region in which he lived and the young boy was fired with an enthusiasm for circus performance, though not necessarily for clowning. As a child, he trained himself in acrobatics and in playing a range of musical instruments. Both of these skills were utilized in his clown entrées in later life. Adrien Wettach became Grock in 1903 when he formed a clown partnership with **Brick** (whose previous partner had worked under the name **Brock**). For Grock this was one of a number of partnerships formed with other circus clowns. Of relevance here, however, is not Grock's experience in circus but his decision to move, for a period of his life, into clowning on the theatre stage. Over the years, Grock's entrée had been developed and extended to the point where it ran for seventy five minutes. This was, of course, far too long to be accommodated by any circus and, consequently, Grock had to leave the circus and reframed his work within a theatrical setting. In doing so he necessarily began to change his audience's expectations. The theatrical frame could more comfortably accommodate the length of Grock's entrée. Another change which resulted from this move into theatre venues was that Grock performed on stage, further away from his audience. Whilst the transition meant that his extended entrée could be the focus of the evening, performing at the Palace Theatre, London in 1911 and 1913 and at the Empire in 1914 (see Willson Disher, 1925 for a fuller account), it also meant that he had to work harder to establish a sense of *complicité* with his audience. With the freedom of time Grock could perform the whole of his extended entrée,which included tricks that had been developed over the years, including moving a piano to a piano stool, juggling musical instruments and jumping over and into a chair. Grock revitalized the idea of theatre clowning, which had foundered from the mid-nineteenth century, and was also responsible for reducing the Auguste's reliance on his Whiteface partner.

> While Grock perfected the entrée form, he also turned it into a one-man show, his musical eccentricities existing virtually independently of the white-face clown. His comic effects were derived from his many props more than from any dramatic conflict with the white-face clown. (Towsen 1976: 233)

Most often his props were musical instruments and his eccentric musical numbers may have influenced later performers such as **Victor Borge** (1909–2000), who combined musical talent with comic skill.

Grock, for example, created an act that centred on his inability to catch his violin bow once he had tossed it into the air (Grock 1957: 145). The audience laughed when Grock dropped the bow so he demonstrated his anger at the bow and his own incompetence. He then went behind a curtain and 'practised' in such a way that the audience saw the bow appearing over the top of the curtain as Grock threw it up. When he returned from practising he dropped the bow again. In line with the types of clown behaviour outlined earlier, Grock is demonstrating failure. However his development of the act little by little and in response to the audience suggests that he was doing what Wright (2006) describes as 'finding the game'. The line between performance and act creation is blurred as Grock develops the entrée in front of the audience in response to his mistake. Grock, in improvising his act, is doing what Sutton-Smith describes as 'Playing with…that ambiguity – whether he really means it or is just playing' (1997: 150). The audience enjoys the act but the frame in which they receive the message of the act is not fixed. They cannot be sure whether Grock's initial difficulty was real or performed and, therefore, they cannot be sure how to interpret the rest of the act. In their enjoyment they are caught between a real frame and a play frame, caught within the characteristic ambiguity of modern clown play.

Grock's act as a whole re-established the idea that the theatre was a place where clowns might flourish and his circus-influenced clowning is a direct fore-runner to acts like Les Witloof, discussed later. This lies in part in the expression in Grock's work of his internal clown. According to Willson Disher, 'Grock, like **Grimaldi**, is funnier the deeper one pries into his soul…His piano is enlarged into man's eternal struggle with fate' (1925: 205). This is also true of Les Witloof, who have all the skill of circus performers but who use their skill to demonstrate the importance of friendship in the struggle against life's vicissitudes. Towards the end of his life, Grock owned and ran his own circus. In this way, his clown returned to the circus but with as much time in the ring as his extended entrée required. His autobiographies offer no real account of his decision to return to the circus but it is likely that it arose out of his life-long desire to be in control of his own fortune and future.

Grock's performance relates to Sutton-Smith's 'rhetorics of play' through frivolity, defined as 'essences of play [which] from this view point are nonsense and inversion' (1997: 201). Elements of nonsense and inversion are present, for example, in the sequence where Grock pulls the piano towards the piano stool rather than vice versa. Perhaps in this way the audience is encouraged to be aware of the place of nonsense in their own lives. The whole process of Grock, the circus Auguste, performing in a theatre also constitutes a form of inversion.

Clown Shows

To return to the present, Les Witloof's *Sous Pression* is a prime example of a *clown show*. Alistair Smith's review of the show (*The Stage*, 2 February 2005) describes its two performers as a 'traditional clown duo'. This labelling demands further interrogation. They are indeed a traditional clown duo in that they work within the status pairing of Whiteface and Auguste, and their performance is an example of a *clown show* in that it is very close in content to the performance of circus clowns. However, their make-up and costume do not conform exactly to the conventions of either circus role. Both **Thierry Craeye** and **Daniel Van Hassel** wear red clown noses but minimal face make-up.

Neither do their costumes point towards the circus clown roles. Both men wear trousers with braces. Craeye combines this with a striped polo shirt, while Van Hassel wears a shirt and

Daniel Van Hassel and Thierry Craeye (Les Witloof) in *Sous Pression*.

tie (with the tie tied very short). In this respect there is no immediate clue for the audience to indicate which clown may take the higher status role. The audience must establish the *particular convention* of this show as it goes on. In terms of action, a running gag about catching glasses of beer makes it clear that Craeye has the Whiteface role. He is able to produce glasses of beer from his brown paper bag, seemingly at will. Van Hassel's Auguste tries very hard but never succeeds in producing a beer which he then manages to drink. The clowns are best described using Wright's terms of *boss clown* and *simple clown*. Craeye's *boss clown* effectively creates a series of challenges (or exploits) for Van Hassel's *simple clown* to attempt but, in line with Wright's definition, Van Hassel plays both in front of and with the audience, signalling a chain of points of bafflement in relation to his repeated failure to do what the *boss clown* finds so simple.

While their makeup and costumes are more contemporary than traditional, the relationship follows a traditional pattern and the sketches which link together to form the show are circus sketches rather than the narrative performance of theatre clowning. A number of the sketches provide Les Witloof with opportunities to demonstrate to the audience their skills in a range of circus arts: illusionist tricks (producing beer from empty bags), physical skill (manoeuvring in a large cardboard box, rope tricks, constructing a house of giant playing cards). Other sketches are reworkings of traditional clown entrées (status interaction with objects, the musical interruption entrée). Interestingly, Les Witloof also experiment with traditional clown anarchy. This is highlighted by the performance space towards the end of the show when Van Hassel brings on a petrol can. Fire as an element of clown performance is always impressive but the sand ring of a traditional Big Top is a less dangerous place to play with fire than a stage. In the Purcell Room, the heads of front row of the audience were virtually level with the stage, at a distance of a metre to a metre and a half. With this spatial relationship between performer and audience, the introduction of fire becomes much more threatening and potentially dangerous. The flaming fencing act that ensues is much more anarchic in a theatre than it would be in a circus because, as De Toro suggests, there is a *general convention* which renders fire in a circus impressive but relatively common. However, the *general convention* of theatre does not usually include fire. In this case the clown's *particular convention* of anarchy with this *general convention* combines to create a *unique convention* for this performance. This *unique convention* will only become *particular* to forms of clown theatre performance if used by enough modern theatre clowns, in the way that, for example, the circus clown's *particular convention* of invading the audience has also become a *particular convention* of clown theatre performance because it is used by many theatre clowns (including Licedei, Mimirichi and Nola Rae).

At this point it is worth analysing one of the show's entrées in more detail. As before, a brief description of the entrée is to be found below, followed by an analysis of the impact and significance of the entrée. The nature of the entrée can also be interrogated in relation to Sutton-Smith's theory of play to establish which rhetoric of play is demonstrated by this sequence and how this relates to the intention and impact of the *Sous Pression*.

In this entrée a number of features of Traditional Circus clowning are in operation. Firstly, the Auguste is engaged in a status interaction with an object, the box, where the object has higher

The Cardboard Box Entrée

A large cardboard box comes down from the flies and covers the Auguste. The box falls over, first in one direction then another. There is a wine glass sticker on the box to indicate fragility and to show whether the box is the correct way up. The White Face clown mimes innocence at the audience. After the box has fallen over a number of times the Auguste goes quiet. The White face is now nearly crying. He takes a sharp knife and sticks it into the box. The Auguste yells. The White face uses the knife to cut a window in the box. He then tips the box forward over the edge of the stage so that it balances, threatening to tip. He then tips the box over and over. All of this is done as an attempt to remove the box so that the Auguste can get out. When the box is removed the Auguste is dressed in reverse. His trousers are where his shirt should be and vice versa. The box is turned again and the Auguste emerges correctly dressed.

status than the clown. The entrée demonstrates a degree of physical skill and timing. The box is moved around rapidly in a carefully choreographed sequence so that when the window is cut, the Auguste is in the correct place. The entrée is anarchic in that the box spills out of the theatrical performance space when it is balanced on the edge of the stage. For those at the front of the auditorium, there seems to be a real risk that the box could slide off. There is also skill in contortion and manipulation when the Auguste appears with his clothes on the wrong way and then, rapidly, the right way. The entrée is strengthened by the contrasting use of noise and silence. The Auguste's distressed cries teamed with the interaction of the Whiteface using *drops* and *clocks* to the audience provoke laughter. When the Auguste is silent the audience is concerned, caught in that space where rationality tells us he cannot have come to any harm but where our emotions are being manipulated by the speed of the sequence and the look on the face of the Whiteface clown. In terms of play, the clowns encourage the audience to enter a liminoid space, described earlier as the space between rationality and emotional involvement. The cardboard box entrée can be seen as an example of the 'rhetoric of power' (Sutton-Smith 1997) because the Whiteface appears to be demonstrating his power over the Auguste. The audience is reminded, through play, that life is full of such challenges. Ultimately, the Auguste emerges correctly dressed and safe, so the significance of which clown has won the power struggle is blurred. This relates to much of the structure of *Sous Pression* because the Whiteface continually triumphs over the Auguste in the matter of producing and drinking glasses of beer. By the end of the show the 'rhetoric of power' that has been established is undercut by the show's final message, which relates more closely to the 'rhetoric of identity', as *Sous Pression* suggests that the play engaged in by the two clowns reinforces the bond of friendship between them.

The mixed message of the show in terms of the value or purpose of play finds a semiotic parallel in the mixing of the performative frames of theatre and circus. Les Witloof rely on performing in a theatre; the show could not easily be transferred to a circus ring. A fly tower is necessary for the paper bags to be hidden and then flown in. The entrée described above can only work on a raised stage so that the box can be balanced precariously on the edge. Circus skills are reframed within the context of the theatre of the venue; even the use of fire gains an extra frisson in the theatre.

A further element of the traditional in *Sous Pression* is that there is no narrative line, beyond the running gag of catching glasses of beer. What the succession of entrées does is to introduce and reinforce the traditional difference in status and ability between the clowns. Significantly, two clowns would never have the opportunity to occupy the ring in a Traditional or Contemporary Circus for 75 minutes. Theatre clowning allows clowns the time to create a performance which uses much, if not all of their material, in a single show. In order to sustain a show of this length, the clowns also have to be able to engage the audience. Craeye and Van Hassel are both particularly good mimes who are able to convey emotion silently but effectively. This allows Van Hassel to appeal for the audience's sympathy as the show progresses.

> Acts of true prowess in the purest tradition like a balance act, a lasso act, a rope act and certainly magic but the whole is never presented as a circus spectacle because it is moulded into the poetic universe of two people.

> (De véritables numéros de prouesse dans la plus pure tradition comme un numéro d'équilibre, un numéro de lasso, un numéro de corde a bien sûr de la magie mais le tout n'est jamais présenté comme un spectacle de cirque car il est assimilé pars l'univers poétique des deux personnages.) (http://www.thea-valdoise.org/spectacle.htm#cc4)

The difference between Les Witloof and Traditional Circus clowns is that they are not demonstrating prowess for the sake of it but in order, according to Craeye, 'to create a poetic universe for two people which is funny, naive, fragile and moving all at the same time' (créer l'univers poétique des deux personnages, à la fois drôles, naïfs, fragiles et émouvants) (http://walrus-productions.com/01.witloff/1.souspression/pdf). There is, therefore, an impetus towards clowning with a purpose beyond that of simply making the audience laugh. The clowns demonstrate the fragility and vulnerability of human existence. Once this is understood, the significance of the song which they sing at the beginning 'Sous Pression' (the punning title of the show referring both to the draught beer which features centrally and to the notion of individuals being 'under pressure') then becomes clear. The most important thing about life, the show suggests, is to 'have a good mate, that's the best thing in the world' (song sheet handed to audience). Despite Les Witloof's claims about meaning in relation to *Sous Pression,* the impact of the piece is created not through the communication of meaning but through the demonstration of skill which engages the audience through its sense of play.

The Catalan clown company Tricicle has developed a show style that takes a central notion or theme and then links together a sequence of sections which have no narrative connection but which are linked by the fact that they demonstrate different aspects of the central notion. In *Slastic* the central notion is sport and all the sections demonstrate one kind of sport. In *Sit,* the show to be considered in more detail here, all the sections focus on sitting. The sections either suggest some of the history of sitting or demonstrate the different places and ways in which sitting might occur. The sections are more overtly theatrical than the style of Les Witloof, and Tricicle are less inclined to include circus skills in their shows. For example, the opening sequence of *Sit* begins in darkness with a voice over intoning 'In the beginning there was nothing. A little later there was (sic) them'. At this point the theatre lights come up to reveal three cave men against a backdrop of the night sky. Initially the cavemen are occupied in finding fleas on their bodies and then eating them. Clown 1 repeatedly fails in this exploit. He cannot find any fleas and when he is given one, he drops it. After this set up (which is arguably longer than it needs to be) a dinosaur is heard offstage left. Clown 1 picks up a log to use as a weapon. When the dinosaur goes quiet, the clown puts the log down and sits on it. The significance of his unwitting discovery is indicated to the audience through the antics of the other two clowns. They notice him sitting and both do a double take. After the double take comes a sequence of looks demonstrated with absolute synchronicity, taking in the log and the clown sitting. The other two clowns want to try sitting on the log. One succeeds while the other knocks the log over. As the log rolls away, the clumsy clown mimes rolling out to the audience. Clown 1 reinforces this with a rolling mime of his own. Clown 3 does a swift but precise mime of driving, including changing gear, checking the mirror, doing up the seat belt and making rude gestures at other drivers. The visual image of a caveman miming driving demonstrates a disregard for chronology which is entirely in keeping with clown logic. Playful connections can be made across the centuries in the minds of the clowns. Whilst the Tricicle clowns include the audience in their playing by establishing a sense of *complicité* through looks and more directly attacking some of them with inflatable tubes, the playfulness is largely established on the stage in a series of settings in which sitting occurs. For the most part, the show remains within *the general convention* of theatre. The skill demonstrated by the clowns is that of mime rather than circus skills, but the lack of narrative thrust or constant characters sites this company firmly within the definition of *clown show,* but one in which the audience is encouraged to observe play rather than engage in it.

An example of a *clown show* which engages its audience more openly in playing can be found in Mimirichi's show, *Paperworld,* which was performed at the Riverside Studios, London in July 2005. Whilst there are enough similarities between *Sous Pression* , *Sit* and *Paperworld* to define all as *clown shows,* Mimirichi's show allows for a more detailed exploration of the nature of play which occurs between the performers and the audience. Three clown characters are established in the show and each can be identified by the colour of his nose (red, green and white).The clowns wear simple costumes in white with coloured details.

These characters are, however, not specific to the performers, as would have been the case in Traditional Circus. For example, the white-nosed clown was played by a different performer in the live performance than on the DVD. In this way the clown characters can be seen as parts to be played, as is the case with the performance of scripted plays. However, *Paperworld* does not have a narrative line and there is no character development. Instead the clowns play with the environment in which they exist, with each other and, importantly, with the audience.

Paperworld interrogates the dynamics of stage space and performer/audience relationships in a variety of ways through the sketches which link together to form the structure of the whole show. Initially, the performers cannot be seen except as shadow versions of themselves which grow and shrink as they are projected onto a screen of paper. In this way, the performers play with the notion of the conventional theatrical frame. They appear to establish the paper screen as a barrier between the performers and the audience but then they enter from the wings to perform in front of it, thus redefining it as a conventional backdrop. Later, it is redefined again when they tear shapes out of it to create character-shaped entrances. Later still, the paper is redefined as a toy when the clowns turn it into paper balls to be thrown at the audience.

One sequence of the show involves the white-nosed clown borrowing a pair of glasses from an audience member. This sequence works on two levels. Firstly, it challenges the notion that there is an invisible barrier between the performers and the audience which protects the audience from the anarchy of the clowns (theatre's *general convention* dictates that there is; circus's *general convention* dictates that there is not). Both the white and green nosed clowns come off the stage and move amongst the audience, swapping people's glasses around. Secondly, the important notion of clown anarchy is introduced and the audience realizes that it is likely to have to take an active part in the performance rather than simply observing it. A by-product of this sequence is that audience members are forced to talk to each other and to establish connections with strangers in order to retrieve their glasses. This goes some way to establishing a feeling of *communitas* amongst the audience.

Later in the show, the notion of anarchy is reinforced when, as part of the action, the clowns begin to destroy the paper screen which has formed their backdrop. The holes which they create at this point are reminiscent of the shadows created at the beginning of the show but now, rather than being ciphers of another world, they form entry and exit points between the two worlds. Eventually the screen is destroyed to such an extent that only one world remains – the world in which the clowns play and in which they also encourage the audience to play.

There are two clear examples of the audience being encouraged to play. The clowns start a paper fight, screwing up bits of paper and throwing them at the audience. At the live performance it took only seconds for them to provoke the audience into throwing paper back at them and at other members of the audience. At this live performance, ironically, the audience established an anarchy of its own when half a dozen small children invaded the stage (which was not raised) to join the clowns in playing with the paper. One of the children even disappeared backstage and had to be retrieved by the stage manager. It took some time for the clowns to get the children back to their seats, hampered as they were by not being able to speak (the whole show is performed without any verbal communication). The more the clowns chased the children, the more the children thought it was a good game. As a result of the glasses and the paper fight, all notions of a performer space and an audience space were broken down. Later, the audience was involved in setting up a football goal and in pulling paper over its head to reach the back of the auditorium. It therefore engaged in a variety of play situations. Sequences throughout the show explored the notion of play and playing. The clowns played with each other and with the audience. In *Slava's Snowshow* the audience is encouraged to play at the end of the show when huge coloured balls are released into the auditorium, but in *Paperworld* the audience plays within the structure of the piece. In this way, the audience is encouraged to return to the play of childhood. However, this is not the play of Sutton-Smith's 'rhetoric of child play', where play is linked to developmental progress. Here the childish play of throwing things at each other is closely linked to the 'rhetoric of play as frivolous', so that the audience is reminded of the importance of playing for the sake of its own enjoyment. As a whole, the show exists very much in the present. Unlike the performances of *clown theatre* explored here and of *clown actors* explored in the next chapter, the audience is not searching for a meaning. The meaning lies in the form and content of the show: 'it is fun to play', echoing Sutton-Smith's 'rhetoric of the frivolous' (1997) even more emphatically than Les Witloof.

Whilst these clown shows are largely silent (except for the clowns' interaction with sound effects), the focus is on circus skills or on various kinds of play rather than on the use of mime to communicate anything beyond a surface meaning. For example in *Paperworld,* one clown makes use of mime to demonstrate to another clown how to find a toilet. The journey is so ridiculous (involving paddling a boat, riding a horse and swimming) that the focus is on the impracticality of this journey to a clown desperate for the toilet rather than on the nuances of mime skills. However, in *clown theatre,* mime skill and the way it can be used to communicate central truths about human nature is vitally important.

Clown use of mime

The use of mime and silence by clowns to communicate meaning connects with Lecoq's concept that an early primitive form of gesture which works symbolically exists to be used when language fails. The immediacy of communication required by a theatrical performance is more likely to occur through gesture than verbal language. Gesture can be used denotatively (**Marceau**, Chaplin, Ingimarsson and Nani) or connotatively (Lecoq and Slava). When it is used connotatively, the audience is drawn into the act of interpretation in which the connotation drawn from the symbolic mime may vary from audience member to audience member. In this way, even more than at the theatrical event reliant on the spoken word, the audience can connect the symbols to their own experience of life. The theatrical frame encourages this act of interpretation, which is supported by the visual semiotics of the set, costumes and props.

The silence of mime and the use of the body to communicate through symbol and metaphor connects with both existential thought and with Jungian notions of archetypes because those 'subconscious symbols would precede culture and be common to all, regardless of social context. These symbols would be connotative in structure' (Felner 1985: 153). The connotative nature of some mime (significantly that of Barrault and Lecoq, which can be defined as 'le mime subjectif') lends itself to communicating to the audience on a visceral or subconscious level. It is evocative in quality and this encourages a subjective response from the audience, according to how it interprets its significance and meaning. The clown's mimed expression of his own Existential struggle can be interpreted by the audience on an individual level.

For this reason, Marcel Marceau's illusionary mime, concerned as it was with communicating a physical representation or simple narrative line, relied on physical virtuosity that has little or no connection to the inner life of the audience. Only occasionally did Marceau use metaphor to convey meaning for example in *Youth, Maturity, Old Age and Death* (a sequence of mimes which express man's journey through life), but even here the metaphor worked at such an obvious level that there was little room for audience interpretation. In fact, the audience's attention was more likely to be drawn to the physical virtuosity in such a way that its response was likely to be focused on the skill of the performer rather than be touched by the emotional or symbolic content of the mime performance.

Felner defines Barrault's orientation in contrast as 'existential, assuming that physiological states occur prior to the emotive' (Felner 1985: 85) and, it could be suggested by extension, prior to the intellectual. In this way, the clown mime communicates physiologically, corporally, that which will speak to the inner life of the audience, communicating through gesture to the emotions in a way that allows clowning to address concepts which relate to existential philosophy. The intellectual response may well not occur until after the performance, as the audience member attempts to process his or her visceral and emotional responses. *Slava's Snowshow* (analysed later) reflects the tendency of Barrault's productions 'to dramatize the inner life of man set against a non-naturalistic background, often rendered by symbolism' (Felner 1985: 88). The set for Slava's show, which indicates no particular place or time, echoes this tendency, using panels of cloth to indicate (depending on audience interpretation) the sky, outside, water, snow or a padded cell.

'No doubt clowns put us in touch with a very profound psychological...dimension' (Lecoq 2002: 158). Through this psychological profundity, which enables the clown to express the inner self, the clown can communicate existentially to an audience. By revealing his own inner self, by offering that self to the audience, the clown is asking the audience *how much of my experience of myself connects with your inner experience of yourself?* Consequently the audience is offered the opportunity to consider the commonality of our human fears and concerns about the nature and meaning of our existence.

In this context, the most relevant of these mime-clowns was **Leonid Yengibarov** (1935–1972) who performed in the circus ring, on stage and in films but whose act relied on a combination of acrobalance and mime. Very little has been written in English on Yengibarov but Towsen describes him as being 'a superb actor and mime, he excelled as a juggler, acrobat and equilibrist. Everything he did combined the world of circus with that of theater' (Towsen 1976: 344). Yengibarov's presentation of himself is worthy of analysis. He eschewed the, by then, traditional colourful make-up of the clown and the more sombre whiteface of the mime, often performing without make-up. His costume made one or two nods towards the circus clown tradition. He is pictured in Towsen's book wearing oversized shoes, dark trousers held up by a single brace rather than by a pair, a stripy tee shirt and a small hat. The simplicity of his costume directed the audience to the content of his act. The everydayness of what he wore contrasted strikingly with the supreme talent he displayed in his act. On the one hand, his costume seems to suggest to the audience that he is not so different from them; on the other, the message is that he may look like them but he certainly does not behave or move like them. What links Yengibarov to the theatre clowns of today is that even when performing a difficult balance, 'Yengibarov was also acting the whole time he did it, using his face and even his body to maintain the characterization' (Towsen 1976: 346). Interestingly, Yengibarov saw his job as being not a simple entertainer but someone who could make his audience 'feel and understand what I am saying' (Towsen 1976: 348). This is a kind of 'play of the self' where the whole purpose of the play is to communicate personal beliefs. His supreme mime talent also relates to Sutton-Smith's 'play as power' rhetoric. Whilst the later Russian clown, Slava Polunin, does not share Yengibarov's ability with acrobatics and balance, he does share the need to communicate a meaning to his audience rather than simply entertaining them. His website, (www.slavasnowshow.com), acknowledges his debt to Yengibarov, amongst others: 'the poetic sadness of Leonid Yengibarov's clownery, the refined philosophizing of Marcel Marceau's pantomime and the humanity and comic poignancy of great Chaplin's films. All of these Polunin considers his major teachers' (programme notes for Slava's Snowshow). Whilst Yengibarov's particular talent lay in the combination of mime skills and acting to demonstrate a kind of 'poetic sadness', similar skills have been employed more recently by other clowns to express both societal and philosophical truths.

Clown Theatre

Performances that can be defined as *clown theatre* tend to use mime to communicate to the audience a deeper message which is more closely linked to the social or political ideas of the performer. This is certainly the case for Nola Rae's *Exit Napoleon Pursued by Rabbits,* which was performed at the Purcell Room, London in January 2005. This performance used its theatrical frame more conventionally in that what took place was recognizably theatre rather than circus. However, the piece played with the notion of the play; a concept that was highlighted by Rae's interactions with the audience.

As the audience members entered the Purcell Room for the performance of *Exit Napoleon Pursued by Rabbits,* they were able to observe the set, which was already lit in a dusky pink and grey wash, towards the centre of the stage. Under a ramshackle tent was a bed on which a person appeared to be lying; all but the foot of the bed, where a pair of boots stuck out, was covered by a blanket. A sound effect of cawing crows was playing, reinforcing the theatrical frame. Nola Rae entered through the same entrance that had just been used by the audience, thereby presenting a challenge to the theatrical frame. She was dressed androgynously in a hobo clown outfit with traditional hobo clown make-up.

She crossed in front of the first row of the audience before climbing some steps to the stage. In this way, the usual stage space of the theatre is disturbed. From the outset, the audience is aware that the performer will not necessarily be contained by the stage. The opening section of the show that follows is a very traditional piece of clown/object status interaction clowning. Rae exits and enters through the tent as if she is not certain where she is. After one entrance, her foot becomes stuck in a chef's hat that is lying on the floor, demonstrating her lower status in relation to the prop which she cannot control properly. Accompanied only by sound effects, the passing of time is indicated by Rae miming being, first, extremely cold and then extremely hot, as if it has passed from winter to summer. Eventually her stomach begins to rumble and she sets about preparing a meal by dusting a potato.

Rae's show develops as a satire on power, charisma and tyranny. Once the initial hobo character discovers that no-one is in fact wearing the boots that protrude from the bed, he puts them on, beginning a process of transformation which leaves Rae looking like Napoleon. A further transformation results in the appearance of Hitler. Without speech, the show's message is conveyed clearly through demonstrations of the behaviour of the charismatic men. The Hitler character goes through public ceremonies. Then we observe him experimenting with different kinds of salute and different ways of marching, all of which are, at the same time, both ridiculous and reminiscent of Nazi goose-stepping and the extended arm of the Nazi salute. An audience member is brought onto the stage and the Hitler character tries, unsuccessfully, to seduce her and then makes her take notes while he plans a speech. Finally the speech is performed to the audience, but the character is attacked from behind by a puppet made from a stick, hanger and coat. The puppet then takes over the speech. Thus one dictator replaces another. Rae's Hitler character fights back. In the course of the fight, the tent is pulled down. Towards the end, Rae's character tips up the bed, creating the effect of a wall and railings. The show ends with the tyrant character apparently behind bars, unable to escape.

Rae's decision to portray male characters raises the issue of the gender conflict of the actor/persona. The audience is aware that Nola Rae is a woman but the part she playing is that of a man. The costume is largely androgynous but a make-up moustache signifies that the character is masculine. When asked during an after show discussion about her tendency towards playing male rather than female characters, Rae offered a number of explanations. The most interesting of these is that she equated the role of the mime-clown with that of a satirist and she claimed that it is easier to 'stick the knife into a male object'. She also suggested that playing men had become habitual for her. As mentioned earlier, there are very few female clowns either in history or performing today, and the two most famous, Rae and De Castro, regularly perform as masculine characters, or as characters costumed and made-up in such a way as to make gender seem insignificant. It could be argued, however, that notions of gender are vital in the consideration of contemporary clown performance. Annie Fratellini suggested that the dearth of women clowns could be put down to women's reluctance to make themselves look ugly, and this may be the case, although many comic character actresses seem happy to do this (Julie Waters, Jennifer Saunders, Joanna Lumley). Perhaps the difference lies in the fact that when actresses make themselves look ugly, they do so to perform a character distinct from themselves. When a clown performer makes up as his or her clown persona, he/she is undergoing a transformation which reveals hidden facets of his or her personality to the audience. What is more significant is that to play the clown means giving away status. Status is only readily given away by those whose status in society is secure. Hence the fact that most famous clowns in western society have been white men (the only exception is the Cuban clown, Chocolat). However, Rae describes her choice to play men so often in societal rather than personal terms, claiming that she finds it 'harder to choose women to satirize' (after show discussion).

What is clear is that there is a purpose to the show beyond entertainment. There is a clear satirical message about the dangers of power and tyranny. Rae described the process of developing this show as having evolved through a number of steps. The concept emerged when it was suggested to her that she should work around the idea of charisma. Initially she considered Rasputin and her reading led on to dictators. It seemed to her that all modern dictators had been inspired by Napoleon and so he became the starting point for the show. Next, Rae identified a number of elements she considered to be common to the dictators she was reading about and which she also felt made 'good clown material'. They had all experienced retreat, which was followed by some kind of vacuum in their lives. They then came to believe that they had a destiny for which they transformed themselves. They were able to control people and experienced a moment of supreme triumph. Each of these elements was demonstrated through the narrative line of the show. The opening section with the struggling hobo demonstrated the time of retreat and vacuum. At one point in the show the hobo holds up a tin can and a light shines onto it and into the clown's face. Rae intended this to represent what she described as 'the light of destiny'. Later, the hobo transforms into Napoleon. The transformation element is emphasized by repetition when Napoleon transforms into Hitler. Most tellingly, Rae demonstrated control by controlling her audience. In doing so, she showed just how easy it is for an individual to gain control over a large group. Initially Rae picked on two male audience members, making them stand up and sit down according to her command. She then divided the audience in two and established a clapping routine which involved the audience following her mimed instructions. There was no point or purpose to the clapping beyond showing that she could make the audience do it. In this sense, it was an example of 'frivolous play' (Sutton-Smith 1997) but as the piece progressed it became clear that play was being used to make a political point about how humans can be manipulated. To that end, any resistance or indecision on the part of an audience member was quickly spotted and mimicked for the amusement of the rest of the audience. In this way, even the most resistant were forced to take part, demonstrating the power of mockery and isolation through play. Thus, the play was transformed from 'frivolous play' to 'play as power' (Sutton-Smith 1997: 10), with play used to communicate a serious social message.

The next two shows to be considered, *The Art of Dying* and *Slava's Snowshow*, use mime and play to explore more philosophical notions about mortality and the meaning of life often connecting with the central tenets of Existential philosophy. The title of *The Art of Dying* closely links the notion of mortality with the notion of craft or performance. Publicity for the show suggested that the piece would explore what happened when one clown (part of a two-clown act) discovered he was dying. In this way, the show indicated that it would be dealing with one of society's significant taboos: death. The narrative of the piece revolves around an increasingly successful clown double act. As the act becomes more popular, one of the clowns discovers, by post, that he is dying. At first he tries to ignore the news by putting the envelope, which contains an x-ray, in the bin. The notion that he is dying prompts him to search for proof that he is alive. He fails to find a pulse and slumps over, seemingly dead. At this point, the narrative takes a leap into the surreal. The clown who is not dying (Clown 1) appears in a costume suggestive of an angel; perhaps we are being offered a vision of clown heaven. Clown 1 discovers the envelope and the x-ray it contains. The dying clown (Clown 2) begins to respond to this proof of his mortality through an extended sequence of alternating tears and laughter until one merges into the other. Finally, reinforcing his earlier denial, he puts the x-ray and envelope back in the bin. Through mime, the dying clown suggests to the audience that he still has things to do; he is not ready to die. In the most general terms, therefore, the piece could be described as existential because it encourages the audience to face the fact of man's mortality. However, the strongly denotative, illusionary aspect of the mime detracts from the potential symbolism. Even the surreal departures do not successfully lift the piece into a deeper exploration of what mortality might mean as a universal theme. The mortality is highlighted by the fact that it is a clown (a symbol of joy, laughter and energy) who is to die.

A more detailed analysis of some of the sequences of the show will explore how far the show truly addresses a serious exploration of mortality, and how the show impacted on its audience. The post-modern performative nature of the piece, in which Nani and Ingimarrson (two clowns) perform for an audience as two clowns performing for an imaginary audience, which, as far as the real audience is concerned, exists backstage, distracts the attention of both the performers and the audience from the more serious matter of mortality. The show plays, therefore, with notions of reality. The audience in the Purcell Room watches the clowns when they are relaxing backstage from a show, or when they are demonstrating part of the show for us. For example, in one sequence, one clown goes through the stage curtains to perform for the imaginary audience. All the real audience can see of that clown is the juggling balls appearing over the top of the stage curtains. Meanwhile the other clown, who is offstage for the imaginary audience, is on stage for the real audience. In being on stage, he is performing being offstage for the imaginary audience. He passes props through the curtains for his partner and catches things which are thrown over the curtains by the clown who is onstage for the imaginary audience. It could be argued that the piece is more concerned with the art of clowning than *The Art of Dying*. The piece plays far more with notions of performance (emphasized by the mime style used, and by the inclusion of circus clown tricks such as catching an apple on a fork) and reality than it does with mortality.

However, the simple fact remains that the two clowns performing have given the piece the title *The Art of Dying* and one of the clowns has died by the end of the piece. For the two clowns, the notions of life and performance are closely connected. The clown cannot live on without the man. Towards the end of the piece the phone is ringing and it is clear that the two clowns are being offered more and more gigs. However the dying clown has no interest in, or enthusiasm for, these gigs. His increasing distance from his clown character is signified through his costume. At this stage, he enters without face makeup, wearing only his trousers and a hat which is not the same as his earlier costume hat. The man is alive but the clown is already fading from existence. This separation of the man from the clown highlights the duality of the clown performer in a way which connects with Heidegger's notions of Authentic and Inauthentic existence. The difficulty lies in establishing whether the man or the clown represents the authentic existence.

The connection of *Slava's Snowshow* to existentialism is much more overt and can be considered on two levels: firstly within each section of the show and secondly, cumulatively in relation to the structure of the piece as a whole. The show begins with Slava making an almost mystical entrance. Music is playing (as it has been since the audience entered the auditorium), the track changes, the lighting alters, and a seemingly small, rather elderly figure with wispy hair moves slowly and silently onto the stage. Slava's costume of a yellow baggy romper suit and red slippers is highly suggestive of early childhood. In contrast, his greying wispy hair suggests age and so, in a single figure who has not yet spoken a word, the audience is presented with an index of the whole of the human journey from childhood to age.

Slava's Snowshow 12/97 at The Old Vic, London. *Slava Polunin And Son.*

Slava's movements also indicate both childhood and age. The shuffling walk is suggestive of both the tottering steps of toddlerhood and the tottering steps of age. Likewise, when Slava makes a quarter turn so that he faces and acknowledges the audience, his gaze has the frankness of a child who has not yet learned that staring is rude and the confidence of an adult able to accept being looked at. From the shrug of his shoulders and the grin it is clear that Slava's clown, Asisyai, is happy to have an audience. Around Asisyai's neck is a rope, carrying with it the full symbolic force of the noose. Simply and directly, the notion of mortality and, perhaps, of life's unbearability (Sartre's 'Anguish') is communicated to the audience. Asisyai stands facing the audience and starts to gather in the rope, which trails offstage. He pulls on the rope for a long time, signalling his exhaustion to the audience through repeated use of *clocks*. Eventually the rope becomes taut and then another clown enters, not level with Asisyai but upstage from him. The other end of the rope forms a noose around the neck of the second clown. The second clown is dressed differently from Asisyai in a long green overcoat and an unusual hat, the brim of which extends about twelve inches on either side of the clown's head but not to the front or rear, indicating that he is a different kind of personality. This different, noosed clown indicates that mortality and angst are common to the human condition; a view propounded by both Heidegger (2003) and Sartre (2003). The rope which connects the two clowns indicates the shared nature of mankind's angst. That both clowns may wish to take their lives indicates that for them life is not joyous but a struggle. Perhaps they are at the point in life, identified by Sartre, where they have realized the meaninglessness of their existence and can no longer bear it. From this point, however, as clowns having acknowledged the audience, they cannot continue with their suicide plan (if that is indeed what it was), echoing, as it does,

Vladimir and Estragon's abortive plan to hang themselves in *Waiting for Godot*. Instead, with the evangelism of the true existentialist, unlike Vladimir and Estragon, they seek to make us understand the truth about human existence. As a result, the audience is presented with a number of sections of performance which blend and blur so that it is not always clear where one sequence ends and another begins. This in itself is symbolic of the way we experience our lives, which can rarely be neatly divided into units.

Later in the show, a sequence occurs which, for the purposes of this exploration, begins when Asisyai walks onto the stage carrying a small helium balloon. The balloon's string has a weight so that the balloon can, in effect, be put down without it drifting into the fly tower. Asisyai communicates his feelings to the audience not by speaking, but by using a clown squeaker. Asisyai takes the balloon to the downstage left corner and leaves it there. Then, as if deciding that this is not the best place for the balloon, he moves it to the downstage right corner. He crosses back to stage left and panics because the balloon has disappeared. His squeaks rise to panicky shrieks and he casts imploring glances at the audience. Finally he remembers that he has moved the balloon and goes to retrieve it. This sequence seems to suggest the futility of much human existence, with an emphasis on the anxiety many of us feel in dealing with our everyday lives. This is an effective demonstration of the anxiety Heidegger identifies in his discussion of our responses to perceived threats.

At this point Asisyai switches squeakers and the audience realizes that in this way, Slava, as Asisyai, can create two characters. From this point, the sequence is open to a dual interpretation. On a simple level, Asisyai creates two distinct characters who are struggling for possession of the balloon. As the struggle becomes more and more intense, they mime their threats to each other. Eventually Asisyai pops the balloon and bursts into tears. The scene, therefore, represents individual ambition and a struggle for possessions which leads only to unhappiness. There is an existential tone to this in so far as it echoes the existential belief that our lives are absurd and devoid of meaning. However, there is a more interesting existential interpretation in which it could be argued that the two characters portrayed by Asisyai represent his 'authentic' and 'inauthentic' selves (as defined by Heidegger in *Time and Being* in *Basic Writings* 2003). In this case, the balloon is symbolic of the way the individual's life may be led in different directions. The 'authentic self' struggles with the 'inauthentic self' for the strength to make authentic decisions rather than accepting what society suggests. Therefore, when one character threatens the other by miming that he is going to get a bigger brother or friend to join the fight, it is possible to interpret this as the emerging 'authentic self' being challenged by the oppressive structures of general and 'inauthentic existence'. This leaves the issue of interpreting the popping of the balloon. It could be seen as the destruction of the 'inauthentic existence' or the 'authentic existence', depending on how you have interpreted the two characters. In this way, the sequence makes the point that for many individuals, understanding whether you are leading an 'authentic' or 'inauthentic' existence can be an extremely difficult issue to resolve.

A similar duality is presented in a telephone conversation sequence where Asisyai once again plays two characters. As before, the meaning of the sequence is ambiguous: the two characters may be the two halves of a telephone conversation or they could be the different ways of

behaving available to one individual. This latter interpretation is reinforce
sketch relies on Asisyai playing both characters rather than having anothe
to perform the other half of the conversation.

Further examples of the individual's attempt to connect with the rest of mankind
other sequences from *Snowshow*. In 'Blue Canary' Asisyai appears between two ...ns,
who are dancing. The dance has no obvious purpose beyond the obvious ple_ɔɾe the two
clowns who can do it successfully derive from it. This is an example of Sutton-Smith's 'play as
frivolity'. All three clowns are wearing similar costumes, signifying some unity. However, Asisyai
cannot keep time with the dance. He appears to be trying to work out life's dance, always a
little out of step. He carries a fishing net, raising the question of what it is that he hopes to catch.
In fact he never catches anything and never gets the dance right. Perhaps this is an enactment
of the individual's attempt to remain in step with society around him, even when the dance
does not come naturally to him. Later in the show, Asisyai enters inside a clear plastic ball. The
metaphor is equally clear: each of us is isolated within our own world. We can never be part
of or truly understand the world or lives of others. The moments of illogicality in the show mirror
the illogicality of existence. We fail to accept the 'Facticity' of our existence: that we exist as
we do because we do, and for no more significant reason. When Asisyai steps from the bed,
which represents a boat, there is a sound effect of footsteps in water. Moments earlier when
the other clown stepped off the boat there was no sound. Asisyai's reaction, communicated
through a *clock* to the audience, points out the illogicality of the moment. No explanation is
offered – as in life, the audience simply has to accept what occurs.

Other elements of the show point to man's struggle against the natural world. Asisyai becomes
entangled in a spider's web, which is then passed out into the audience. Members of the
audience willingly pass the web over their heads to those seated behind. In this way, the
audience is reminded that the entanglements of life affect us all, not just the performers on stage,
and the activity also encourages the audience to participate in the beginnings of play. The
activity is taking place in *limen*. The audience has no way of knowing whether the spreading
of the web to the back of the auditorium is in any way necessary for the show to continue or
whether it is simply a frivolous activity. This also occurs before the more anarchic elements of
the show, so the audience has not firmly established the *particular conventions* (De Toro 1995)
of the performance.

An element of anarchy is present at a number of points throughout the show. The green-coated
clowns venture out into the audience carrying trays of glasses of water and wearing umbrella
hats, which sprinkle water on the audience. In the 2004 performance at the Hackney Empire,
these clowns walked around the edges of the balcony, high above the audience in the stalls
who were drenched each time a clown tipped his umbrella or his tray. Members of the
audience sitting in the front row of the dress circle were coerced into holding the clowns' free
hands, seemingly to make them balance. Thus the audience is drawn into the immediacy of
the moment; there is a palpable sense of danger as the clowns are not harnessed in any way.
The activity, therefore, appears to be an example of Geertz's 'deep play' but the play frame
of the theatrical performance, combined with the fact that audience members would be hurt

clowns fell, suggests that it cannot be. Once again the audience is caught between the world of fantasy and the world of reality. The clowns demonstrate the excitement to be gained from taking risks, from stepping beyond the expected bounds – this is existentialist clowning at its most evangelical. The clowns show the audience a different way of living.

Equally, the snowstorm at the end of the show blasts out into the auditorium. On stage, Asisyai battles to stay on his feet amidst the noise, wind and snow. The audience is likely to feel exhilarated by the energy of the spectacle. Perhaps at this moment we are able to be authentic, to live in the moment, reacting to what occurs before us. In this way, the existentialist clown encourages us to free ourselves from the usual constraints of society. When the huge balls that signal the finale of the show are launched into the auditorium, adults play like children, eager for a touch of the brightly coloured spheres, and finally the play frame is very clearly established. The audience engages in 'frivolous play' and a sense of *communitas* and bonding is established as the balls are knocked backwards and forwards.

The show as a whole serves as a metaphor for the journey of life. In relation to Heidegger, 'Authenticity' relates to the realization of both the isolation of the individual's existence and the inevitable termination of that existence in death. Asisyai expresses this understanding through the clown's vision of the world, which is intrinsically authentic. The clown understands that there is no grand plan beyond his own journey towards death. Slava seeks to express this with the allegorical/metaphorical journeying in *Snowshow* – signalled by trains and departures. The sorrow of parting, the pain of striving for connection, and failing, are represented in the parting scene when Asisyai plays both parts of a couple separating on a train station. This vision of the world connects with the evangelical slant of the existentialists. It seems important that there is often no programme for *Snowshow* and when there is, the programme notes offer no hints as to the meaning of the show. The 1999 performance at the Piccadilly Theatre was accompanied by a programme but the 2004 performance at the Hackney Empire was not. The audience experience in *Snowshow* parallels that of life – we have to work it out as we go along – and who knows, it may all mean nothing.

Benedict Nightingale's review of Slava's *Snowshow* in *The Times* on 30 January 2004 demonstrates how the show is open to interpretation, although it appears that Nightingale rather misses the point in his analysis. 'I laughed a little at his St Sebastian parody and rather more at the episode in which he mistakes his hand for a groping stranger's but never a lot' (Nightingale 2004: n.pag). Nightingale has clearly come to the theatre expecting circus clowning and instead he gets existentialist clowning, which encourages the audience to evaluate their approach to life rather than just laughing at the clown on stage. What Nightingale describes as a St Sebastian parody demonstrates how tightly man clings to life, even with several arrows through him. Slava's depiction of the farewell at the station was diminished by Nightingale's description of a groping stranger. What is depicted by Slava is the pain of parting from someone with whom you feel as one, parts of a whole – as is demonstrated by Slava, who plays both halves of the relationship with consummate skill. This example of illusionary mime unusually works on two levels. The audience is likely to feel admiration for his skill, which convincingly creates a parting between two people when we know only one is present. The audience is also likely to experience pain/sorrow/recognition of the inevitability of the human condition – that ultimately we must part from those we love and we will be alone (the very thing which Didi fears so much in *Waiting for Godot*). As with *Waiting for Godot*, the critics seem uncertain as to what to make of a theatre show that appears to abandon many of the conventions of the current dominant form of realistic theatre.

As well as highlighting man's ultimate isolation, the anarchic sections of the show deliberately work to bind the audience together, reminding individuals of their connection with other humans. Sometimes such connections are demonstrated physically as a result of the clowns' actions, as Paul Taylor notes in his review in *The Independent* on 2 February 2004: '[a]t the end, two people near me were still trying to sever their accidental partnership.' Paradoxically, as Slava reminds us of our ultimate isolation, he encourages an atmosphere in which strangers are forced to make contact with each other in a way which is not common in a city like London, where tube travellers will do anything to avoid making eye-contact with each other. These accidental partnerships, which are formed as the audience members are tangled in spider's web or help anarchic clowns balance or play with over-sized balls, sum up the meaning of the show and suggest Slava's view of life, where happiness can depend on the success of the random and accidental partnerships we form with others. This also demonstrates the elements of play theory, which suggest that part of the essence of fun is that it should be '*characterised by attention to means rather than ends*' (Sutton-Smith 1997: 188, italics in original), and that 'play is supposed to be non-productive and not to intend serious consequences' (ibid: 189). Equally, it seems likely that Sutton-Smith would view Slava as a good player who 'can "flow" and can get others to flow' (1997: 207). In encouraging his audience to play, purely for the fun of playing, Slava acts as a bridge between the usually constrained adult world and the world of fantasy and play. It is significant that there is no clear grand narrative to hold the show together. The audience is presented with thematic connections which encourage us to consider what we experience as we journey through life. Again, this lack of narrative suggests a similarity to Beckett, whom Slava claims as an influence.

Licedei's *Semianyki* offers a different example of *clown theatre*. Its performance style typifies what the company claims are distinctive features of its work: dumb clown-mime performance, poetic clownery, no clearly emphasized national orientation, capable of being enjoyed by both adults and children, dealing with simple emotions and truths. This performance was seen in The Assembly @ St George's as part of the 2006 Edinburgh Fringe Festival. The performance created by Licedei has only the simplest of narratives, perhaps only a setting, and from this starting point a piece of theatre is developed which incorporates solo and group sketches framed within the situation of the home life of a grotesque family. In *Semianyki* there are solo sketches (the equivalent of traditional circus entrées) which involve the Father drinking vodka whilst his arms are fixed at right angles to his body by a pole, the son conducting an orchestra, involving members of the audience as instrumentalists, and the baby, in a darker sketch, decapitating dolls. Group sequences include one in which the son mimes chalking on imaginary walls that are then observed by a number of the other clowns, who read the writing until one of them simply crashes through the imaginary wall. Another sequence involves the family around the dining table, where they each demonstrate some particular skill. Necessarily, the notion of a narrative is limited. As far as a plot can be defined, it is that a chaotic family exists with an alcoholic father, a pregnant mother and four children. The father regularly threatens to leave. He is persuaded to stay several times before he finally departs, abandoning the family to even greater chaos, during which time the mother gives birth. Towards the end of the show he returns and the family is happily reunited.

The piece has a number of strengths: its visual style, its engagement of the audience and its accessibility. The audience is encouraged to play at a number of points in the piece, as has been identified earlier. Additionally, at the end of the show, when small reels of paper unwind at speed above the stage, the clowns push them out into the audience, who become entangled. As a result of these actions, play occurred on two levels within the performance. One level of play took place on the stage between the clowns and the second took place by breaking the usual audience/stage boundary so that play occurred between the clowns and their audience. In terms of Sutton-Smith's Play Theory, the play created had strong connections to both the 'rhetoric of the imaginary' and the 'rhetoric of frivolity'. In relation to the 'rhetoric of the imaginary', *Semianyki* demonstrates 'play as an example of metaphysical chaos' (Sutton-Smith 1997: 128). The play that occurs on the stage is increasingly chaotic, demonstrating the disintegration of the family. The boundaries between reality and fantasy are blurred by sequences such as the one discussed above in which the son writes on imaginary walls. In this way, play is used to express the instability of life. The playful content of *Semianyki* is also an example of what Sutton-Smith defines as the way in which literature and play interact when the literature (in this case the theatrical play) 'contains explicitly playful content as part of the art form itself' (1997: 137). Teatr Licedei's work is also an example of play's frivolity, because the play in *Semianyki* is predominantly play for the sake of play. Its purpose is to emphasize the importance of play and to encourage the audience members themselves to play by demonstrating the fun to be had simply in playing. When the mother forms a connection with a member of the audience through *complicité*, the play which ensues is purely frivolous as she flirts with and leers at him. This relationship also creates a moment of what Turner (1982) describes as 'pure potentiality'. The performer has no way of knowing how the audience member will react. A sense of 'spontaneous communitas' (Turner 1982) is created amongst the audience as a whole when the individual responds to the clown performer. It is not necessary to the structure of the piece but it enhances both the atmosphere and the audience's engagement with the performers. Two factors make this a good example of clown theatre: that it takes place in theatre rather than circus spaces and, importantly, that the performers play different characters in each production rather than maintaining an individual clown identity throughout. The playing of different characters moves Teatr Licedei's performers towards the clown actors who are the focus of the next chapter.

4

CLOWNS WHO ACT: ACTORS WHO CLOWN

There are two traditions that can be traced through the appearance of clowns in dramatic texts. The first, as exemplified by Grimaldi, Kemp, Armin and De Castro, involves existing clown performers being written into dramatic texts for a variety of reasons which echo the functions of clowns established at the beginning of this book. Shakespeare introduces clown characters into the plays to help vary the dramatic pace. In some plays (*The Tempest* and *A Midsummer Night's Dream*) they act as light relief; in other plays such as *Lear*, the fool fulfils the clown's traditional role as truth-teller, like the court jester. Sarah Woods' *Only Fools (No Horses)*, commissioned by Angela De Castro, takes three of Shakespeare's clowns (Touchstone, Feste and Lear's Fool) and uses them to make a comment on contemporary society's need for clowns and fools. A variant on this tradition is Dario Fo who writes the texts himself (often in collaboration with his wife Franca Rame) which initially he performs but which, like the other texts listed above, are then available for other performers. The second tradition relating to the appearance of clowns in dramatic texts is when a playwright has been influenced by clowning and creates characters that are not intended to be performed by any particular clown but which make use of conventions of clown behaviour and performance to enhance the purpose of the drama. Brecht and Beckett both make use of this kind of clown character in their work. Examples can be identified in Brecht's *Baden-Baden Cantata* and *Man Equals Man* and in Beckett's *Act Without Words 1, Act Without Words 2* and *Waiting for Godot*. Also considered here are those theatre performances (either devised or text-based) in which the performers can primarily be defined as actors but who make use of clown techniques to create theatre that might be described as *clownesque*. In this kind of theatre the playful nature of the performance is created by combining techniques from acting and clowning, but the performers would not define themselves as clowns. This eclectic performance style has become increasingly popular throughout the United Kingdom and Europe since the late 1960s. This chapter, however, begins its consideration much further back in clown performance history with Joseph Grimaldi (1778–1837).

Grimaldi's clown character, known as Joey, developed within the narrative structure of pantomimes written by Hughes and Dibdin, but Joey remained a constant character in much

Joseph Grimaldi 1778–1837 As a clown in the pantomime of *Mother Goose*. "Sir, I'll just trouble you with a line".

JOE GRIMALDI,

As CLOWN in the Pantomime of Mother Goose.

"Sir, I'll just trouble you with a line."

the same way as circus clowns of the period created a constant clown persona. However, Grimaldi was the first clown to do this in the theatre and as a result he can be viewed as the father of modern theatre clowning.

While Joseph Grimaldi seems to have had the ability to make people laugh from a young age, he did not appear on stage as a clown until 1800, when he worked as part of a double act at Sadler's Wells playing Guzzle, the drinking clown, to Baptiste Dubois' Gobble, the eating clown (Findlater 1978: 79). What was most significant about Grimaldi was the contribution he made to the way the clown looked, and he was an important influence on the later, common use of face make-up. Contemporary sketches and engravings show Grimaldi wearing startling face make-up that consisted of a white base with a red, curved triangle on each cheek. His eyebrows also appear to have been darkened. Various reasons can be given for the design of Grimaldi's make-up. One interpretation is that the red triangles echo the bright colours and geometric shapes of the Harlequin costume. However, it is not clear why Grimaldi's make-up should have been influenced by a pantomime character he did not play. It is possible that Grimaldi chose the two contrasting colours because they would define his features and could be seen clearly from the poorly lit stage to the back of the auditorium. Another possibility, more in keeping with the parodic element of clowning, is that his make-up was intended as a satirical comment on the dandies of the period, who were regular attenders at Sadler's Wells.

Sketches and engravings show his hair in a variety of styles. In the illustration above, Grimaldi has blue hair (whilst other images show him with red hair, which could be seen as influencing the unruly red hair of the later Auguste clowns). The strong lines of his make-up are clearly visible on his cheeks. His costume is in bright colours and the lines of the costume are clearly designed to facilitate Grimaldi's acrobatic sequences. Other contemporary sketches and engravings show Grimaldi in a range of costumes, according to the part he was playing in the pantomime. In this way, Grimaldi differs from the circus clowns who would follow in his footsteps. Theatre clowns have been keener to make use of the signifying qualities of costume, by changing their outfit according to the nature of the piece being performed, than circus clowns, who define their make-up and costume and retain them throughout their careers. Grimaldi could, therefore, be described as an early clown actor. His routines were individually developed but could be moulded into the setting of whichever pantomime the theatre management decided would draw in an audience. Grimaldi changed his costumes as required. Findlater describes his clown costume for *Mother Goose* as

> ...red-white-and-blue motley. He wears a red shirt, frilled and decorated with blue and white facings, which is cut away at the chest and waist to reveal an ornamented shirt beneath; his blue-and-white-striped breeches end above the knee, with a red-white-and blue crested wig, his whitened face is daubed with red triangles on either cheek. (Findlater 1978: 116)

Other illustrations (Findlater 1978: 140–1) from productions of *Harlequin and Asmodeus* (1810), *Harlequin and the Red Dwarf* (1812), and *Harlequin and Padmanaba* (1813) show him in a red, white and black costume; in a red and white costume with a small amount of blue trim; and in a costume of white breeches, blue cummerbund and white and blue patterned jacket. In some illustrations his hair is blue, in others red. Therefore, semiotic analysis of his costumes is less useful in establishing an understanding of his clown character than it would prove to be with later clowns, who develop a costume style and then maintain it or relate it to the show they have devised, where it can be read semiotically as an indicator of character. However, the constancy of the make-up, regardless of the changing costumes, demonstrates a deliberate choice on Grimaldi's part to retain his individual persona as a consistent element of his performance, rather than being completely absorbed into the writer's character.

That Grimaldi's make-up should be a satirical comment on contemporary society is hardly surprising when consideration is given to the satirical nature of a number of his routines. A range of topics were satirized, such as greed, the military (around the time of the Battle of Waterloo) and the theatre. 'The clown himself was, in some respects, a satirical mirror of the times: his guzzling, for instance, was a parody of Georgian greed – a further reason why audiences found him so wildly funny' (Findlater 1978: 158). During the period when Grimaldi was performing, the aristocracy and gentlemen farmers indulged hearty appetites, so, when Joey guzzled pies and strings of sausages, he was commenting on the excess observed in society. Similarly, when he costumed himself in a coal scuttle and kitchen utensils to represent the uniform of the Hussar in *Harlequin and the Red Dwarf*, he was demonstrating both his observation of folly and his ability to mock that folly. To do so, Joey wore a costume in which 'two black varnished coal-scuttles formed his boots, two real horseshoes shod the heels, and with jack-chains and the help of large brass dishes or candlesticks or spurs, equipped his legs in a uniform almost as clattering, unwieldy, and absurd, as the most irresistible of our whiskered propugnatores' (*The Times*, quoted in Findlater 1978: 142). In doing so, Grimaldi draws attention to the ridiculous nature of the Hussar's uniform. Grimaldi, through actions rather than words, was able to insert satire into the loose narrative line of the pantomime. In this way, as well as having a primary function as an entertainer, Grimaldi also functions as a social commentator; a parodist. As has been illustrated, two hundred years later, clowns like Nola Rae would similarly be creating whole narratives which satirized elements of their own society in shows like *Exit Napoleon Pursued by Rabbits*.

The play in which Grimaldi engages is limited by the restrictions of the plot within which his character exists, but much of his play is skills-based. His physical exploits, as he tumbles through openings in the set, are reminiscent of the rough and tumble of childhood, but they are also a way of commanding respect and demonstrating his power through the high standard of his acrobatics.

The characters of the Harlequinade, in which Grimaldi so often took the role of Clown, were distant descendants of the Commedia dell'Arte characters of Pantalone, Colombina and Arlecchino. The influence of Commedia can be seen not in Grimaldi's clown character (which has no direct correlation), but in the lazzi-like nature of his routines and, it could be argued, the satirical nature of some Commedia scenarii. For example, Findlater (1978) gives details of a routine in which Grimaldi creates a man out of vegetables which echoes lazzi (highly rehearsed sequences of physical comedy) in which Commedia characters would pretend to be vegetables (Gordon 1992: 11). Grimaldi's routines also contained a considerable amount of violence and cruelty, typical contents of clown performance. A review from *The Times* referring to the 1812–13 pantomime *Harlequin and the Red Dwarf* notes that for Grimaldi: 'serious tumbles from serious heights, innumerable kicks, and incessant beatings, come on him as matters of common occurrence' (quoted in Findlater 1978: 140). This sounds very similar to the comic violence lazzi identified by Gordon (1992), such as the beating of Arlecchino, most often by Pantalone but also by a range of other characters.

Another significant element of Grimaldi's contribution to clowning is his mastery of transformations and trick work. However, such tricks have been taken up more by the American three-ring circus than by clowns in the theatre. For the audience of Grimaldi's time, this trick work was the equivalent of today's computer-generated images. The audience could marvel at the visual effect even though they might know how it was created. Grimaldi used star traps and vampire traps to appear and disappear magically. Over-sized heads and cloaks were used to allow for the transformation from the pantomime characters to the Harlequinade characters. There is no real equivalent for this in today's theatre clowning. Perhaps the use of illusion in Les Witloof's *Sous Pression* comes close when one of the clowns repeatedly extracts a glass of beer from a seemingly empty brown paper bag. In Grimaldi's day, as now, the audience marvelled at the skill involved in pulling off a trick which would have been far beyond their own capabilities. In general, Grimaldi's performance links most closely to Sutton-Smith's rhetorics of 'play as imaginary' and 'play as frivolous'. There is a strong element of fantasy and imagination in Grimaldi's work, particularly in his creation of the vegetable man. Unusually for a clown, there is also an element of 'play of the self' in the sense of Geertz's 'deep play'. Findlater's book (1978) details a range of injuries suffered by Grimaldi as a result of falls and malfunctioning tricks, and Grimaldi must have been aware of the risks he was taking. Grimaldi's clowning, therefore, was highly physical and the parts he performed were tailored to his particular skills.

Further back in theatre history, Shakespeare created clown characters that were often written with a particular actor in mind. These clown characters were used in a variety of ways in a number of his plays. What is common, however, to all is that they occupied a liminal space, creating a bridge between the theatrical world of the play and the real world of the audience. This bridging function also occurs within the plays. Many of the plays with significant clown parts have two worlds established, with the clown acting as a link between them. Often he is the only person to move between the two worlds. Thus in *Twelfth Night,* Feste moves between the world of the courtly lovers, where he mocks and parodies Olivia and Orsino, and the world of the more earthy characters, Toby Belch, Andrew Aguecheek and Maria, where he is co-opted to take part in the plot against Malvolio.

Shakespeare wrote parts for specific actors who specialized in clown performance. The most important of these clown actors were Will Kempe (for whom the parts of Bottom, Dogberry and Falstaff were created) and Robert Armin (Feste, Touchstone and Lear's Fool). The clowns and fools in Shakespeare's plays make use of a range of clown techniques that are recognizable from other clown performances. Some of the clown roles call for displays of physical skill, such as dancing and singing (Feste). Many of the roles make great use of word-play and the delivery of doggerel (Feste, Lear's Fool); still others create opportunities for slapstick (Trinculo and Stefano). The different techniques can be closely linked to the different performers: so Armin's roles are written to demonstrate his skill in singing and in delivering word play. It is true that the role of Feste also demands a high level of physical skill, particularly in the scene where the actor has to switch rapidly between performing as Feste and performing as Feste performing Sir Topas. Parts written for Kemp, such as Bottom, were more physical in their creation of comedy.

The minor clown roles, such as Peter in *Romeo and Juliet,* the clown in *Titus Andronicus;* and the Porter in *Macbeth,* can be defined as minor because in these plays the clown's only function is to mark a turning point in the play. So the clown in *Titus Andronicus* provides a pragmatic counterpoint to Titus. He opens Titus's eyes to the insanity of his actions and provides the audience with a release of tensions. He also acts as a go-between for Titus and the court. He appears in only two scenes: Act 4, scenes 3 and 4. In the first scene, he enters with his pigeons on the way to the court. He engages in clown word-play by mistaking Titus's reference to Jupiter as a reference to a gibbet-maker and demonstrates a simplicity of mind throughout his speeches. In the second scene, the clown enters briefly, delivers Titus's letter and is told he will be hanged. Taken together, these scenes offer first a release of tension and then a reinforcement of the closeness of death in a world governed by Saturnius. However, the very brevity of his appearance limits his potential impact. Clowns with repeated entrances not only have the opportunity to make more of an impact on the audience but also to fulfil a function of a higher order, such as mirroring a major theme or commenting on the actions of their superiors. A group of such clowns can be found in *The Tempest*. These clowns, Stefano and Trinculo, together with their follower, Caliban, provide a comic version of a major theme of the play – that of kingship and what it means to rule a community. Together these three characters represent a combination of the Island (Caliban) and the world outside (Stephano and Trinculo) and all three take a step away from their usual servitude. These clowns are much more closely involved with the plot than the previous example. They are also different from many of the other major clowns in that their humour is resolutely physical. They draw laughter from the audience with their physical antics. First there is physical humour in the scene in which Stephano discovers what he believes to be a four-legged monster under the gabardine. This sequence has the same potential for humour as any circus clown entrée. Similarly, in Act 1, scene 2, the action with the clothes line provides the opportunity for a range of object interaction clowning in which the characters become entangled in the clothing before finally managing to dress themselves in a most ridiculous manner. All this lunacy, enacted in Stefano's belief that he can be an adequate king, provides the audience with a comic contrast to the power struggle Prospero has created. Stefano's foolishness also provides a comic contrast to the qualities that are required in a leader. In this way, the audience is made to laugh but a valid point about kingship is also demonstrated. According to Videbæk, the clown plot to murder Prospero 'comically counterbalances the political one' (1996: 21); the audience learns from the resonances created between the comic plot and the serious one.

Other major clown roles, such as Bottom, Feste, Touchstone and Lear's fool, have less of the physical about them. There is obvious visual humour in Bottom's ass's head, and Titania's wooing of him connects with the common clown theme of finding humour in sexual matters. Bottom is also a prime example of clown anarchy: he causes chaos wherever he goes. In the rehearsals organized by Quince, Bottom wants to play all the parts and has to demonstrate, badly, how all the parts should be performed, revealing clown naivety. This scene also connects with the clown's inherent metatheatricality. In some cases this is shown by the clown's direct address to the audience but, here, the Mechanicals' rehearsal highlights the difficulty of depicting things on stage, such as moonshine and a wall. This scene also provides the opportunity for the insertion of physical comedy and stage business as the Mechanicals try to work out how to present the characters and elements of the scenes. Bottom, in presenting each role, has the chance to parody a range of bad acting techniques. In the fairy world (with the help of Puck's magic) he causes chaos by attracting Titania's romantic and sexual attention. This relationship is created by Shakespeare as a parody of courtly love. Moving as he does between the various groups,

Bottom links the world of the Mechanicals with the world of the fairies, and finally to the world of the court and the romantic young lovers. The potential physicality of much of Bottom's stage business points towards Will Kemp's particular skills as a clown performer.

The final two clowns to be considered (Feste and Lear's Fool) are wordier in nature; more reliant on parody and word-play. The role of Feste also contains many songs and some physical action. Feste's primary function in the play is to guide the audience's responses to the other characters. Whilst he does become involved in the plot action towards the end, for a great part of the play he stands outside the main plot and this distance enhances his function as commentator. He is also able to adjust his clowning to suit the group he is with. Thus his clowning with the courtly Olivia and Orsino is reliant on word play and parody. The song he sings in Act 2, scene 4 is an ironic comment on the sentimentality of Orsino. Orsino asks for a song which 'dallies with the innocence of youth' and Feste sings 'come away, come away, death'. With Toby Belch, Andrew Aguecheek and Maria his humour is much more earthy. He joins them in their drunken revelry demonstrating his musical skill once again by singing 'Oh mistress mine, where are you roaming?' There is also a dark side to Feste's clowning, which is revealed in his treatment of Malvolio towards the end of the play when he takes on the role of Sir Topas and torments Malvolio by switching between roles.

In *King Lear* Shakespeare moves the clown character in a new direction. Lear's Fool's physical skills are devoted not to slapstick but to mirroring the King's decline. His word play relies on doggerel and puns, which he uses to try to help Lear. Here the fool becomes a truth-teller in that he becomes an extension of Lear. He reveals to the audience various aspects of Lear's character and helps us refocus our attention on the king when watching his struggle becomes difficult to bear. Lear's Fool is anachronistically like a modern theatre clown. He can reveal the pain of existence. He is not on stage simply to make us laugh but to make us understand what it is to be human and to be flawed.

In a modern context, in *Only Fools (No Horses)*, Angela De Castro uses clown play to suggest a serious point about society, and the role of fools and clowns in society. De Castro's performance as Lear's Fool in this play provides an example of the contemporary *clown actor*. The importance of words and word play is indicated by the title, which works in a number of ways. The word 'fools' is prominent in the title and appears to suggest the focus of the play but there is also a half reference to the popular television series *Only Fools and Horses*. The origins of that title are obscure but the lyrics of the television series theme tune make the meaning clear 'why do only fools and horses work?' In the piece, commissioned by De Castro and written by Sarah Woods (2005), the Fools are the three characters of the play: the Fool, Touchstone and Feste, drawn from Shakespeare. Lear's Fool spends the play wishing to die and even trying to kill himself. Eventually, he chooses a method of suicide which is to be buried up to the neck and trampled by wild horses, but there are no horses – hence the title of the play. The implication is, therefore, that only the fools are working, which elevates their importance. In commissioning the play, it was De Castro's intention that a piece of theatre would be created which allowed for the three fools to be on stage, considering the possibility of finding an end to their stories (De Castro, interview with the author, 2006). In its final version, the play is much more complex than that. It is so full of references to Shakespeare and to other writers on fools and fooling that it becomes very difficult to follow. Also the predominance of the text reframes the physical comedy of the clown as only a small part of the performance, rather than its focus. Equally important is the fact that only one of three performers (De Castro) is a clown, the others are actors. The director, John Wright, is experienced in clown theatre and playful theatre but, together, they failed to create a convincing piece of *clown theatre*. There are various reasons for this.

Firstly the set was overly complex. It consisted of grass covered curves which created the sense of an eye. Where the pupil should be, there was a video screen. When the Fool ventures out into the real world, his experiences are shown on the screen. At frequent intervals throughout the show, one or more of the performers was rigged to fly, as the notion of defying gravity was central to the play. However, the significance of this device was not adequately communicated to the audience. The costumes were equally complex, with De Castro's Fool in purple velour and a crown. Touchstone makes his first entrance inexplicably dressed as a carpenter, and Feste appears at one point dressed as a Japanese Geisha.

De Castro's ability to connect with and play with the audience is hampered by the complexity of these elements. The truest moment of clown performance arose from De Castro's spontaneous insertion of comments and looks within the show. Early in the performance, strands of hair began to come loose from the wig she was wearing. She ignored the first two but on the third she held the strand up to the audience, pulled a face and sighed. In her ability to play spontaneously with an unplanned element she was able to make a connection to the audience, which she struggled to do within the confines of this text.

The opening sequence of the play creates the opportunity for clown performance. The Fool is trying to commit suicide. The entrance with a noose around his neck refers both to Beckett and to *Slava's Snowshow* (in which De Castro appeared in 1999). The crown he carries allows a conversation to develop in which De Castro plays both parts (with the crown she is Lear, without it she is the Fool). The humour here arises from the rapid switches from one character to another. At the end of the conversation, the Fool climbs onto a higher area of the stage and jumps. The atmosphere is without gravity (De Castro is rigged to fly) and the Fool fails in his exploit. Here the connection to clowning is clear. The Fool has a task he wishes to complete (to commit suicide) and no matter how hard he tries, he cannot succeed. This objective runs throughout the play to the point at which the Fool and Feste have a conversation about how the Fool might kill himself. The Fool's responses to Feste's suggestion demonstrate both the clown's vulnerability and his unusual logic. So the suggestion that the Fool might kill himself by jumping from a great height is answered by the response, 'I'm very bouncy' – a comment which draws attention to De Castro's rotund build. The suggestion that dehydration might be a route to death is met with 'My mother is a camel', demonstrating clown illogicality. Finally the decision is taken to bury the Fool up to the neck so that his head can be trampled by a wild stallion. In true clown fashion the Fool fails to complete his exploit because there are no horses.

The show contains a number of sequences that rely on traditional clown behaviour. The concept of failure has already been dealt with in the Fool's attempt to kill himself, and this is emphasized when the Fool tries to get either Touchstone or Feste to help him by holding the end of the rope, but they are too concerned with chasing each other to do what the Fool asks. There are several incidences of violence. Early in the play Feste nails Touchstone's ear to a table. Later on, Feste and Touchstone throw stones at the Fool when he is buried up to the neck. The idea, drawn from Wright and Lecoq, of the importance of play is demonstrated in the section where Touchstone tries to creep up on Feste as he eats his sandwich. What occurs on stage is reminiscent of a game of Grandmother's Footsteps.

The Fool provides an example of the clown/fool's potential for wittiness and wordplay when he negotiates that Touchstone must pay for the smell of Feste's sandwich with the sound of his money. Another example occurs towards the end of the play when the Fool challenges Touchstone to find the answer to his riddle. After a lengthy exchange, the answer is revealed to be 'You are a fool. Without a master', which is, of course, central to the situation of the play.

Later in the play there is an example of clown transgression of social conventions when Touchstone removes a crown from a silver platter and puts it on his head. The transgression of claiming the crown is mild in comparison to what follows. Touchstone excretes onto the silver platter so that a pile of excrement takes the place of the crown. This situation is pushed even further when Feste discovers it and tries to persuade Touchstone to eat it, eating half of it himself in the process. The sequence appears to have little connection to the plot beyond highlighting the privilege of the fools to transgress the usual conventions of social behaviour. Finally, as the meaning of the play becomes clear, the audience realizes that the Fools are trapped by the fact that nobody wants to hear the truth, and telling the truth is the Fool's job.

The complexity of Woods's text reduces the opportunity for clowning in its performance and, consequently, there is much less opportunity for play. De Castro acknowledges that the play was not what she intended it to be: 'I wanted something very simple, accessible, just telling the story, the point of view of the fools on what happened to them' (De Castro, interview with the author, 2006). In a simpler version, there would have been opportunity for the clowns/fools to play at trying to find for themselves the resolution that Shakespeare failed to provide. Despite the experience of *Only Fools (No Horses)*, De Castro remains convinced that '[i]t's a mistake to think a clown can only do their (sic) own devised work' (De Castro, interview with author 2006). For De Castro, the clown can do anything, and that includes working silently, working with words, devising his or her own work and using the texts provided by writers. It is likely that a clown will bring a different perspective to text work from a more conventionally trained actor. De Castro suggests that this is because 'actors look for perfection, clowns celebrate imperfection and that makes it more real' (De Castro, interview with author 2006).

If the fools in *Only Fools (No Horses)* are fictional truth-tellers, there remains one individual in the western Europe who, whilst being an example of a clown actor, might also be reasonably described as connecting with the truth-telling tradition of the court jester (dealt with in the next chapter). He is to be found in Italy and his name is Dario Fo. Fo was born in 1926 in Lombardy in the north of Italy. Mitchell identifies the influence of growing up in this area on the kind of theatre Fo went on to produce: 'Fo referred to the stories of the *fabulatori* as a "structural storehouse", a model and constant background source of reference for the satirical stories, fables and tales which form the background of his monologues' (Mitchell 1999: 49). Fo is internationally recognized as an actor, director and playwright, and much of his solo performance work uses clowning to present a socio-political message. Indeed Fo uses the Italian word *giullare* to describe himself. There is no direct English translation for this word, but the closest is jester. When he was awarded the Nobel Prize for Literature in 1997, the press release described Fo as one who 'one emulates the jesters of the Middle Ages in scourging authority and upholding the dignity of the downtrodden' (www.nobelprize.org). Thus it can be seen that Fo is widely recognized as fitting within the jester's tradition. 'He if anyone merits the epithet of jester' (www.nobelprize.org). Indeed Fo's Nobel Lecture was entitled 'Contra Jogulatores Oblequentes' (Against jesters of irreverent speech) and, in effect, it is Fo's manifesto for comic theatre. According to Farrell, '[t]he harlequin behaved as a harlequin to proclaim the mission of the harlequin' (Farrell and Scuderi 2000: 203). In preparing his speech, Fo behaved as a true clown by rejecting the conventions of behaviour and offering an alternative instead. Thus, he did not create a complete lecture which could be translated and issued prior to the ceremony, instead Fo gave a 'semi-improvised monologue delivered on the basis of a series of sketches, scrawls and cartoons' (2000: 203).

Fo's connection to the jester tradition can also be identified in his performance style and writing. Indeed, in much of Fo's work, it is difficult to separate the text from Fo's performance of it, and *Mistero Buffo* is the work where the both the text and Fo's performance can be seen to have the clearest connections both to jesters and to clowning. Brian Glanville's comments on the workshops run by Dario Fo and Franca Rame in London in 1983, coinciding with Fo's performance of Mistero Buffo at the Riverside Studios, highlight the similarities between Fo's techniques and the techniques of clowns analysed elsewhere in this book. 'Like Max Wall or Tommy Trinder, he'll make use of a latecomer...Like Roy Hudd, he may crack a "difficult joke", and pretend that one part of the audience has got it, the other hasn't' (cited in Mitchell 1986: 275). The importance of the performer's connection to his audience can be seen here, together with the clown's ability to play, to respond spontaneously to whatever occurs.

Fo also makes use of what Wright defines as the *drop*. When writing about *The Pope and the Witch*, Scuderi describes the way in which Fo performs the *fou* pope, which involves him dropping in and out of character, using direct address and a wink to signal to the audience when he is the Pope and when he is the actor playing the Pope.

> Then before his next line, the stage directions read 'He gets back into character'. The change in and out of character accompanied by the metatheatrical wink to the audience evinces both the *verispellis* and the paradoxical *finto tinto* qualities that underlie the clown's subversive power. (Farrell and Scuderi 2000: 50, italics in original)

From this it can be seen that the clowning technique of coming in and out of character is used by Fo to highlight a satirical comment. The aside and the wink serve to indicate to the audience that, whilst he is presenting the Pope to them, Fo's identification is with the peasants. Other clown techniques can be observed elsewhere in *Mistero Buffo*. In *The Resurrection of Lazarus*, for example, Fo displays considerable skill in playing the whole of the crowd who are witnessing the event. Here Fo uses mime to create a whole range of characters.

An examination of the text of *Mistero Buffo* raises the question of whether Fo should be considered first and foremost as a writer or a performer and, for the purposes of this argument, the text is considered not as a piece of dramatic literature but as a guide in considering how Fo performs the play. Evidence is also drawn from other critical material and, as has been seen above, from reviews of Fo's performance of the piece. There are, of course, similarities between Fo and the *clown actors*, such as Angela De Castro, and the performers of *clown theatre*, such as Nola Rae. The difference lies in the material available to the critic of their work. As might be expected, given their mime form, Nola Rae's performance pieces do not exist in a textual form. Fo's work (like the play performed by De Castro) exists in textual form and, as is the case with much theatre criticism, performance can, to some extent, be deduced from that text. Fo's understanding of clown techniques such as slapstick, direct address, dropping in and out of character and mime, is written into the texts (particularly the monologues in *Mistero Buffo* and *Obscene Fables*). This also gives a clear indication of the required performance style to anyone other than Fo who wishes to perform them.

A number of extracts from *Mistero Buffo* can be analysed in terms of what they reveal about Fo's performance style and his political viewpoint. One such sequence is 'Boniface VIII'. In this sequence Fo's mime skills are displayed in the dressing of Boniface, where each item of clothing is demonstrated through its impact on the physicality of the wearer and through his mimed interaction with other characters who are not physically present on the stage. Fo's political standpoint expresses a view on the inappropriacy of wealth and luxury in the Catholic Church. This is similar to, but more extensive than, Brecht's Cardinal Barberini dressing and transforming into Pope Urban VIII in *Galileo* (1986). The historically distant character of Boniface VIII is used to enable Fo to comment simultaneously on the Catholic Church's past and present ostentation. Jesus is depicted as a poor man and Boniface's response to him is 'Look, look what a terrible state he's in! Now I see why they call him "poor Christ"' (Fo 1997: 82). Historically, of course, a meeting between Jesus and Boniface VIII could never have occurred but Fo collides the two periods of history to make his point about how far the Catholic Church has moved from its humble founder.

In Fo, politics and religion become so closely entwined that his work as a clown actor often comments on religion to make a political point. His most common technique is satire, through which he focuses on the gulf between the wealthy churchmen, who are his targets (such as Pope Boniface VIII), and the peasants, with whom he sympathizes. In this sense, Fo's creations serve a similar purpose to the jesting of **Will Somers** and his attacks on Cardinal Wolsey, discussed later. Both Somers and Fo attack individuals who can be seen as representing the negative face of religions.

More overtly, political comment can be seen in the character of the Maniac in *Accidental Death of An Anarchist*. In the original Italian text the character is called Matto, the Italian word for fool. Fo's choice of this word signals the connection between the character and the outspoken jesters of the past. According to Scuderi, '[t]he attributes that define this character are derived from the subversive clowns of earlier comic forms' (Farrell and Scuderi 2000: 42). Scuderi recognizes both the clown tendency of the character and its historical precedents. The translation as 'maniac' deprives the English audience of this link and does not point to the real nature of the character.

The content of *Accidental Death of an Anarchist* is designed to reveal the absurdity of the official version of the death of Giuseppe Pinelli, who is alleged to have fallen out of a window while in police custody. In Act 1, scene 2 and Act 2, scene 1, the Maniac repeatedly reveals flaws in the account of the Anarchist's death:

> Unless this officer was very quick about it, and went rushing down to the second floor, stuck his head out of the window as the anarchist was coming past, put his shoe back on mid-flight, and then shot back up to the fourth floor just in time for the body to hit the bottom. (Fo 1997: 172)

This speech is full of clownish absurdity. Only a clown, working from an internal world view in which conventional logic has no place, could present such a plan. The absurdity is clear to the audience. This is one example of many ridiculous explanations that the Maniac presents which encourage the audience to realize how ridiculous the official explanation of the real event was. In terms of clowning techniques, there are a number of slapstick moments in *Accidental Death of an Anarchist*. The Maniac's glass eye falls out, the character Sports Jacket slips and falls on it, it is placed in a glass of water and the Maniac swallows it. Another slapstick sequence revolves around the Maniac's false hand, which repeatedly falls off when it is shaken by another character. There is also an extended sequence of comic violence when the characters hit and kick each other.

The use of clown techniques and comic violence are some of the means by which Fo might be identified as a clown, while Jenkins, in his article 'The Roar of the Clown', aligns Fo with Brecht in terms of the political content of his work: 'Fo blends politics and art with an effortless eloquence that makes him a Brechtian clown' (Jenkins 1986: 173). For Fo, content and style of performance are closely linked. His use of montage demonstrates, and is reliant on, his physical skill and his ability to play a multiplicity of characters in quick succession, and it also creates an episodic structure which discourages emotional empathy in a way similar to that utilized by Brecht.

Like Fo, Brecht's clown characters in *Man Equals Man* make use of mock violence. The first example of this can be found in scene 4 – 'The Canteen of the Widow Leokadja Begbick'. In this scene the soldiers rush Galy Gay and force him to undress. At this early point in the play violence is used as a source of slapstick comedy. The audience is not encouraged to empathize with the victim or to condemn the perpetrators. This is an example of *spass* (fun); the performers can have fun performing and the audience can have fun watching. Combined with the mock firing squad, these episodes emphasize the central ideology that often in society man lacks individuality and can be replaced by another. Brecht's play mounts to a climactic episode of violence which demonstrates the dangers of losing sight of humans' individuality. Gay's transformation into Jip renders him inhuman and his repeated shots at the fortress, encouraged by Widow Begbick, are not comic. The gestus of violence is used to demonstrate comedy and anti-comedy, underlining Brecht's political and ideological message.

In establishing Gay and the soldiers as types of clown, Brecht creates characters who can easily break with mimetic traditions. Images of Brecht's 1931 production of the play (see Thomson and Sacks in the *Cambridge Companion to Brecht* 1994: 71), which was designed by Caspar Neher, demonstrate how the eccentricity of the soldiers and Gay was reinforced through costumes and even through the use of false noses (the clown's archetypal trademark). Visually, Gay became more of a whiteface clown as the play progressed because the actor playing him, Peter Lorre, 'whitened his face powder during the play' (Schechter, cited in Thomson and Sacks 1994: 71) to demonstrate in an epic manner his increasing fear of death. Traditionally, in the circus, clowns have difficulty submitting to authority. They have a natural affinity with anarchy, which suits the actions of the soldiers particularly well as they use Jip's passbook as evidence that Gay is Jip and they undermine their sergeant, Bloody Five. Whether or not we agree with their behaviour, the soldiers and Gay are men of action. They do not remain passive; they adapt and transform as is evidenced by Gay's transformation from harmless porter to a mechanized inhuman killing machine.

A number of other clown techniques can be identified within the text of *Man Equals Man*. There are sequences of slapstick humour. Gay demonstrates comic naivety bordering on clown stupidity. There are examples of internal illogicality in Gay's actions or actions perpetrated against him. The clearest example of slapstick humour is found in scene 2 when the four soldiers attempt to get into the Pagoda. This scene is reminiscent of a circus entrée in which a group of Augustes attempts to complete an exploit that is doomed to failure. Here the clown soldiers attempt to gain access to the Pagoda in the hope of stealing money. In a series of interactions in which objects prove to have higher status than the clown soldiers, Uriah loses his helmet, Jesse traps his hand, their uniforms are ripped, Polly gets his foot stuck through the roof and Jip gets stuck by his hair to the doorframe. Everything that they attempt demonstrates their incompetence. Brecht's insistence that theatre should be *spass* increases the likelihood that such scenes would be played in such a way as to maximize the humour. The clown's traditional transgressing of the mimetic conventions found in naturalistic acting can be seen as being in line with Brecht's theories of *Verfremsdungeffekt* and *gestus*. Each slip, trip or fall signals a punctuation mark in the action, giving the audience time to laugh but also time to reflect on the unlawful actions of the soldiers. If the four soldiers can be seen as Augustes, then Galy Gay is the dimmest Auguste of them all. In scene three, the soldiers trick him into revealing information about himself by pausing to let him fill in details and then presenting those details to him as though they knew them all along, provoking Gay to ask 'Oh, have you met me already, as you know that? Or my wife perhaps?' (Brecht 1979: 12).

In scene 9 number ii, Galy Gay is charged with stealing an elephant and with attempting to sell a phoney elephant. These two charges are, of course, mutually exclusive: he cannot have stolen an elephant if it is not really an elephant at all. This episode is a clear example of clown logic. An even clearer example is to be found in scene 9, iii, where Uriah shouts 'Fire! So that he can hear he's dead!' (Brecht 1979: 54). Only a clown would be convinced of his own death by the sound of gun fire rather than the impact of the bullet. Until the point of his mock death, Gay and the other soldiers have been established as Augustes, but, with their elaborate plotting, the soldiers move towards the kind of cunning more usually associated with White face clowns. When Gay rises again as Jip he is no longer a clown and becomes instead a grotesque version of himself; an incarnation which is far more dangerous than the original harmless Gay. In this way, Brecht makes use of the clown characters to establish a clear political point about the nature of man's individuality and about the horrors and injustices of war.

Given his political approach to the use of clowns, Brecht was frustrated by Beckett's use of clowns in *Waiting for Godot*. According to Mayer, 'The sham abstraction of the clowns in Beckett's play displeased the Marxist dramaturg Brecht' (Mayer 1979: 73). Brecht's intention was to rewrite Beckett's play in such a way as to increase its political message. His notes indicate that he intended to turn Vladimir into an intellectual and Estragon into a proletarian, allowing for dialogue which would have echoed that found in Brecht's *Conversations of Refugees*. Beckett's purpose, however much Brecht may have disapproved, was far from political. In fact, he uses his clown characters to create a philosophical message which relies heavily on existentialism. The contrasting uses made of clown characters by Brecht and Beckett demonstrate the versatility of the clown.

Beckett used clown characters (both mute and speaking) to create pieces of theatre designed to reflect, and to encourage the audience to reflect on, what it means to be human. It is significant that, having used talking clowns in *Waiting for Godot*, when Beckett returns to clowns as metaphors for human existence four years later, he renders them silent. However, it seems that whilst Didi (Vladimir) and Gogo (Estragon) talk, Beckett uses their words to confuse rather than to clarify meaning. By the time he came to write *Act Without Words 1* and *Act Without Words 2*, Beckett abandoned the spoken word, preferring to rely on mimed performance that would communicate visually with the audience without the complication of words. As Beckett is communicating on the human condition metaphorically, he seems to have decided that image-based metaphors would be more successful than verbal ones. These two pieces offer slightly different philosophical responses to what the purpose of life is and how mankind might deal with the business of being alive in a seemingly random, if not hostile, environment. In *Act Without Words I*, Beckett explores the notion that man adapts to the world in which he finds himself. Thus, the man is thrown on stage three times before he realizes that responding to the whistle is not a good idea. The silence and stoicism of his response (he does nothing more than pick himself up and brush himself off – echoing the words of the song 'I'm gonna pick myself up, dust myself off and start all over again') draws the audience into a relationship with him, establishing what Lecoq would identify as *complicité*. Through this relationship, Beckett encourages individuals in the audience to interpret the man's experiences in the light of their own experience. No comment or gloss is offered by *Act Without Words I*; the notion of what the piece means is left (as in life) to the individual. Beckett offers the suggestion, through the man's physical actions, that life is relentless in its attack on us (reflecting notions of existential angst) and that one possible way forward is to learn to adapt to what life throws at us. It is necessary for the audience to decide what is signified by the whistling. Whistles occur from both wings and from above, indicating omnipresence. There are two obvious interpretations available. One is that the whistles signify the force which rules the universe. For Christians this would be God but it could equally be interpreted as Karma, where the man's struggles are a punishment for previous wrong-doing. Alternatively, the whistles indicate the presence of other antagonistic humans. The nature of human relationships and what consolation they offer us for the pain of existence is explored throughout Beckett's plays (*Endgame*, *Waiting for Godot*, *Act Without Words 2*, and *Play*). The audience member will interpret the connotative symbol of the whistles in the light of his or life experience and world view. Whatever the significance of the whistle, the man takes a long time to learn that nothing good will come of responding to it. He repeatedly tries to reach a carafe hanging down from the flies and repeatedly fails in that exploit in typical clown fashion, despite adapting to whatever means are offered him. A number of the items which fly in can be interpreted as vital to the continuance of life, connecting the piece more strongly to notions of existence. The tree (somewhat arbitrarily) provides shelter, the carafe contains water, and the rope has the potential to become the means to ending existence. In this way, Beckett is suggesting that, as individuals, we try to adapt in order to survive. However, the lack of success of the man's attempts to survive indicates that such attempts are examples of the way humans seek to live by external, socially imposed, values. Ultimately, the man chooses not to respond to the whistles and the offered objects. Here Beckett offers the audience a symbol for authenticity, for a life based on Good Faith, but the symbol is not a happy or attractive one, which suggests the existential pain of man's ultimate and unavoidable isolation.

This adaptation equates to what Sartre identified as inauthenticity and bad faith and ultimately it fails us. At the end of *Act Without Words 1*, the man realizes that it is best not to respond at all. However, when he does nothing at all, nothing happens, and the performance ends. In this way, Beckett seems to suggest that inaction in the face of life is not a viable course of (in)action. In *Act Without Words 2*, he goes on to present alternative strategies for coping with life. Here each 'Player' (and what exactly does that choice of label signify?) has created rituals to help them deal with the meaningless of life: one prays repeatedly whilst the other relies on physical exercise. So Beckett is addressing the concept at the heart of Sartrean Existentialism, that of the meaningless of human existence. Sartre suggests that when man recognizes this lack of meaning, he experiences angst. The players in *Act Without Words 2* have developed ways of avoiding this angst. Their responses lead them into Bad Faith and Inauthentic existence. The angst is not addressed by their rituals; it is blocked out by the fact that they leave themselves no time in which to feel it. There is no indication that the rituals provide them with a response to the meaningless of life. They simply find a way to pass time but there is no productive outcome from these rituals, as is indicated by the structure of *Act Without Words 2*. All that has happened by the end of the piece is that the players have moved further across the stage. Beckett's device of ending the piece with a repetition of the opening suggests to the audience that these rituals are never-endingly cyclical in their nature. They are no more useful than the endless waiting of Didi and Gogo in *Waiting for Godot*.

The two Players' rituals are, however, different in nature. Player A relies on medication and religion for support whilst Player B relies on clock-watching and exercise. The lack of communication between the two highlights man's isolation in life. Both Players brood – an indication that they are constantly reflecting on the meaning of life and the brooding provides a punctuation similar to what Wright (2006) identifies as a separation. The piece demonstrates that there is no meaning to life. Beckett appears to share Sartre's view that man is isolated, that life is random and without meaning. It seems as if Beckett is searching for a resolution to this existential angst but he fails to provide an answer in *Act Without Words 1*, *Act Without Words 2*, or *Waiting for Godot*.

In *Waiting for Godot*, Beckett presents Didi and Gogo potentially as clowns (indicated by the costumes normally adopted which are reminiscent of Chaplin's clown, and by the clown-like names).

> Blin's first idea was to present the characters as clowns and construct a circus ring onstage...he claimed that it was the relationship between Vladimir and Estragon, the rapid-fire cross-talk dialogue that made him think of clowns. (Bradby 2001: 58)

Peter Hall had the same initial response as Roger Blin (the French director who directed the world premiere of *Waiting for Godot* in January 1953 at the Théâtre de Babylone in Montparnasse) when he began rehearsals of the play for *his* production which opened at Arts Theatre, London on August 3 1955. However, neither director portrays the characters as typical circus clowns. Both pull back towards tramp clowns, reminiscent of Chaplin and the double act of **Laurel** and **Hardy**. These clowns explore the same existential issues as the performers in the later mime pieces but they are able to draw attention to their situation with words. Through their communication, Beckett presents the audience with a picture of how little we communicate with those around us. We misunderstand each other, argue for the sake of arguing but are drawn back together rather than be alone.

> *...Estragon pulls himself free, exit right.]* Gogo! Come back! *[VLADIMIR runs to extreme left, scans the horizon. Enter ESTRAGON right, he hastens towards VLADIMIR, falls into his arms.]* There you are again!
> ESTRAGON: I'm in hell!
> VLADIMIR: Where were you?
>
> (Beckett 1990: 68–9)

There remains the question of why Beckett chose to use clown characters in order to explore notions of human existence. Perhaps he was relying on the ambiguity of clowns. The audience laughs at the clowns (for example in the hat-swapping sequence) but at the same time, they may be laughing *with* the clowns, internalizing elements of the experience and exploring the parallels between the clowns and themselves. *Waiting for Godot* is not necessarily a particularly funny play but the iconic significance of clowns establishes the potential for laughter in the minds of the audience. Then, when the characters behave in non-clown-like ways (discussing suicide), a tension is created between what the audience expects of the clowns (societal norms and, therefore, inauthentic existence) and what they actually appear to feel (existential angst). Running beneath this is the audience's awareness of the commonly-held notions that beneath the make-up, clowns are generally sad individuals, so that, when Didi and Gogo discuss suicide, they bring to the surface a stereotypical view of clowns.

There is no indication in the cast list that Didi and Gogo should be played as clowns but the inclusion of a number of physical clown routines point strongly to the need for them to be performed as such. Gogo's initial difficulties with his boots, as well as serving to highlight physical suffering, are a clear pointer towards the traditional clowning element of the clown struggling to establish supremacy over an inanimate object. Later in the play, the hat routine can also be likened to circus clowning. These elements were highlighted in Luc Bondy's 1999 production where '[t]he scene of the trying on of the boots in Act 2 was built up into an elaborate game with much giggling and Estragon rolling around on his back' (Bradby 2001: 203).

By the mid 1950s, the notion of a tramp clown or hobo clown (in the USA) had been firmly established, beginning with Chaplin and tracing a line through Joe Jackson to Emmett Kelly and Otto Greibling. So it seems clear that Beckett alludes to this tradition in the actions and names of his characters. Indeed Bradby suggests that 'Beckett's choice [for the part of Estragon] would have been for the much more restrained and sad-faced clowning of **Buster Keaton'** (Bradby 2001: 91). Beckett clearly has in mind, not the traditional circus pairing of auguste and white-face for Estragon and Vladimir, but the more restrained clowning of those who clowned on film such as Keaton, **Langdon**, Chaplin and Laurel and Hardy. Blin thought that 'to see Vladimir and Estragon as clowns was a false trail' (in Bradby 2001: 58). However, it is clear that Beckett had a strong notion of a particular kind of clown in mind when he wrote the parts of Vladimir and Estragon. He wanted the kind of clowning where the sadness of the clown and the futility of his attempts to control his world highlight the tragic-comedy of life. Blau described Vladimir and Estragon as 'simply two *performers* stripped of traditional notions of character' (in Bradby 2001: 98). Here, Blau provides a pertinent description of the art of clowning. When the clown performer stands before his audience, he does so revealed in his clown persona, not hidden behind an externally created character. The actors who play Vladimir and Estragon as clowns will not be helped by Stanislavskian approaches; they need to allow connections to form between the fears expressed by Vladimir and Estragon and the fears they carry within them as individuals. The revelation of this inner fear through the futile words and actions of Vladimir and Estragon brings alive the existential clowns created by Beckett.

Beckett's plays, along with those of other writers of what Esslin described as the Theatre of the Absurd, began the process of changing the face of European Drama irreversibly. From the mid 1950s, the range of theatrical performance style broadened considerably and this range was increased still further by the theatrical developments of the 1960s. From the mid-sixties, Britain experienced a period of theatrical experimentation. What follows is a brief summary of key developments and key companies that influenced the development of theatre clowning in Britain. The Happenings, Assemblages and Events of those years established a model of theatre in opposition to the tradition of text-based realism. Thus a form of theatre began to be created which encouraged the audience to interpret the meaning of a theatrical performance that was not communicated primarily through words. The creation of an environment and the incongruous use of props was a step towards the imaginative world of clowning. Following on from these experiments, in the late 1970s a new kind of theatre company could be seen developing in Britain which focused on creating theatre not from text but from the performers' exploration of their own experiences, through their bodies. The People Show, founded in 1966, can be seen as one example of this kind of theatre which challenged its audience by constructing sequences of movement with no obvious literal interpretation. By the 1980s, devising had become a common method of working across small touring theatre companies. Physical theatre, which had appeared in the late 1960s under the influence of Grotowski and Artaud, now re-emerged amongst actors and directors trained by Lecoq.

Without doubt the influence of Lecoq-trained graduates such as Simon McBurney (founder of Complicite), returning from Paris to Britain, was central to the development of these new companies. Complicite and other companies were interested in exploring the ways in which the performers' bodies could be used to convey both narrative and emotion. As a result, much emphasis was placed on the expressive and mimic potential of the human body. Drawing also on the clown training offered by Lecoq (introduced in the 1960s), these companies were also alive to the possibilities of physical humour. Following on from the work of companies such as **Kaboodle** (1978) and **Mummerandada** (1985), who began creating what could be described as popular theatre, often performed outdoors in public spaces, companies like Complicite challenged conventional theatrical form whilst continuing to perform in conventional theatre spaces. In combination, these companies instigated the development of new playful theatrical forms.

Complicite's A Minute Too Late, focusing as it does on death and bereavement, might seem an unlikely context in which to find play. However, McBurney, Houben and Magni play with what Billington describes as 'our inability to cope with the rituals of death' (The Guardian January 28th 2005), creating an example of the clownesque. Clownesque theatre uses elements of clown technique in the rehearsal and/or performance of a piece of theatre and McBurney's performance as a man whose wife has died is both funny and touching, using clown techniques as a way to approach the all-too-often taboo subject of death. The play was originally created in 1984 and re-created by the original cast (McBurney, Jos Houben and Marcello Magni) at the National Theatre in 2005. The initial show was inspired by the death of McBurney's father and focuses in particular on the social embarrassment which can be felt around death; people do not know what to say to the bereaved. The notion of embarrassment, of not being certain how to be, of finding humour in the ceremonies and rituals of death, is one of the ways in which this show connects with clowning. The clown is often a failure; he never knows what to say or do and, faced with death, he recognizes his own ignorance and social ineptitude even more clearly. This way of being is taken up by the central character played by McBurney, but McBurney is performing in a blurred space where it is difficult to define whether he is performing a character (acting) or revealing some element of himself (clowning). Even more than this display of incompetence, two facets of the performance link this piece of theatre to clowning: play and physical control. 'It wasn't a play, it was play' (Phelim McDermott in the programme of A Minute Too Late, 2005). The piece plays with notions of death. It makes it acceptable for the audience to laugh at death. The actors play with each other through fragments of scenes which lead the audience on a journey through the various rituals surrounding death. We are shown a graveyard, a funeral service, the registrars' office, a high-speed ride in a hearse and a man alone in what was the marital home. The high-speed chase in the hearse, which is created using light, movement and sound effects, has its genesis in the logic of a clown. We are shown the one event least likely to occur whilst travelling in a hearse.

The performance style is clearly indicated to the audience at the opening of the show. Magni and Houben come onto the stage and begin moving props around. The audience is told that the show has not started yet and they are invited to talk amongst themselves. Houben and Magni then introduce themselves as individuals rather than as characters. They explain to the audience that the show will be performed in English, in their mother tongues (Italian and Flemish), and in the language of mime. In this way, the theatrical nature of the event is highlighted. The audience's attention is drawn to the boundaries between the real and the theatrical and it becomes clear that as the performance progresses there may be moments where we, as the audience, are uncertain whether we are watching reality or theatre. Even the attitude that the audience is to take is indicated for them. Houben tries to introduce the subject matter of the show: 'what matters is what this show is about -' but he is interrupted by the arrival of McBurney, who trips onto the stage, apologizing for being late. Houben pauses then continues: 'We are ready: one last thing, the show is about death. Off we go!' From this opening sequence, the audience is introduced to a postmodern performance style in which the performers draw attention to what they are doing as performers, and also draw attention to themselves as individuals, not as characters. The performance style is introduced and McBurney's status in relation to the other characters and to the plot is established. From the minute he enters, we are aware of his incompetence and we are given permission to laugh at his ineptitude.

The importance of physical control is evident from the opening scene in the graveyard. In their training with Lecoq, the trio of performers would have been introduced to the notion of the clown's *exploit* (the task which the clown attempts to complete). Here, McBurney attempts to step over the graves without standing on any of them. There is comedy in the detail of the physical action as McBurney takes high sidesteps in trying to avoid the graves. Houben and Magni are tending other graves. Houben puts flowers on a grave and leaves. McBurney steals a flower to put on the grave he is visiting. Houben returns, having only gone for water. In this short sequence we see the *clownesque* at work. McBurney has demonstrated physical skill; he has shown himself to be incompetent, as he does not have flowers to put on the grave; and he transgresses social convention in stealing a flower from another grave. While this happens, Magni and Houben are mime-acting. As the piece progresses, they each play a number of roles. Shortly after the flower sequence described above, Houben re-enters as a different character who bumps into McBurney and, apparently, falls down dead. This, in turn, leads into a sequence of physical play that brings to life possible taboo imaginings about what happens to a dead body. As rigor mortis appears to set in, Magni and McBurney attempt to cover Houben with a blanket that proves to be too short. Their solution is to make Houben smaller, but when they apply pressure to his legs to make them bend, his torso shoots upright. Each time they press on one part of Houben's body, another shoots up wildly. Such a sequence addresses universal fears about the bodies of the dead. The *clownesque* allows theatre to address such dark subjects in a light way.

What also connects the humour of the piece to clown humour is the fact that both rely on incongruity, but the sequence of incongruous events has a connection in that they all reflect the clown's logical (or illogical) view of the world. Once you have entered a clown's world, anything can happen. Thus gravestones fall apart, people drop dead in graveyards, and hearses drive madly through the streets. This lunacy then creates an emphatic juxtaposition with the moments when McBurney overtly physicalizes his emotional response to being told that his wife's illness is incurable. Having laughed with, and at, McBurney earlier, the audience is drawn into his emotional world in a way that is distressing. If we laugh with him, it seems we must also feel pain with him. Earlier, we have shared his social incompetence as he tries to deal with the unfamiliar situations into which his wife's death has placed him. We watch as he copies the other people present at a funeral service, as he does not know what to do. The element of play reasserts itself towards the end of the piece when McBurney returns to his empty home and Magni and Houben perform as household objects in quick succession, with Magni drawing a huge response from the audience as he plays being a lamp and the bulb in his mouth lights up.

In using *clownesque* techniques, companies like Complicite arouse the audience's awareness of their inner life and encourage them to contemplate the truth of their existence. In this way, the work of these performers reaches out beyond the boundaries of theatre buildings. There are also clowns, particularly although not exclusively in western society, whose work exists only outside of theatres in institutions where the public might not expect to come into contact with clowns.

5

THE TRUTH TELLERS: CLOWNS IN RELIGION AND POLITICS

The concept of performing truthfully is common in clowning, as has been seen in the emphasis on the use of the self within clowning, and the need for the clown to be entirely present in the moment. In these ways, the clown's performance should be truthful to his or her personality. However, the clowns under consideration here are also communicating greater 'truths' and these truths relate to their perception of the world either spiritually or politically. These spiritual and political concerns indicate a link to other periods in history when fools and jesters have had the responsibility of helping society see the truth. These clowns, fools and jesters operate outside conventional performance frames which inevitably changes their position in society and their audience's response to them. Play used as a way of deflating the mighty or parodying their behaviour, in both the Church and in royal courts, has existed for centuries. Therefore, discussion of the holy fools of earlier times and the court fools and king's jesters of the thirteenth to sixteenth centuries will help to clarify the role of the clown ministers of contemporary society and today's political clowns, of whom there are just a few.

Holy Fools
The academic discipline of Fool Studies provides useful literature for establishing the historic existence and the function of holy fools. Often, as is the case for Welsford (1968), Billington (1984) and Otto (2001), a consideration of the holy fool is incorporated into a much broader examination of the history of the fool (as the titles of their books indicate: *The Fool, his Social and Literary History* (Welsford); *A Social History of the Fool* (Billington); and *Fools are Everywhere* (Otto). Other writers such as Cox (1969) and Saward (1980) are more concerned with the place of holy fooling within the Christian Liturgy. Neither field of study is particularly broad but, taken together, they enable comparisons to be drawn between fool activity of the thirteenth to sixteenth centuries and present day clowning, and from this comparison useful conclusions can be drawn about the nature of the connection between fools or clowns and religious faith.

The central argument of Otto's book, as the title suggests, is that the fool 'is not the product of any particular time or place' (2001: xvii). Indeed, as the broad historical and geographical existence of the clown has already been established, Otto reveals that fools have existed in both eastern and western societies for hundreds of years. The connection can be found between clowns and fools (whilst different labels are used) in their kinds of activity, in their appearance and in their position in society. Both can be identified by costumes that clearly distinguish them from the other members of the society in which they live. They make their impact, variously, through word play and physical skills such as juggling and tumbling, and both have the ability to diminish any member of society who is pompous or self-important.

The activity of fools in relation to religion in the thirteenth to sixteenth centuries can be divided into a number of categories: socially-endorsed; individual satire; and fooling within the Church. Firstly, there were societally-endorsed occasions where fooling could occur in relation to the Church, for example in the medieval Feast of Fools. The purpose of the Feast of Fools was to invert (a purpose it has in common with much later clowning). This inversion consisted of 'putting down the mighty from their seats and exalting the humble and the meek' (Billington 1984: 5). This was achieved by the peasants and lower classes being permitted to take over the roles of the bishops and churchmen for a limited (and clearly defined) period of time. In this way, the process served as a release valve for society by allowing behaviour which, at another time, would be punished. Secondly, court fools or king's jesters were able to comment satirically on the churchmen of their day. In this later example, the satire tended to focus on the individual rather than on the church as a whole. This is certainly true of Will Somers' attacks on Cardinal Wolsey during the reign of Henry VIII. As Otto asserts, the fools 'did not set out to overthrow a religious institution, and they generally mock those who corrupt religion, not religion itself' (2001: 172).

In the Middle Ages, folly for Christ's sake was evangelical. It affirmed God through weakness, failure and suffering. This is related to the concept of Christ as a fool whose life is full of examples of 'foolish' behaviour. Christ told a truth that was unacceptable at the time (of the existence of a merciful God); he behaved in ways that were not acceptable (he went into the desert for forty days and forty nights, he threw the merchants out of the temple). From such behaviour is drawn a justification for later Christian fooling based on the idea that, if the life of a fool was good enough for Christ, it is a worthy path to follow. What is clear from Saward's (1980) writing is that the holy fool is the odd man out. As such, he is very similar to the clown wherever he occurs. In theory, then, as a natural outsider, it should be easier for the clown to find spiritual detachment.

The medieval attitude to fooling was clearly defined. Two types of fool were recognized: the natural fool and the artificial fool. The natural fool (an individual with a low level of intelligence or some mental disability) was entitled to the protection of the Church, whilst the artificial fool was viewed as an associate of the devil. This mixed view of the fool or clown in relation to the Church still exists today in that some churches welcome clown ministry and others regard it as unworthy of a place within the liturgy.

Fools and Theology

Academic writing on the connection between fooling and theology began in the 1960s, but, of course, the place of folly in religion can be traced back to the Bible (and many modern clowns take the notion of holy folly as a justification for their existence). In the Bible, folly can be seen in the unconventional behaviour of the prophets who transgress (as clowns do) the normal conventions of behaviour within their society. So Isaiah walks naked (Isaiah 20:2) and Ezekiel eats excrement (Ezekiel 4:12). The tradition of holy fooling is firmly established by Saint Paul who raises the notion of being fools for Christ's sake. Saward's book *Perfect Fools* (1980) also deals with the idea of Franciscan folly and, together, Saint Paul and Saint Francis provide a basis for the holy fooling that existed from their time through until the sixteenth century, in which being a holy fool brought the individual closer to Christ through the assumption of the self-abasing role of the fool. Historically, holy fooling falls into abeyance at this time and was only resurrected in the 1960s when clown ministry movements were established, first in the United States of America and then in the United Kingdom. There is very little Clown Ministry in Europe and what exists is often an offshoot of an American Clown Ministry organization.

The connections between the Bible and fools are manifold. The examples of Isaiah and Ezekiel have been cited earlier but there are a number of other more fundamental features that should be taken into account. Saward (1980) pays considerable attention to Paul's writings on holy folly where a clear contrast is established between the wisdom of the world and God's wisdom: 'if the wisdom of the world is folly to God and God's own foolishness is the only true wisdom, it follows that the worldly wise, to become *truly* wise, must become foolish and renounce their worldly wisdom' (Saward 1980: 4). This mission of ensuring that the world recognizes the folly of what it believes to be wisdom (self-protection, self-aggrandizement, and the pursuit of wealth and power) was the task of the early holy fools, and is the task of the modern Christian clowns. According to Sutton-Smith, the use of play in religion is appropriate because 'play is a metaphoric sphere that can conjoin what is otherwise apart' (1997: 93). In this way, clowns and fools in the church provide a link between the spiritual and the secular.

Clown Ministry

Such literature as exists on clown ministry is written by those directly involved in the movement. There is yet to be any published critical evaluation of the function of the clown ministers, either in relation to the early holy fools or to contemporary society. The clown ministry movement began in the United States of America in 1968 when the term was first used by **Floyd Shaffer** in a church newsletter. His book, *Clown Ministry* (co-authored with Penne Sewell), was published in 1984 and offers a history of the founding of the movement together with instructions on how to become a Christian clown. Much of the literature in this area takes the form of 'how-to' manuals. This is particularly true of the books written by Litherland, *The Clown Ministry Handbook* (1989) and *Everything New and Who's Who in Clown Ministry* (1993) which contain descriptions of clown types (drawn from the circus taxonomy) and skits for performance in church. In the introduction of his book, Shaffer does, however, identify some themes central to clown ministry. These are *servanthood, the vulnerable lover, being childlike* and *being authentic*. These notions recur in other clown ministry writing and offer a limited theoretical base for an examination of clown ministry. In England, clown ministry began in the early 1980s and the most significant contribution to clown ministry literature in this country has been made by **Roly Bain** who co-founded Holy Fools (a loose association of British Clown Ministers) in 1992. He has written more extensively than anyone about British clown ministry in *Where Fools Rush In* (1993), *Clowning Glory* (with Patrick Forbes in 1995) and *Playing the Fool* (2001). Bain has also made available DVDs of clown ministry performances (*The Gospel According to Roly, Only Fools and Heroes, Slack Ropin' USA*). His writings are more analytical than those of the American clown ministers and much of the following analysis of the theory and practice of clown ministry is drawn from his writing.

Bain identifies a number of key issues in the theory of clown ministry. Like Shaffer, he recognizes the significance of the *vulnerable lover* and like Saward writing on holy fools, he explores the notion of God's Foolishness. He considers the importance of playfulness (similar to Shaffer's childlikeness) and truthfulness (Shaffer's authenticity). Importantly, Bain also writes on the concept of resurrection in connection with clowning, and on bringing the liturgy to life: 'it is a circus tradition that whatever happens to clowns, a bucket of whitewash in the face...an exploding car or a collapsing ladder, the clown always rises again, gets up and continues. For this reason, clowns are rightly seen as resurrection figures' (Bain and Forbes 1995: 59). This approach to the connection between clowning and resurrection highlights the similarity between clown behaviour and Christ's life, death and resurrection. An important feature of clown performance is clown failure. The clown succeeds in entertaining the audience when he emphatically fails to achieve what he set out to achieve. Similarly Christ's crucifixion would have been the ultimate failure had he not risen again. The clown rises again when the pay-off of an entrée or skit allows him to demonstrate success where previously there was failure. Thus a convincing argument for use of clown ministry is to be found in the comparison of the clown and Christ: 'clowns and fools share a calling to make resurrection visible, possible for others' (Bain and Forbes 1995: 106). For Shaffer 'the clown's historic make-up is a symbol of death and rebirth' (1984: 14) because the whiteness symbolizes death and the colour added to this signifies rebirth and new beginnings.

The concept of the *vulnerable lover* is raised by both Shaffer and Bain. For Shaffer, vulnerability is about being willing to risk rejection (as indeed was Christ) and it is about loving unconditionally as God loves mankind. For Bain, vulnerability brings the clown closer to Christ (who was at his most vulnerable on the cross) but more importantly it serves a wider societal purpose because 'when we embrace and carry that vulnerability within ourselves, we live a question mark against the high, the mighty, the proud, the pompous, the self-important, the self-righteous' (Bain and Forbes 1995: 129). 'The vulnerable lover accepts all his imperfections and weaknesses, acknowledges his own absurdity' (Bain 1993: 33). This is equally true of Christ and the Christian clown, strengthening the connection between Christ and those who clown for his sake.

For both the American and British schools of clown ministry, the concepts of authenticity and childlikeness/playfulness are closely related. These concepts are central both to Christianity and to Clowning. Earlier chapters have stressed the importance of authenticity in clowning, that the clown must be connected to the true self of the performer. Now it can be seen to be equally important in Christian clowning. Elsewhere this book has highlighted the importance of

The Holy Fool, Roly Bain. *Image taken by Brian Pancott.*

play: for readying a clown for performance; as occurring between clowns; and between the clown and his audience. In clown ministry, the purpose of play functions in much the same way. According to Bain, the importance of play lies in the way it 'increases trust, excites wonder, stimulates questioning' (Bain and Forbes 1995: 97). The relevance of this to religion is clear as belief is founded on trust. Wonder is an important element of worship and questioning is a part of an individual's process in establishing his or her relationship with God. This also relates to Sutton-Smith's 'rhetoric of play as identity' because 'both religion and play...make life worth living and make everyday activities meaningful, because of the transcendence that they propose, one eternal and one mundane' (1997: 67). As both play and religion can bring about transcendence, it is logical that the two can be combined to facilitate this. However, Sutton-Smith does not recognize that the clown ministry movement is re-establishing the connection between religion and play.

> One wonders whether the moment in history has arrived when the uneasiness between play and religion will be revised; whether the time has come when the joyfulness of play and the awesomeness of religion will be transcended in some new form of human enjoyment and devotion. (1997: 164)

It is just this form of human enjoyment and devotion which can be found in clown ministry.

Whilst there are similarities in the theoretical underpinnings in clown ministry on both sides of the Atlantic, they are different in their delivery; just as American and British Circus and Theatre clowns have developed differently. From the evidence of the skits in Litherland and Shaffer's books, American clown ministry is closely related to extrovert circus clowning and street performance. All the information on make-up and clowning is similar to common circus clown types. The skits fall into two categories: those which are based around a circus routine and those which could just as easily be performed by a Christian drama group as by clown ministers. While many American clown ministers are practising Ministers of Religion (Shaffer, for example is a Lutheran pastor), their clowning appears to be more about performing than engaging with the liturgy, and their make-up follows the garish circus Auguste tradition. Roly Bain's style of make-up is more in keeping with the European clown mime tradition. His red nose is painted on and, otherwise, only his cheeks and lips are made-up. His cheeks are reddened and onto each cheek a cross is drawn in black. His costume incorporates his clerical collar together with brightly coloured trousers and a baggy brightly checked jacket, suggestive of an Auguste character.

Whilst Bain's costume and make-up style is similar to that of European Theatre Clowns, his performance style is closely based on circus. This is probably as a result of his training at Circomedia in Bristol.

Framing
Whether the performance style is American or European, clown ministers perform in settings where clown performances would not usually take place. De Toro's general conventions proved useful earlier (chapter 3) and his concepts are once again helpful. The particular conventions

of a service vary from church to church but *general conventions* in western society indicate that the service will be led by an ordained minister; a sermon will be given; and there will be readings, prayers and hymns. The presence of clown ministers clashes with this convention. Some worshippers may be glad to have the service made more fun and joyful whilst others may be offended on the grounds that religion should be a serious business.

According to Litherland, a good place to start with clown ministry is in outreach settings and she suggests locations as diverse as prisons and shopping malls. Performing in such places avoids the possible clashes with church traditionalists but allows the clown minister to 'reveal faith, hope and love, in unique ways' (Litherland 1989: 40). It also leads to clowns performing in locations where there is no established frame for their work. In Litherland's opinion, a congregation needs careful preparation before clown ministers can take part in worship, let alone lead whole services. This is a critical difference between clown ministers and the holy fools mentioned earlier. Part of the holy fool's mission was to parody and satirize individuals and religious practices. If modern clown ministers creep into church only when they have permission and the way has been paved for them, they are unlikely to be able to make critical comment about the church that receives them. Instead, the emphasis appears to be on making worship accessible and more fun. The central purpose of clowns within the church has, therefore, changed. Their role now is less about inversion and parody and more about making Christianity accessible through the techniques of circus, and occasionally, theatre clowns.

Content of skits and services

In *The Clown Ministry Handbook*, Litherland (1989) offers a skit entitled 'The Calling of the Disciples'. This skit provides a clear example of how American clown ministry appears to have lost contact with the heart of clowning. Whilst the literature they produce offers comments on the particular relationship between clowning and Christianity, this skit could as easily be performed by an amateur drama group as by clowns. There is no inherent connection between the identity of the performers as clowns and the content of the skit. In the skit, the clowns sit in small groups occupied, according to the stage directions, in a variety of activities. Significantly, none of these activities, which include fishing, reading and sketching, are related to clowning. The voice of Jesus is heard and he engages the clowns in conversation, persuading them to become his disciples. Apart from the fact that the stage directions describe the performers as clowns, there is nothing to indicate this. None of the elements of traditional circus or modern theatre clowning are present. There is no evidence of parody or transgression, as the scene is a relatively literal presentation of Jesus recruiting disciples. There is no demonstration of physical skill: a number of the clowns claim to be magicians or balloon-modellers but their skills are not demonstrated. There is no linguistic transgression. The content of the scene is conveyed verbally and no use is made of mime. There is no interaction between the clowns and the audience. In this example it appears that the American clown ministry organization is simply using clowns to make the Christian message appear a little more fun or accessible. What occurs misses the heart of clowning, which has already been identified as being closely linked to vulnerability, authenticity and a readiness to play. There is no spontaneous play in this skit; rather it is the performance of a drama text.

Elsewhere in the same book is a skit called 'The Clown Healer' in which a clown tries to help a girl who is very upset. This skit does contain more clowning as the clown performer mimes throughout in response to the words spoken by the girl. It is also closer to the central concepts of Christian clowning identified above in that the clown repeatedly tries to help the girl, despite being rejected. In this way, the clown allows his vulnerability to show. He is prepared to fail repeatedly in the hope of making a connection with the girl. There is still very little in the way of interaction with the audience and the only examples of skill are in the miming and in the cutting of a snowflake from a piece of paper. A parallel can be drawn between the clown's approach to helping one in need and the assistance offered by Jesus to those who were lonely or ill.

While such skits may be entertaining, and may therefore make the act of worship enjoyable, it is hard to identify ways in which they are examples of pure clowning due to the fact that most of these skits could be presented equally successfully by non-clown performers. The examples given so far have been of skits that might fit within the structure of a service led by the Pastor or Reverend of the church rather than by clowns, where the skit might connect with the theme of the sermon or act as an illustration of the reading. Litherland (1989) also provides an example of a complete clown ministry service. This service is a Tenebrae service. The Tenebrae service is a recognized part of the Christian liturgy and it has parallels with the Quem Queritis which also gives physical and visual form to part of the liturgy. The Tenebrae service usually takes place on Good Friday and charts Christ's journey to the cross and his crucifixion. Traditional Tenebrae services end in darkness and the congregation leave, returning on Easter Sunday for a service that celebrates Christ's resurrection. It is also possible for the service to include the relighting of Christ's candle so that it ends on a note of hope, and this is what happens in the clown ministry version of the service. The Tenebrae Service is regarded as a reversal or inversion of the Easter Vigil and it therefore is a particularly appropriate service for clowns to lead.

In the clown ministry version of the Tenebrae Service, the clowns are silent and readings are spoken, according to the stage directions, either by a narrator or the Minister. This serves to separate the action from the readings in a way which may be intended to highlight the behaviour of the disciples. Each time there is a reading, the clowns mime the content of the reading. In this way, the content of the readings is made doubly accessible because it can be seen and heard at the same time. Also the need to focus on the clowns' actions as the candles are extinguished highlights the increasing darkness more than might be the case if the focus were only on the spoken word. Each reading tells a different stage of the Passion of Christ and after each reading a candle is extinguished. At the end, to offer hope, Christ's candle is lit again and, from that, all the other candles are relit. However, apart from the possibility of viewing this service as an inversion of the Easter vigil, there is little that is specifically clown related. The clowns play all the characters (both those who betray Jesus and those who came to tend to his dead body) so it is not possible to interpret the betrayers as clowns who did not understand what they were doing. The portrayal of Jesus as a clown connects with points made earlier about the concept of fools for God. From these examples, it is clear that in American clown ministry the act of clowning has not been fully integrated into the liturgy. Despite the aims identified above, clown ministry does not appear to make use of the clown's potential for failure, vulnerability and authenticity in ways which illuminate the liturgy. It is likely that using clowns simply to increase accessibility diminishes the potential power of both Christianity and clowning. The limited nature of clown activity in the skits cited makes it impossible to analyse what happens against any play theory.

However, in the United Kingdom clown ministry is used in quite a different way. What follows is an analysis of an example of Roly Bain's clown ministry performance based on his DVD *Only Fools and Heroes* (1998). Bain's performances demonstrate that for him, there is a very close link between clowning and Christian liturgy and bible stories, combining traditional clown sketches and traditional sermons. Two such sketch sermons will be analysed here, the first of which is 'Adam the Imperfect'. The piece is filmed in an orchard and Roly Bain enters, chasing a balancing ball; then carrying it; then being chased by it; then finally rolling on it by sitting on it. Finally he stands on the ball, verbally revealing that the trick 'unlike the Church, is to keep moving'. Here the clown minister is able, through gentle parody, to offer a criticism of the Church. There is, therefore, a link both to traditional holy fools and to the parody which takes place in circus clowning.

The next element of clown performance utilized by Roly Bain is physical skill, as he juggles two balls and an apple whilst balancing on the walking ball. The apple clearly represents the apple in the Garden of Eden and the connection is pointed up by Roly Bain's comment that 'every time I try and eat the apple, I fall', which accompanies his attempt to take a bite from the apple whilst juggling. Having fallen off the ball, Roly Bain moves into the more traditional sermon element of his performance in which, in a storytelling style, he relates the temptation of Eve, and Adam and Eve's fall from grace. Despite repeatedly falling from the ball and repeatedly failing to bite the apple, Roly Bain draws the conclusion that no one is perfect and the important thing is to keep trying. Unlike the American clown ministry sketches, the content of the sketch sermon is closely linked to Roly Bain's identity as a clown. Even his costume indicates the connection between the two: he wears a stripy Victorian-style swimming costume with stripy socks, over-sized boots, a back to front baseball cap and a loose clerical collar. The semiotics of the costume highlight the combination of the religious and the clown. The points of the sermon which emphasize a Christian message are supported by clown action that is either demonstrating physical skill or demonstrating failure.

The clown element is even clearer in the sketch sermon entitled 'Moses the Magnificent'. This sequence opens with Roly Bain riding a bicycle along a country road. When he stops cycling, the handlebars come off in his hand. This is the introduction to an extended physical routine in which the bike falls apart and is put back together incorrectly, but in such a way that it can still be ridden. This relates to Wright's notion of the *exploit*. Here Roly Bain's basic *exploit* is to stop his bicycle. Once it begins to fall apart, the more complex *exploit* is to put it together again. The sequence is entertaining but lacks an obvious connection to any biblical message. The connection is made, rather clumsily, with the claim that the bike once belonged to Moses. From here, Roly Bain moves into the sermon section of the performance but he uses the elements of the picnic he has brought with him to support his telling of the story of Moses: his picnic rug becomes the Red Sea; the bicycle basket is like the one in which Moses was placed in the bulrushes; the water bottle becomes the tree struck by Moses to get water; the picnic stove is the burning bush; and the sandwich is manna from heaven. Once the elements of the picnic are set up, Roly Bain plays a scene reminiscent of Commedia Dell'Arte's 'Lazzo of the Fly' in which he responds to the sound of an unseen fly. The fly represents all the plagues sent by God which are eventually squashed by Roly Bain, using a fly swatter. He then removes ten plastic knives from the basket to represent the Ten Commandments. The number of knives quickly becomes excessive (perhaps indicating the increasing guidance offered by churches regarding appropriate Christian behaviour), their proliferation stopped only by Roly Bain telling of the arrival of Jesus. Bain then removes a large wooden fork and a large wooden spoon to represent what are, according to him, the two most important commandments 'Love God' and 'Love Thy Neighbour'. Whilst the props *support* the telling of the sermon, there is little that is specifically clown in the way in which they are used. Indeed the use of props suggests a non-conformist service for children. The sketch sermon ends with further interaction between Roly Bain and the bike in a classic example of clown status interaction with objects.

The link between Christianity and clowning is stronger in Roly Bain's work than in the sketches drawn from Litherland. As 'Adam the Imperfect' demonstrated, the message of the sketch sermon would be significantly altered were it not performed by a clown. This is less true of 'Moses the Magnificent' because the clown routine and the sermon are linked more clumsily. However, both provide an example of what Sutton-Smith (1997) defines as play forms being used for the purpose of enhancing and reinforcing a sense of community. He classifies this kind of play as fitting within the 'rhetoric of identity' which, in turn, connects with Turner's notion of 'communitas'. According to Sutton-Smith, 'identity rhetoric has its historical basis in community traditions; its players and advocates are adults, male and female; and their play is usually some kind of festival' (1997: 107). This description fits clown ministry, which uses play to reinforce the Christian message and to strengthen the bonds within the Christian community.

The Court Jester – A Political Commentator
Just as the development of clowns can be traced in relation to the Christian Church, so the incidence of clowns who focus on making satirical or religious comment can be tracked elsewhere. As was the case for Christian fools, for court jesters and political clowns there are periods of popularity and considerable activity and periods when the role seems to have all but disappeared from society.

Most of the writing on court jesters, as with holy fools, is to be found in the discipline of Fool Studies. In this Billington, Otto and Welsford are again useful sources of information, with each of them considering the incidence of court fools (the term can be used interchangeably with court jesters) in Europe and in Asia. It is important to acknowledge that, particularly in Europe, two kinds of fool were recognized, as has been mentioned above. In courts throughout Europe, it appears that both kinds of fool were popular and Welsford notes that the records that exist often make it difficult to discern whether an individual fool was 'artificial' or 'natural'. The focus of this section will be on the artificial fools because it was only they who had enough wit to make pointedly satirical or political comments on the society of which they were part. Welsford identifies the period of most common incidence of court jesters as falling between the twelfth and sixteenth centuries, with the fourteenth and fifteenth centuries being a time in which jesters or court fools were particularly commonplace; 'there is no doubt that the court fool was a regular institution in fourteenth and fifteenth century England' (Welsford 1968: 116). Her work focuses on identifying sources of historical data to prove the *existence* of court fools, while the focus here will be on the *activity* of the court jesters, in particular the nature of the relationship between the jester and his lord or lady. There is little if any documentary evidence of female jesters, although Welsford does describe two Italian female fools, Giovanna Matta and Caterina Matta (as mentioned earlier Matta is the Italian word for fool). Indeed, the naming of fools across Europe seems to follow this generic pattern; thus **Claus Narr** and John le Fol. However, both Giovanna and Caterina were natural fools and are not, therefore, of concern here.

The similarity between fools in this period and what are now recognized as clowns is highlighted by Billington: 'Those fools who enhanced the reputation of the profession, Tarlton, Kempe and Armin, moved in all circles...For the most part their skills were the clowning arts of dancing, tumbling and singing' (1984: 42). It appears that fools engaged in a range of behaviour and techniques to enhance and secure their popularity. Thus sometimes the jester is little more than a court entertainer whilst at others he becomes truly political in ways which involved risk both to his livelihood and life. German fools of the sixteenth century 'were clever, observant men, deeply engaged in the religious controversies of the time' who could also be 'used at times as a convenient tool in the hands of politicians' (Billington 1984: 139–40). This view is supported by Towsen, who asserts that 'Often the fool was a daring political jester who took advantage of his free license as a buffoon to engage in satirical comments on affairs of state' (1976: 26). This is certainly true of Henry VIII's jester Will Somers' attacks on Cardinal Wolsey. Given the role of Wolsey in the royal court of the time, Somers's attacks on him are as much political as religious, and appear to have been instrumental in advancing the Cardinal's disgrace by revealing to Henry VIII a store of gold which Somers discovered in Wolsey's cellars. The jesters' relative freedom of speech made them particularly useful when it was necessary to voice an opinion in opposition to the actions or ideas of the monarch or noble to whom they owed allegiance.

Otto (2001) identifies an important function of the fool /jester as his ability to impart the truth, citing the jester of French king Philippe VI, who was the only member of the court who dared to tell the king that the French army had been defeated. Jesters could also be used to persuade the king to attend better to affairs of state, as was the case with Tom Killigrew. Killigrew's close relationship with Charles II meant that he could persuade the king to attend a meeting. Otto (2001 121) relates how Killigrew bet a chief minister, Lauderdale, £100 that he could get the king to the meeting within half an hour. Killigrew knew that the king strongly disliked Lauderdale and, when he explained the situation, the King attended the meeting so that Lauderdale would be out of pocket.

Thus it can be seen that the jester's role in society is a combination of entertainment and truth-telling, together with an ability to manipulate his master as a result of their close relationship. Billington suggests that, far from being immoral or blasphemous, fooling or clowning can 'easily act as a social preservative by providing a corrective to the pretentious vanity of officialdom' (1984: 321). It could be argued, therefore, that the fool, jester or clown fulfils much the same function as the carnivalesque in providing an outlet for behaviour or views that would otherwise contribute to civil unrest. Despite this seemingly universal usefulness, there have been times when the fool or jester has not occupied a central position in society.

The political role of the clown diminished with the demise of the court jester in the seventeenth century. Billington recognizes that 'by the end of the eighteenth century respectability was the key code of behaviour and, not surprisingly, this influenced the attitudes to the Fool and even his own view of himself' (1984: 81). The popularity of foolishness as a mode of behaviour was on the wane. As has already been established, Grimaldi was a relatively rare example of a theatre clown during the eighteenth century, and his popularity lay in his physical skill and trick work rather than in political comment.

The opportunity for political clowning seems to have remained scant throughout the nineteenth and twentieth centuries, with only isolated occurrences of political clowning. Indeed, Eastern Europe was one of the few geographical locations where clowning with a satirical or political edge continued to exist. There were also risks associated with political clowning in the USA, as Chaplin discovered when he proposed The Great Dictator in 1937. The film portrays Chaplin's anti-fascist stance by parodying Adolph Hitler through the character of Adenoid Hynkel. The film was made in 1940 at a period when America was still at peace and pursuing a policy of isolationism, with which Chaplin disagreed because he felt he understood the danger that Hitler posed. When the film was first proposed, Chaplin met with resistance in both America and Great Britain. In his article 'Anglo-American Anti-fascist Film Propaganda in a Time of Neutrality: The Great Dictator, 1940' (2001), Cole provides a clear overview of the difficulties Chaplin encountered, including a clandestine battle waged to prevent the film even being produced. However, despite these objections, Chaplin did succeed in making the film. Its plot centres on Adenoid Hynkel (Hitler) and a Jewish Barber (both played by Chaplin) who bear a startling resemblance to each other. The Jewish Barber fights in World War One and is wounded rescuing a Tomanian pilot, Schultz. In the film, Tomania represents Germany. The Jewish barber loses his memory and only returns to his barber's shop twenty years after the end of the war. His shop is in the Jewish ghetto because Hynkel, assisted by Garbitsch (Goebbels) and Herring (Goering), has begun his persecution of the Jews. Whilst Hynkel tries to extract money to attack nearby Osterlich (Austria) from Epstein (a Jew), the Ghetto enjoys a period of relative calm. When Epstein refuses to loan the money, events escalate. Schultz tries to warn Hynkel that his actions are excessive and is sent to a concentration camp, as is the Jewish barber. The two escape wearing Tomanian uniforms and the barber is mistaken for Hynkel. Meanwhile Hynkel, having been taken for the barber, has been arrested. This inversion, in which the powerful man is replaced by the truth-telling clown, follows a well-established convention. According to Cole, 'Barber and dictator as doubles were a metaphor representing the duality of good and evil, the reality that human nature can be tyrannical and tyrannized with equal ease' (2001: 146). The use of symbol and metaphor in clowning has been discussed earlier, and the use of disguise in performance is a common medium for revealing deeper truths. Towards the end of the film, the barber, as Hynkel, stands to make a speech and what follows is Chaplin's own impassioned plea for humanity and liberty. This speech constitutes an extended political message in a way that is unusual for clowns.

A number of traditional clown techniques are used in Chaplin's portrayal of Hitler in the character of Adenoid Hynkel. The character's name closely resembles Hitler's but is clearly ridiculous. Near the beginning of the film Chaplin delivers a speech, as Hitler, using Yiddish and mock German, which relates to the clown tradition of transgressing the usual language conventions. The parody here is emphasized by the comments of the official translator, which are clearly not a translation of what has been said. In this way, Chaplin makes a pertinent point about the control and dissemination of information. Mussolini is also parodied as an overweight, rather stupid individual, Benzino Napoloni. In one scene Hynkel and Napoloni engage in a food fight, which is an example of traditional clown activity to the extent that a journalist receives a custard pie in the face. There are also examples of comic violence, the most slapstick of which occurs when Hannah (played by Paulette Goddard) leans out of a window and hits storm troopers on the head with a frying pan in an attempt to help the Jewish barber. Chaplin is offering a clear political message when Hannah says 'that's what we should all do, fight back. We can't lick 'em alone, but we can lick 'em together' (*The Great Dictator* 1940). In making *The Great Dictator,* Chaplin highlighted the use of film as propaganda, and emphasized the potential of using clown characters within that frame.

Working outside a recognized performance frame, The Clandestine Insurgent Rebel Clown Army (CIRCA) was founded on November 2003 as an alternative protest organization which uses clown techniques and clown appearance to demonstrate in a non-violent way at national events. Almost nothing has been published on CIRCA, either in the national press or in academic journals. Their own centrally organized website is, therefore, the main source of information about them. The website of another protest organization, Shut Them Down, has published a collection of articles on protest in the United Kingdom, which are available for download on their website (www.shutthemdown.org). Another useful source of information is a BBC4 documentary called *Can You Hear Us?* which follows the activities of CIRCA (together with those of a Communist and a Green Party activist) in July 2005 at the time of the Make History Poverty march and the G8 summit at Gleneagles.

The CIRCA website (www.clownarmy.org) offers a clear description of the movement's aims and describes techniques used by CIRCA in training clowns and preparing and delivering protests. Each word of the organization's title carries significance in relation to their style of protest. For example, their clown names and costumes render them anonymous, hence 'clandestine'. They are insurgent because they 'have risen up from nowhere and are everywhere' (www. clownarmy.org). They are rebels and clowns because they feel that this is the only viable form of existence in a world. Finally they are an army, not because they advocate violence as a solution to the world's problems but because 'alone clowns are pathetic figures, but in groups and gaggles, brigades and battalions they are extremely dangerous' (www.clownarmy.org). Whilst they are not bouffons, this echoes Lecoq's understanding that clowns become more dangerous in groups. In terms of organization, CIRCA has a number of clown gaggles (groups) that are described as battalions, unions or regiments. These are located around the United Kingdom in Central England, Scotland (particularly Glasgow), London, Sheffield, and South Devon. Each gaggle decides on its own name and offers training to new recruits. The language used by CIRCA parodies the language and titles that are used in the armed forces. So, despite the fact that the gaggles are organized horizontally and co-operatively, individual clowns have names like Major Mishap, Private Parts and Captain Klepto. One element of their training, 'Marching and Drilling', continues the military parody. In this way, the very structure and labels that CIRCA uses parody the armed forces, which they see as being part of the problem in a world that is constantly waging war. Paradoxically, this satirical modelling provides the various clown gaggles with a common language so that, in the middle of a demonstration, any clown rebel (in line with the absence of hierarchy) can shout a change in activity. For example, a cry of 'let's fish' will be understood by all clown gaggles, as the technique of 'fishing' is taught as a universal rebel clown activity in the two-day training that anyone wanting to join CIRCA must complete. Clowns are taught 'fishing' (the art of synchronized movement, rather like a shoal of fish), 'socking' (where a gaggle of clowns moves backwards and forwards, like a sock being pulled inside out) and 'marching'. These manoeuvres allow clowns from different gaggles to merge quickly when they attend national-level demonstrations.

CIRCA site themselves firmly in the tradition of court jester and political commentator. 'CIRCA aims to make clowning dangerous again, to bring it back to the street, restore its disobedience and give it back the social function it once had: its ability to disrupt, critique and heal society' (www.clownarmy.org). Working in a subversive, anarchic style, these clowns operate in larger groups than are seen elsewhere in clown activity in modern society, and their aims are much more wide-ranging. They are attempting to reclaim traditional areas of Clown behaviour. Pictures on CIRCA's website reveal individuals in brightly-coloured costumes, some wearing wigs, all wearing some form of face paint. CIRCA clowns do sometimes use language to make their political points, frequently using high-pitched voices or funny accents, but at other times the protests are in the form of silent sit-ins, and sometimes they sing. In terms of behaviour, their protests are similar to the demonstrations of other protest groups (they use techniques such as leaflets, invitations, they go to speakers corner in Hyde Park, they organize sit-ins). The style and mood of the protest, though, is significantly altered by their clown status. According to 'Kathy Camouflage' (a CIRCA clown) in a radio interview for Indymedia, in a protest leading up to a larger demonstration at Gleneagles in July 2005 the clowns were 'playing with the police to distract and amuse them' (http://radio.indymedia.org). The game was Wizards, Giants and Elves, which involves two teams pretending to be one of these mythical creatures, marching towards each other chanting and then chasing each other. This game is a physical version of rock, paper, scissors in that giants beat elves, elves beat wizards and wizards beat giants. Depending on the combination of creatures chosen, players either have to chase their opponents or be chased by them. It is difficult to imagine another protest group trying to involve the police in a game more usually found in playgrounds and drama workshops. According to Kolonel Klepto and Major Up Evil, there was a moment 'when for a few seconds the police forgot which side they were on' (Harvie et al. 2005: 253). The nature of this kind of play (associated with childhood) is that it breaks though traditional binaries and reminds each of us that we are individual human beings, not simply part of a side. What is demonstrated, though, is the centrality of play to CIRCA's way of working and, while the game may be fun, the purpose of the play is very serious. CIRCA are attempting to communicate a message that expresses their rejection of globalization in an inventive, creative and non-violent way. 'Behind its whiteface façade of stupidity, it is a serious attempt to develop a form of civil disobedience that breaks down the binary and oppositional thinking that is still so inherent within protest movements' (Harvie et al. 2005: 244). By using the ancient art of clowning as part of civil disobedience, CIRCA are trying to change the very nature of protest and demonstration. Their theory is that if they are making the police laugh (or struggle not to laugh), the demonstration is less likely to escalate into violence and arrests. Four videos are available over the internet for download or streaming which allow CIRCA's activities to be analysed. One video shows a clown gaggle targeting Leeds Labour Party Headquarters and an Armed Forces recruitment office. These demonstrations took place around the time of the hand-over of power in Iraq, hence the targets of the Labour Party and the Armed Forces. The clowns' appearance, as described below, parodies Army uniforms.

Their dress is basically camouflage gear with additions of brightly coloured fur trimmings (in pink green, orange and yellow), which subvert the intention of wearing camouflage by making them highly noticeable. The clowns carry feather dusters as weapons and wear colanders (again trimmed with bright colours) as helmets. On reaching the Labour Party Headquarters, the clowns rushed into the building hooting and whooping. This tactic of making a lot of noise, and thereby disrupting the normal business of whichever organizations they are targeting, is a common one for CIRCA. In keeping with their non-violent policy, when the clowns are stopped at the top of the stairs (the Labour offices are on the first floor) they simply stage a sit-in on the

The Clandestine Insurgent Rebel Clown Army holds its first protest ahead of the G8 Summit at Gleneagles in 2005.

stairs, laughing and singing and making jokes about going to the Labour MP's home for tea and doughnuts. In response to the clown's activities, the Labour Party employee, whose job it is to mind them until the police arrive, seems torn between irritation and amusement. The gaggle is moved on by the police, who treat them as trespassers (which they become when they refuse to leave when asked to do so). Once outside the building, the clowns change tactics and begin to parody and undermine the police. One policeman talking into his radio is followed by a clown who copies his every move while declaiming into an imaginary clown radio: 'Mum I've become a police man!' At the same time, another clown is using a feather duster to clean the outside of a police car. In this way, the power of the police is diminished as they are treated as objects of fun. The police in Leeds handle the situation with a light touch. The clown gaggle moves away from the Labour Headquarters, marching along to cries of 'Left. Left, left'. At the Armed Forces Recruitment Office their tactics are much the same. The gaggle (comprising of about a dozen clowns) enters the recruitment office and begins milling about. According to the video footage (taken by one of the clowns), it takes less than two minutes for the police to arrive. During this time the clowns have cleaned several soldiers with their feather dusters and asked if they can join the Army. When the police arrive, the clowns form a line, shouting 'form an orderly queue, form an orderly queue'. One general tactic of the clowns is that when a suggestion (such as forming a queue) is made, the idea is taken up by all the other clowns, who join in, repeating the idea. This rapidly increases the noise levels and, therefore, the disruption caused. Members of the public present in the office look bemused by the clowns' actions. The police ask them to leave, which they do. As soon as the clowns are out of the office, one of the soldiers pulls the metal shutters down, closing the office. The clowns have secured their aim: they have caused significant disruption without violence and they have prevented the army continuing with its usual business. In terms of making a political point it has taken the combined might of the Army and the police force to remove the clowns. Neither organization comes out of the clown activity looking particularly powerful. The clowns hang a closed sign on the Recruitment Office and set up a table with a 'join here' sign. They then proceed to parody the Army's aims. One of the clowns claims that the clown army is a true force of liberation but that they liberate with 'love and jelly babies' rather than by killing people. While such activity may be enjoyable for the clown gaggle involved and while it disrupts those it targets, this kind of action has a very limited impact. Some of the general public will have witnessed the events but it is highly unlikely that either clown action had any lasting impact on the Labour Party or the Armed Forces.

The series of demonstrations which CIRCA staged in the lead up to and around the actual G8 summit had potentially more impact for a variety of reasons. Firstly, CIRCA went on a nine-week tour of the United Kingdom, ending in Scotland. This brought Rebel Clown activity to a number of areas where it had not been seen before, and allowed CIRCA to launch a recruitment drive. This tour was funded by the Arts Council for England. In Scotland, CIRCA connected with a number of political organizations and took part in demonstrations which made the national news, connected as they were with the Make Poverty History March and the G8 summit. Additionally, CIRCA's activities were filmed and televised by BBC4. Despite this relatively high profile, the level of any lasting impact of CIRCA's actions needs to be considered. The similarities between CIRCA and the Armed Forces they parody can be seen in their G8 Briefing and Operations Information which details all the meetings and training available in Edinburgh in July 2005. One marked difference, however, is the emphasis CIRCA places on being horizontally organized: 'we have no leaders, no centralized command – everyone is an officer, a general and a private' (G8 Briefing and Operations Information in Harvie et al. 2005: 8). This seems to connect CIRCA with anarchist rather than democratic organizations working for social and political change. Equally, it seems to align them with the Hippie and more politically aware Yippie movements of the 1960s. The term Yippie originated in the United States of America to signify the radicalization of the Hippies. Like clowns, Yippies looked different from the rest of society; believed in the power of counter-cultures; and challenged authority theatrically before the news cameras.

CIRCA identified two operations to be carried out by the national organization, with as many clown gaggles joining in as wished to do so. Clown gaggles were also free to develop their own initiatives and demonstrations, in connection with, or quite separate from, the main demonstrations. The two operations were Operation Brown Nose, which coincided with the Make Poverty History March, and Operation HaHaHa, which began on July 6th 2005 during the day of action and blockades, to which many organizations contributed. Performances given around the country in the lead up to these events included a parody of army planning meetings, with clowns using a map, miniature cannon and a clown doll to demonstrate how they intended to launch clowns into Gleneagles.

During the Make Poverty History March, the CIRCA clowns marched with other organizations to protest at the West's attitude to the issue of African debt. However, it is clear from the BBC footage that the clown army had become too big to make collective decisions, and gaggles splintered off from the main march to pursue individual aims. One group, followed by the cameras, came across a group of fellow anarchists being held by the police. The clowns wanted to help but did little more than talk to the police. Later in the day (with a Section 60 order covering the whole of Edinburgh, giving the police the power to stop and search anyone suspected of concealing a weapon) the clowns were stopped by the police and searched. Their only weapons were their feather dusters but this did not stop the police from surrounding them and making them empty out their bags. It is clear that clown gaggles' operation in Edinburgh met with more aggressive policing styles than the Leeds gaggle described earlier.

The most significant example of CIRCA causing disruption through non-violent civil disobedience was their brief closure of the A9 road between Edinburgh and Gleneagles. Their intention was to disrupt the G8 summit by preventing delegates from reaching Gleneagles. The clowns were marching along a minor road towards their objective when they were cut off by a line of police approaching from the opposite direction. The clowns headed across a field and with good fortune realized they were heading towards the A9. Police tried to intercept the clowns but each time a clown's way was blocked, he or she simply changed direction and then kept moving, keeping their objective in sight. Once they reached the road, they placed traffic cones across the road and stopped the traffic. They then danced and sang in front of the traffic they had blocked. One pair of clowns even used their feather dusters to clean the windscreen of the coach at the front of the stationery queue of traffic. The police herded the clowns off the road and set the traffic moving. The police then surrounded the clowns who, in response, played within the circle created for them by the police. They also interacted with the police, helpfully pointing out where there were gaps in the circle containing them. Later they marched at the circle of police shouting "left, left, left" in squeaky voices and some of them marched backwards (incorporating the clown tradition of inversion and contrariness). The policing style shown on the video became more aggressive at this point, with a number of the clowns being pushed roughly by the police. It is important to note that the clowns never retaliated and when they were warned that unless they move off, they would be arrested, they marched noisily back towards Edinburgh.

CIRCA's activities are linked almost entirely to the notions of subversion and parody, which are primarily expressed through their costumes and their satirical modelling of their organization on the Army. The setting of their action makes it difficult for them to effect any structural interruption because their actions take place within the frame of everyday life rather than within discrete ceremonies or performances. So, in terms of the style of transgression used, they are confined to linguistic transgression (in CIRCA's case, silly voices) and, more significantly, behavioural transgressions. Even in this area, their transgression is limited because they are no more transgressive than many politically or socially motivated demonstration groups. Their behaviour is disruptive (as was demonstrated when they closed the A9) but their disobedience is very limited. Indeed, the BBC footage shows one unidentified clown complaining that their civil disobedience was too obedient.

In terms of framing, CIRCA regard themselves primarily as performers rather than as demonstrators. Elements of their touring programme included a show that fits well within the traditions of popular theatre. They use clowns in a series of short sketches, which incorporate audience participation, visual aids such as maps, and direct address to the audience. However, when they are taking part in a demonstration, it is very difficult to identify a fixed relationship to any potential audience. This, in turn, makes it hard for CIRCA's clowns to establish a connection with the audience.

The connection between the CIRCA and play theory is very interesting. CIRCA's activities are derived from a strong ideological position in much the same way as is true for clown ministers, and this position is reinforced by the gaggles, which help the individual clowns to feel connected to the organization. This has close links to Turner's notion of *communitas*, particularly as it is expressed in *The Ritual Process* (1969). In this book, Turner suggests that 'the values of communitas are strikingly present...in the behaviour of what came to be known as the "beat generation", who were succeeded by the "hippies" ...who "opt out" of the status bound social order' (1969: 99). In much the same way, *communitas* is present amongst the rebel clowns, whose alternative vision of society rejects usual status identifiers in favour of a consensus approach. From this approach develops a notion of 'communitas' similar to Buber's definition of community 'being no longer side by side (and, one might add, above and below) but *with* one another of a multitude of persons. And this multitude, though it moves towards one goal, yet experiences everywhere a turning to, a dynamic facing of, the others' (Buber 1961: 51). From this sense of communitas, it is possible to make a connection to Sutton-Smith's 'rhetoric of power' and 'rhetoric of identity'. Both these rhetorics explore the relationship between play and conflict either on a social or individual level. According to Sutton-Smith, the 'rhetoric of play as power' can make 'use of play as the representation of conflict' (1997: 10). The rebel clowns use play as a way of highlighting conflict, for example the conflict between their view of how the world should be run and how it is run. At the same time, in the Leeds situation, play becomes a way of diffusing the potential aggression of conflict. When Sutton-Smith locates the sites of 'play as identity' he discusses parades, celebration and carnivals, but the demonstrations which CIRCA takes part in are to be found on the same continuum. The sites of 'play as identity' identified by Sutton-Smith may be more positive in intent than political demonstrations but, in Edinburgh, play is still used as a way of creating and reinforcing a sense of identity amongst the rebel clowns which creates a binary opposition between them and the authorities they challenge.

The confrontation with the police in Edinburgh also reveals elements of Geertz's 'deep play' in the rebel clown activity in that the play, which, according to Turner, takes place in the liminal space between the real and the imaginary, can have significant consequences in the *real* world. If any clown, in his or her playing, breaks the law, then the consequences could include custodial sentences or fines. CIRCA's awareness of this risk is clear in their training advice to rebel clowns, who are given the name and contact number of the organization's solicitor. Each gaggle is also advised to carry a first aid kit and have at least one member who is trained in first aid. Clearly there is the potential for physical harm. In the videos viewed as part of this research, rebel clowns were pushed by police and, in parallel demonstrations, demonstrators were beaten by police using batons. Thus, the potential risk attached to the play might be deemed as out of proportion to the benefit of the play. Perhaps this is because the clowns 'sometimes invert these play forms to express their own hidden rhetorics of resistance or subversion' (Sutton-Smith 1997: 74). For CIRCA, clown play is highly politicized and expresses political ideas through parody and subversion.

The key features of CIRCA's clowning, then, are a commitment to political and social protest (particularly against globalization); the appearance of clowns (make-up and brightly coloured costumes); and rebellion. This final element links them closely to the ancient tradition of clowning in which the clowns operate outside the normal conventions of their society, and to the more recent tradition of court jesters where the jester traditionally speaks the truth which the ruler, whether king or government, may not want to hear. For example, at the G8 summit at Gleneagles, CIRCA's plan was to surround Gleneagles, block roads and thus 'keep the ministers of the G8, the eight most dangerous terrorists in the world behind the fences at Gleneagles, where their brand of insanity can cause no more harm' (Harvie et al. 2005: 133). This view that the supposedly sane politicians are in fact the insane, whilst the supposedly crazy clowns are the ones speaking sense, is a political parallel to St. Paul's view of the worldly wise as foolish in comparison with God's wisdom. Sanity and insanity are subject to perception rather than rationality and CIRCA operates from an alternative viewpoint to much of society. Perhaps they are telling a truth the world needs to hear, which without them would go unspoken.

For both religious and political clowns, the ideology comes from the mind and is expressed through the body. For the clowns considered next, the motivation lies in the heart, but the clowning makes use of many of the already established techniques.

6

CLOWN HEALERS

This chapter explores the contribution made to society by clowns who work in a psycho-social way rather than in a purely performative frame. Clowns who use their skills in order to help with the healing process can be found in hospitals across the world and, more recently, clowns are venturing into refugee camps and to sites across the world where people are suffering as a result of war, political upheaval or natural disaster. Despite the variance in the framing of the clown event, it will be demonstrated that while the clown healers have a different purpose to clowns who perform in circuses and theatres, they still have much in common, particularly in terms of technique, the way in which they build a relationship with the people with whom they work and the way in which play is a central element of their work. In theoretical terms, the nature of clown-doctor play relates to Sutton-Smith's 'rhetoric of play as child play' because interventions with children often emphasize the link between play and development. The therapeutic nature and intention of play with sick children suggests a relationship to the principles of play therapy. However, whilst clown play may be therapeutic, the relationship between the clowns and the patients is not based on a therapeutic contract and, whilst the patients have some control over the clowns (agreeing to engage with them, directing the play), they do not have the ability that a child in play therapy would to choose the toys which are used as a vehicle for play.

Clown-doctoring is a relatively complex area of study, requiring not only an historical and contemporary understanding of the development of clown-doctor programmes and the processes and techniques they use in hospitals and community care settings, together with the theories outlined above, but also an awareness of theories of the beneficial effects of humour and laughter on health.

A clown-doctor is a specially trained professional artist who works in a healthcare facility providing therapeutic humour to patients. They are not simply entertainers – they serve as an integral component of the healthcare delivery process. (http://web2.uwindsorca/fools_for_ health).

Clown-doctors are usually individuals with a background in professional performance (often as actors, singers or musicians rather than as circus clowns). These individuals are trained by one of the major clown-doctor organizations world-wide to enhance their skills in improvisation, storytelling, mime, singing or playing an instrument. They are also encouraged to develop the ability to listen and to conduct themselves with sensitivity and professionalism. Emotional stability and resilience are also necessary, in much the same way as these are vital for doctors and nurses, because the clown-doctors often work with people who are seriously ill, and they also have to learn to cope with the death of patients. The clown-doctors are rarely qualified medical doctors (although this is the case for **Patch Adams** and **Dr Fruit-Loop** a.k.a **Dr Peter Spitzer**) but they are taught about 'hospital procedures, infection control, a range of physical and psychological illnesses, and the structure of hospital paediatric services' (www.theodora.org. uk). Having developed these skills, they are able to approach patients with sensitivity and adapt their performance to the needs of the individual. In most of these organizations the clowns work in pairs, providing each other with both inspiration and support. Common techniques used by clown-doctors will be discussed when contemporary clown-doctor practice is examined later.

The concept of modern clown-doctoring was created by Patch Adams. Adams trained as a medical doctor at the George Washington Hospital in Washington D.C. in the United States, beginning his studies in 1964. As Adams (1998a) recounts in *Gesundheit! Bringing Good Health to You, the Medical System, and Society through Physician Service, Complementary Therapies, Humor and Joy*, he immediately felt himself to be at odds with the system within which he was training. He found his tutors to be arrogant and aloof and their attitude to patients was reductive: 'people were called by the names of their diseases, as if the disease were more important than the human who suffered from it' (Adams 1998a: 10). Adams realized that he would never fit into the contemporary American health care system and he set about thinking of alternative ways of practising medicine, influenced no doubt by the Hippie movement and communes which were establishing themselves across the United States during the 1970s. In 1983 Adams founded the Gesundheit Institute, a commune-style health care setting which provides free health care (unusual in the United States) and which encourages patients to participate in all areas of the commune's life. As early as 1984, Adams began running workshops teaching doctors and medical students 'how to be a nutty professor'. To do this, he dressed the participants in 'leotards, deelyboppers, angel wings, and rubber noses and introduced them to juggling, clowning, and slack-rope walking' (Adams 1998: 22). The first of these workshops took place at the Harvard Medical School.

Although Adams' introduction of clown-doctors is relatively recent, Van Blerkom (1995) argues compellingly that there is also a strong link between modern clown-doctors and shamanism and complementary medicine. Her article focuses on the work of Big Apple Clown Care and establishes a number of clear links between the ways in which shamans worked and those in which modern clown-doctors operate. Similar links can be identified between the practice of shamans and clown-doctors and the techniques used by clowns in non-health care settings. 'Both clowns and shamans mediate between order and chaos, sacred and profane, real and supernatural, culture and anticulture or nature' (Van Blerkom 1995: 463). The liminality of clowns and their ability to move between polar opposites has been explored earlier. Just as ritual clowning and religious clowning can be found both in primitive societies and modern western society, so clown healers can be found in Native American cultures and in western society. According to Van Blerkom (1995), clown figures with healing functions can be found amongst the Yaqui and Mayo Indians of Sonora, the Iroquois and the Laguna Koshare. The resemblance between shamans and clown healers is clearest in their use of music, drumming, singing, sleight of hand, magic tricks and the inversion of the usual cultural order. According to Van Blerkom, '[s]hamans and other healers manipulate symbols of their societies' medical systems' (1995: 469). The same manipulation can be found in the costume and work of clown-doctors. Most clown-doctors base their costume around a parody of the doctor's white coat, and medical equipment is employed in unexpected ways. For example, medical tubing can be used for making music, for blowing bubbles or for tying up clown-doctors. The clown-doctors provide psycho-social support in a manner akin to shamans. The ancient roots of inversion, parody and humour in healthcare are clear.

The concept of clown-doctoring is now established around the world (Big Apple Clown Care, New York; Theodora Trust, United Kingdom, Switzerland, China, Belarus, France, Italy, South Africa, Spain and Turkey; Clown-doctors UK and Le Rire Médecin, France; Dream Doctors, Israel; Doutores da Alegria/Doctors of Happiness, Brazil; Cliniclowns, Europe). However, it is important to remember that at the time Patch Adams was struggling to introduce a different kind of health care in which clowns played a part, he was viewed as a maverick and a rebel. As a doctor who wanted to clown, he was, appropriately for a clown, challenging conventions of social behaviour. At the time, hospital wards, even children's wards, were serious places where people came to be cured or to die, not to be entertained and made to smile and laugh.

Big Apple Clown Care

Around the same time that Adams was establishing the Gesundheit! Institute as his way of responding to what he saw as a lack of humour in healthcare, The Big Apple Clown Care programme was founded in 1986 by Big Apple Circus co-founder, **Michael Christiansen**. Whilst the Gesundheit! Institute offered an entirely different approach to healthcare; Big Apple Clown Care was the first organization to take clown-doctors into general hospitals. Since then, the Big Apple Clown Care programme has expanded and now offers a range of services that include one-to-one bedside visits in a range of healthcare settings. The ninety Big Apple clown-doctors work in intensive care units, in accident and emergency departments and with both inpatients and outpatients, making around 250,000 visits each year. According to their website, part of the clowns' purpose in hospital is to

> use parody to help demystify and simplify complicated medical procedures by performing their own 'highly technical' clown medicine that includes red-nose transplants, kitty cat scans, chocolate milk transfusions, plate spinning platelet tests, and prescriptions of laughter. (www.bigapplecircus.org)

In addition to working with children in hospitals, Big Apple also runs a Vaudeville Caravan programme which provides interactive, room-to-room entertainment to elderly residents of Chicago-area nursing homes. This was introduced in 2002 and encourages performers to use their skills with senior citizens whose lives might otherwise be dull and boring. Whilst the Big Apple Circus website offers an outline of their provision, it offers little in the way of analysis regarding their working methods and offers no evaluation of the success of their interventions. Its focus, though, is on the clown-doctors as performers and entertainers rather than as therapists.

Theodora (England)

The London-based Theodora Children's Trust, which has its home at the Great Ormond Street Hospital, is part of an international organization, The Theodora Foundation, founded by Jan and André Poulie in 1993 in memory of their mother, Théodora. The international sphere of operation of this organization means that there are 131 Theodora clown-doctors working in nine countries, across three continents. The organization is committed to making clown-doctors available to hospitals around the world. The United Kingdom branch has recently expanded its provision to include the Sheffield Children's hospital (visits beginning in 2006); taking the number of hospitals it is involved with to eight. The Theodora trust website identifies the following objectives:

1. to have a positive effect on sick children in hospital and their families
2. to collaborate with hospital staff to complement their work
3. to run a clown-doctor training programme in partnership with a medical school
4. for the training to be recognized by health authorities for its professional standards and specialized role
5. for hospitals in the UK to sign up to the clown-doctor programme through the Trust. (www. theodora.org.uk)

Similar objectives can be found on the websites of Clown-doctors UK and the Humour Foundation.

Hearts and Minds (Scotland)

Other websites, like Hearts and Minds (Scotland) for example, focus on what they perceive to be the benefits of clown-doctoring, such as participation, empowerment, demystifying medical procedures, distraction and simulation. The Hearts and Minds' clown-doctor programme was established in 1999 and its clown-doctors visit the Edinburgh and Glasgow Royal Hospitals for Sick Children and Royal Aberdeen Children's Hospital twice weekly. They also visit Rachel House Hospice in Kinross on a weekly basis. Other units (the Raigmore Hospital and Ninewells Hospital, Dundee) receive less frequent visits. Unusually for the United Kingdom, where the focus of clown-doctoring appears to be that it is a service most relevant to children, Hearts and Minds also have a programme of clown-doctoring aimed specifically at the elderly. This programme is known as Elderflowers and was founded in 2001.

Le Rire Médecin (France)

The French organization Le Rire Médecin was founded in 1991 by Caroline Simonds (who had worked for three years as a clown-doctor with Big Apple Circus Clown Care) and Anne Vissuzaine. Together they first worked in L'Institut Gustave Roussy and l'Hôpital Louis Mourier.

Now the organization makes more than 55,000 visits to children, their parents and their carers. Their aim is to give those they meet 'la possibilité de rire, de rêver et d'oublier la maladie' (the chance to laugh, to dream and to forget their illness) (www.leriremedecin.asso.fr). In common with the other clown organizations discussed here, the clowns respect the patient's right to refuse a visit from the clown-doctors. According to Le Rire Médecin 'l'enfant dicte les règles du jeu et peut d'un souffle léger chasser les clowns de sa chambre' (the child dictates the rules of the game and is able with just a light breath chase the clowns from the room) (www.leriremedecin.asso.fr).

Cliniclowns (The Netherlands, Belgium and Austria)

Information about the Cliniclown organization is difficult to find in English language publications or on English language websites. However, the organization is highly significant in Europe, particularly in the Netherlands where between fifty and sixty clowns work regularly with hospitalized children. The Austrian branch was founded first, in 1991, followed by the Dutch branch in 1992 and the Belgian branch in 1994. Cliniclowns, unlike many other clown-doctor organizations, tend to have either a medical or pedagogical background, to which improvisational and clown skills are added. Cliniclowns work exclusively with children either in hospitals or in special schools for the long-term sick. Their purpose, according to the founder of the Dutch organization, Tom Doude Van Troostwijk, is to give back to ill children the possibility of play, which in turn enables them to develop more normally. There is a clear link here to Sutton-Smith's 'rhetoric of play as progress' whereby play has a developmental purpose and value.

The Humour Foundation (Australia)

The Humour Foundation was the vision of two men, Jean Paul Bell and Dr Peter Spitzer (a general practitioner) who were inspired by Patch Adams, Big Apple Circus Clown Care and the Theodora Trust. A pilot study to assess the impact of clown-doctors was launched at the Royal Hobart Hospital in 1996 and, following the success of this, the Sydney Children's Hospital became the first hospital in Australia to regularly host clown-doctors in 1997. The Humour Foundation focuses its work on adults as well as children and also works in palliative care units, where their aim is 'to provide ways of dealing with death', and where, 'paradoxically people frequently share their feelings. Clown-doctors take risks in balancing lightness with the profound. Caring clowning can speak the language of the heart and bring a sense of profound connection and consolation' (www.humourfoundation.com.au). The Humour Foundation takes research into the value and effects of clown-doctoring very seriously and their website is a useful resource in this area. Later, consideration will be given to the ways in which clown-doctor practice might be evaluated with reference to The Humour Foundation website, which provides a detailed account of its pilot study and its findings.

Fools for Health (Canada)

Fools for Health is a Canadian organization which was founded in 2001 by Bernie Warren, following the model established by the Big Apple Circus Clown Care programme and Le Rire Médecin. Initially the organization worked within an adult rehabilitation unit at the Western Campus of Windsor Regional Hospital. In the five years since their founding their provision has expanded and they now identify a number of programmes beyond the clown-doctors who work in hospitals. They also run a 'Down Memory Lane Programme' (which has some similarities with Hearts and Minds', Elderflowers). The contacts which clown-doctors have with the elderly are often longer and at a slower pace than the contacts with younger patients. When working with an elderly person, particularly those with cognitive problems, the clown will 'sit with a patient at length, skilfully using arts-in-health memory therapies' (http://web2.uwindsorca/fools_for_health.htm). They also run a 'Travelling Clown-doctor Programme'. Clowns working within this programme visit rural hospitals and even make home-visits. The 'Jr Clown-Doctor Programme' works to improve children's self-esteem and teaches them how laughter can help with healing in even the most difficult situations.

Clown Doctors UK (Newcastle)

This organization is the newest of the clown-doctor programmes. It recruited and trained its first clown-doctors in the summer of 2006. Applicants were required to have a minimum of five years experience as a professional performer, experience of working with children, and had to demonstrate in a workshop setting the ability to work spontaneously with other clown performers. The organization presents its aims as including social involvement, participation and access to the arts. The intention is that clown-doctors will demystify medical procedures and jargon that can be frightening for children. The organization currently works only with children. According to their website, '[t]he programme offers a new form of therapeutic treatment, replacing medicine with merriment and offering young patients a way of contributing to their own recovery through humour and play' (www.clowndoctors.co.uk). The emphasis, therefore, is on the therapeutic aspects of the encounter rather than emphasizing the clown-doctor's skill as a performer.

A significant point of comparison between the various organizations is whether the clown-doctors are considered to be entertainers or, in some sense, therapists. For example, despite requiring its trainee doctors to have at least five years experience as a professional performer, Clown-doctors UK insists that the clown-doctors are more than simply entertainers. On the other hand, Le Rire Médecin maintains that 'Les clowns du Rire Médecin sont des artistes et non des thérapeutes même s'ils s'adressent aux enfants malades' (the Rire Médecin Clowns are artists and not therapists even though they are aimed at ill children) (www.leriremedecin.asso.fr). This difference of opinion lies at the heart of the work carried out by the clown-doctors. The case studies looked at later will examine how far the concepts of entertainment and therapy can be separated, with reference, also, to the field of play therapy. What actually happens when clown-doctors work on hospital wards is best summarized by the Theodora Trust:

> The clown-doctors begin their hospital visits with an impromptu session in the outpatients department and then move on to the wards, where they are briefed by the nurses on those children who would benefit most from a visit. They then wait to be invited by the child before proceeding. The clown-doctors use their improvisation and entertainment skills to involve each patient as much as possible, ensuring that the child is not confined to the role of spectator but can participate in the magic and the activities. With tact and sensitivity, the clown-doctors also involve the families and the medical staff in these sessions. (www.theodora.org.uk)

There remains the question of why clown-doctors might have a positive impact in healthcare settings. Some answers to this question are offered by research which has been carried out into the therapeutic effects of laughter and humour since Norman Cousins' ground-breaking work *Anatomy of an Illness* in 1976.

In this area of research, some work is defined as humour therapy and some as laughter therapy. It could be argued that humour therapy occurs where the client or patient is actively involved in the creation of humour whilst laughter therapy takes place when the client or patient is provoked to laughter by another person or an external source, such as a video or humorous book. However, the distinction between the two therapies is not so clear cut. In the article 'Taking Humor Seriously', Lawson claims that 'the distinction between humour therapy and laughter therapy has not been made sufficiently clear' (2003: 19). Indeed she goes on to offer a definition of American Humour Therapy which derives from what she defines as the 'entertainment axis...so patients are the recipients of humour therapy in much the same way that audiences are the recipients of professional humour' (2003: 19). From this it could be inferred that humour therapy is more passive than might have been previously thought. The terms 'humour therapy' and 'laughter therapy', therefore, have to be defined and clarified in the context of whichever study or article they are found. Norman Cousins' *Anatomy of an Illness* (1979) reports in detail the effects of watching humorous videos (such as the Marx Brothers and *Candid Camera*) in reducing the pain caused by ankolysing spondylitus. His detailed observations of the benefits he perceived as a result of prescribing laughter therapy for himself have been followed by others, examining in detail the measurable and perceived effects of laughter and humour therapy. A selection of this research, including Mahoney (2001), Pearce (2004), Hoare (2004) and Godfrey (2004), is examined here in order to establish a background against which clown-doctor interventions might be analysed.

Much of the research in these closely-connected areas seeks to establish what the benefits of laughter and humour might be to those suffering from a variety of problems, including stress, pain, chronic illness, hospitalization, invasive treatment and terminal diagnosis. Two key areas of possible benefit exist: the physiological and psychological, and, to confuse matters further, there are common links between the two areas. In 'The Best Medicine' in *Nursing Standard*, December 2004, Joe Hoare defines psychoneuroimmunology as a 'discipline that studies the relationship between psychological states and the immune response – reveals that laughter is a complex and health-inducing phenomenon' (2004:18). This emphasizes the close connection between physical health, the individual's perception of their state of health, and psychological well-being.

The first group of effects which are sometimes considered as beneficial outcomes of laughter and humour are those that are physiological. However, even within this area, there is disagreement between scientists as to the physical effects of laughter and humour. The range of effects claimed includes the reduction of stress chemicals such as serum cortisol (Goodman in Godfrey 2004; Pearce 2004), and the release of endorphins (Pearce 2004). Lawson suggests that '[l]aughter reduces the level of stress hormones such as cortisol and adrenaline and stimulates the production of endorphins. Our brains are wired in such a way that they cannot generally produce stress hormones and endorphins simultaneously' (2004: 19). However, in contradiction, Mahony (2001) argues that no empirical study has been carried out which proves that laughter increases the production of endorphins. Both Pearce and Goodman (in Godfrey 2004) argue that laughter has beneficial effects on the immune system: 'the immune system (increase on T cells) appears to be activated' (Godfrey 2004: 476). There are also suggestions that laughter increases circulation, blood pressure and heart rate, thus providing a form of aerobic exercise.

As well as creating physiological benefits, laughter and humour have a positive impact on our psychological state. In popular thought laughter is recognized as being beneficial and this popular notion is supported by scientific study. These benefits can vary according to the source of the humour and the level of the stimulation provided. Mahoney's 2001 study looks at the link between expectation and reality in relation to laughter and humour. We expect to feel better and less stressed if we are exposed to something humorous, particularly if it is humorous enough to make us laugh out loud. Some of the benefits of laughter may arise, therefore, because we expect them to occur. This can be likened to a placebo effect. In fact, the results of Mahoney's study

> ...suggest that some of the successes of the wide variety of humour and laughter interventions currently being used in applied settings, may be due, in part, to the interaction of existing beliefs about the value of humour and laughter and the potentiating messages, either stated or implied by the very existence of the intervention in a clinical setting, that the intervention will be successful. As with any placebo effect, the benefits are real enough. (2001: 226)

Drawing on the research of Hudak et al (1991), Mahoney suggests that 'individuals having high humour traits coped well with pain with or without the assistance of an induced humour state, but that individuals having low humour traits were more vulnerable and less able to cope' (Mahoney 2001: 226). The analysis of the work of Le Rire Médecin, in which clown-doctor contact is traced over a period of weeks and months, seems to demonstrate that repeated clown visits can enhance the humour trait of sick children, making them more responsive to humour and leading to the child experiencing increasing benefits from the stimulation of humour states.

Overall, however, it is difficult to define whether clown-doctor intervention is humour therapy or laughter therapy. This difficulty, in part, arises from the range of interventions which may be made by skilled clown-doctors. There can be times, therefore, when the patient is a passive recipient of the humour created by the clown-doctors, either by inclination or as a result of physical incapacity. At other times, patients interact with the clown-doctors, even setting the rules for the games played and thus controlling the clown behaviour. Additionally, some patients may join the clowns in making other patients laugh. In this case their connection with the clowns is most active. In involving them in active play to the extent that their illness allows, the clown-doctors are encouraging activity that relates to the developmental theories underlying Sutton-Smith's (1997) 'rhetoric of child play', which emphasizes the function of play in relation to the way a child interacts with and understands the world. Sutton-Smith recognizes that 'play is said to be the best way in which [adults] can communicate with children to assist them toward recovery' (1997: 43).

Other studies consider the source used to provoke patient humour or laughter as a distraction. The underlying assumption is that individuals feel pain less, or are able to endure it better, if they are able to focus on something other than the pain. Thus it might be expected that reading, doing a crossword puzzle or watching a film would enhance the patient's ability to endure discomfort. Mahoney's research indicates that the effectiveness of any distraction is inextricably linked with expectation. As there is an 'already existing cultural belief that laughter ameliorates pain and discomfort' (2001: 221) it is to be expected that providing a humorous distraction will have a beneficial effect on discomfort thresholds.

There is, therefore, a difficulty in assessing to what extent the positive effect of clown-doctors on patients (if indeed they have a positive effect) is due to physiological changes brought about by laughter or to the simple fact of the patient being distracted by the clowns. There is very little available material which scientifically assesses the effects of clown-doctoring. Therefore, much of what follows is based on descriptions of clown-doctor interventions together with observed changes in the patient's state. The Humor Foundation of Australia provides an example of clown-doctor evaluation of work carried out at The Northern Hospital based on a scientific model, while Clown-doctors UK also carried out a detailed evaluation at the end of their first year.

The Northern Hospital (TNH) report has a full title of 'Humour for Good Health in The Emergency Department and Child and Adolescent Health Unit (Marcon 2005)' and will be referred to here as 'The Clown-doctor Project Final Report'. The report documents the 'methodology and findings of the Humour for Good Health project [which] funded the employment of two professional performers to work as clown-doctors and interact with patients and families in the emergency department, waiting room(s) and CAHU' (Marcon 2005: 4). The project employed consideration of the evidence-based therapeutic effects of laughter to examine whether the clown-doctor interventions could provoke positive emotions and have a beneficial effect on patient health. TNH used two qualitative methods to measure the success of the Clown-doctor Project; Independent Observation and Focus Groups. The independent observer evaluated two separate sessions, each lasting between one and one-and-a-half hours. On each occasion the observer kept a record of how many separate episodes the clown-doctors were involved with, the age of the patient involved, the techniques used, and the response of the patient. The clown-doctors were observed working in the waiting room and in the treatment rooms of the Emergency Department. 64 per cent of the children involved were ten years old or younger. The most common age group for clown-doctor interaction was the under-three age range, which accounted for 43 per cent of the interventions. There seems to be an indication, therefore, that the clown-doctors, who initiated all but one of the interventions, are drawn to working with younger children. It is not clear from the study whether this is because of a preconception that younger children are more open to clowns; a reflection of the make-up of the patient population at the time of the observation; or because the younger children appeared to the clown-doctors to be more interested in what they were doing. The activities observed were using bubbles, telling jokes, music, dancing, clumsy play, props, caring talk and massage and, commonly, some combination of these. What is most significant about the report is not the statistical detail about the number and character of the clown-doctor interventions but the nature of the response to them. According to page seven of the observation report 77 per cent of patients and their families rated the clown-doctor experience as excellent, and there were no adverse responses. Clearly the clown-doctor activity was well-received by its target audience. Very little of the clown-doctor activity observed independently was seen by medical staff. In the Emergency Department, it appears that the clown-doctors judged the timing of their interventions so that they occurred before and after treatment or assessment rather than during it.

The other method of evaluating the clown-doctor intervention was through staff focus groups, which were led by an independent evaluator. The questions posed in the focus groups were much more open than the patient evaluations (which allowed the respondent to rate the clown-doctors on one of five levels). As a result, the findings of the focus group are expressed much more subjectively. 'There was a general consensus that the project was positive for the Emergency Department' (Marcon 2005: 9). Comments by the focus group indicated that the project was of benefit to staff as well as to patients, which indicates a positive response to its aim of reducing stress levels amongst staff. The only problem that arose in the project was from the clown-doctors working too close to a recently bereaved family. It does not appear to have been standard practice for the clown-doctors to be briefed by medical staff prior to going onto the ward, while such briefings are common elsewhere in clown-doctor practice. A briefing session may have avoided the clown-doctors' unwitting intrusion.

The report concludes that the Clown-doctor Project was a success and recommends its continuation. However, the nature of the praise that 'clown-doctors distracted patients and families from the monotony of waiting' (Marcon 2005: 12) undervalues the potential positive impact of clown-doctors by framing them as a distraction rather than as part of a therapeutic team. It is clear from *The Clown-doctor Chronicles* that clown-doctors are able to do much more than simply distract patients.

Clown-doctors UK commissioned an independent evaluation towards the end of their first year of delivery. The evaluation report was produced by Esther Salamon, Cultural Partnerships & Developments, August 2007. This evaluation used a similar methodology to the TNH study. The evaluation offers background information on the Clown-doctors UK project, including useful information about the principles guiding Tin Arts, an organization based in Newcastle which facilitates and delivers a range of arts projects and services, including a clown doctor programme. One key purpose of the provision is identified as:

> To stimulate and engage with individual patients and their families in order to demystify often painful, distressing and confusing medical procedures. (Salamon 2007: 4)

Esther Salamon who carried out the evaluation observed two patient sessions and also carried out separate focus groups with the Clown-doctors and Health professionals. The inclusion of a focus group with the clown-doctors is a notable difference from the TNH evaluation and useful information was gathered about the experience of the clown-doctors in terms of training, support and practice. The nature of the comments in both focus groups is qualitative rather than quantative (there is no numerical analysis offered of interventions, age of patients or positive and negative outcomes). This lack of numerical analysis reflects an assertion by Tin Arts that 'the quality/nature of the engagement is paramount...numbers don't figure...we are not playing a numbers game' (Salamon 2007: 16). What the evaluation reveals is that both clown-doctors and health professionals are, as might be expected, aware of positive and negative aspects to the delivery of clown-doctor provision. A number of significant points are identified. The importance of a strong working relationship between the hospital staff and the clown-doctors is highlighted by both groups, with the clown-doctor focus group emphasizing that support from the hospitals 'makes/breaks the effectiveness of delivery' (Salamon 2007: 24).

The centrality of the relationship between hospitals and clown-doctors occurs again and again in such literature as exists on clown-doctoring. Related to this is the matter of whether it is better for clown-doctor pairs to work consistently in one place over a long period of time to develop relationships with staff and patients, or whether it is better for clown-doctors to rotate, working in different wards and different hospitals. The evaluation carried by Esther Salamon reveals a range of opinions in this key area. In a section of the clown-doctor focus group headed 'Desired Changes to the nature of support being offered', some clown-doctors wanted to see greater rotation of the clown-doctors so that they worked in different pairings more often. On the other hand, the health professionals' focus group offered the view that it is beneficial for families if children are able to 'develop relationships with the Clown Doctors, particularly if [the] child has a long-term illness' (Salamon 2007: 37). The final comments of this focus group highlight a division of opinion in this area, with requests both to rotate clown-doctors less so that they do not form bonds and then get moved, and to rotate them more because children sometimes want to see a clown-doctor again who has not been assigned to their ward for some time.

Tin Arts and the hospitals they are working with are developing ongoing evaluation and appraisal systems, such as Comments Book (filled in by staff, patients and their families), artists' monitoring forms and short observations submitted by hospital staff. Whilst observation of two sessions was carried out as part of the evaluation process, no comment is offered on these sessions in the evaluation report. Tin Arts, like other clown-doctor organizations, are aware of the need to develop monitoring and evaluation methods in this under-researched area. Clearly, there is a need for a much greater degree of research into the effects of clown-doctor interventions on patients, family and staff. The practice of clown-doctor intervention is relatively young and much of its current reputation is based on observation, anecdotal report and through its indirect link with humour and laughter therapy.

The only detailed account of a sustained clown-doctor programme is to be found in *The Clown Doctor Chronicles* (Simonds, C. and Warren, B. 2004). The book recounts the experiences of Caroline Simonds (Dr Giraffe) of Le Rire Médecin over the course of a few months in 1999–2000, working on a children's haematology ward. Usually Simonds works with her clown partner Nadine (La Mouche), but there are also accounts of her working with a variety of other clown-doctors.

Like many of the clown-doctor organizations, Le Rire Médecin has a code of ethics which outlines the ways in which the clown-doctors are expected to perform their duties. The intention of the code is to 'maintain the quality and professionalism of their work – without limiting the creativity of the artists' (Simonds and Warren 2004: 173). This code of ethics resembles those which govern the work of other therapists, such as the British Association of Counselling and Psychotherapy, the British Association of Dramatherapy and the American Psychotherapy Association. Issues common to all these codes of ethics are confidentiality, relationship boundaries with clients/ patients, and maintenance of skills. Indeed, such fundamental concepts govern most people who work in clinical or therapeutic settings. Other items in the Le Rire Médecin Code of Ethics relate more specifically to the work of clown-doctors. Article Three states: 'The artist never works alone at the hospital. He works as part of a duet and is always accompanied by a partner' (Simonds and Warren 2004: 173). While this is a principle adhered to by other clown-doctor organizations, such as Clown-doctors UK, Theodora Trust and Fools for Health, *The Clown Doctor Chronicles* does contain an example of a clown-doctor working alone.

Simonds and Warren identify a number of reasons why working in pairs is helpful. It allows the relationship to develop around the traditional pairing of Auguste and Whiteface, with both clowns usually able to play both roles. Also, in relation to the hospital setting, the use of clown pairs means that there need not be any pressure on the child to be part of the act. Some children become clown assistants, but this is always by choice. A pair of clowns provides a wide enough range of possibilities for a patient to watch without having to be actively involved. Without a partner, 'there is no one to suggest other ideas; initiate a new piece of business, create improvisational conflict, help reset the volume if he is too "loud" or "soft", or at the end of the day to discuss the day's events' (Simonds and Warren 2004: 55). Thus, between them, the two clowns are able to meet the needs of the child and to support each other. Given that many clowns work with children who are terminally ill, and therefore have to deal with death on a regular basis, such support can prove invaluable.

Another important article of the Code of Ethics details the need for the safety of the patient to be paramount. This may seem rather obvious but when use is made of transgression and mock-violence, it is clear that clown-doctors have to balance the desires of the child with the need not to worsen his or her medical or psychological state.

> Clown-doctors do not make a medical diagnosis or write a case history, rather they create their own prescription, one that does not focus on the patient's illness but instead on those parts of the individual that are healthy. They help parents and the rest of the medical team realize that a patient is not simply his illness. (Simonds and Warren 2004: 19)

In order to be able to provide the intervention needed by the child, clown-doctors must have a range of skills. The importance of professional performance experience has been highlighted earlier and many clown-doctors also sing and play an instrument. Other techniques, such as juggling, puppetry, balloon-modelling, are also common. Such a range of skills, together with expertise in improvisation, enable a clown-doctor marriage (the term used by Simonds to describe a pair of clown-doctors who regularly work together, regardless of gender) to respond differently to each patient they deal with. This level of individual tailoring of the act to the patient distances the art of clown-doctoring from circus clown performance, despite the superficial similarity of the skills. A pair of clown-doctors usually works with one patient at a time. This is very different from the idea of entertaining a ward full of children.

Clown-doctors serve a range of purposes in a hospital or hospice setting. Their freedom of movement from patient to patient (observing ward hygiene regulations as they go) is similar to that of the doctors and nurses. They can provide a connection from one child to another in wards where the patient is not well enough to be mobile. They bring energy and anarchy to what is often a very serious setting, demonstrating the clown's ability to transgress the usual societal norms of behaviour. Clown-doctors on wards do this in a number of ways: they often make a lot of noise; they bring in musical instruments; they dance and encourage those children who are able to dance with them; they blow bubbles; they rearrange the furniture; they carry out 'red nose transplants', persuading nurses, doctors, parents and children to wear red noses; and even pour water over each other. Of course, such behaviour also means that 'from time to time, they act as scapegoats for the children, their families and the medical staff' (Simonds and Warren 2004: 80).

Simonds and Warren also comment on the ways in which the clown might function as what Winnicott (1991) calls a 'transitional object' and also aid in 'personal play' (Slade 1995). When a child suffers from a serious illness, he may have difficulty in seeing himself as separate from the illness (in much the same way that a very young child does not see himself as separate from his mother). 'As a result, the clown-doctor plays an important part in enabling the child to separate his illness from himself' (Simonds and Warren 2004: 137). Slade identified 'personal play' as children becoming objects, using the whole of their body to play at being something else. Many seriously ill children are too ill to play in this way any longer, or may never have been able to play like this. Rather than playing themselves, they play through the clown-doctors. The children dictate the pace and nature of the play:

> ...the child can control the clowns directly, through language or gesture...or indirectly with the compliance of one of the clowns...So, although they may be powerless to control their illness or the hospital procedures that are done to them, in their play the sick child is empowered because they have control over their clown toys. (Simonds and Warren 2004: 138–9)

In this way, the child has an outlet for asserting his or her individuality. Each child interacts with the clowns differently, therefore, making them respond individually to his or her wishes. In becoming part of the clown team, the child establishes a new role and a new identity for him or herself. In turn, this helps parents and medical care-givers to view the child from a different perspective and perhaps treat him or her differently. This in turn enables the child to cope more readily with the illness and the hospital environment.

The clown-doctors can help children to vent their anger at the situation in which they find themselves. Often this occurs through mock-violence. Louie was a seven-year-old boy who was visited repeatedly by Dr Giraffe and La Mouche and who established a game, based on the Lara Croft video game, in which he controlled whether the clowns lived or died. The violence of the game permitted Louie to express his anger, and it also allowed him to approach the concepts of death and how dying people might be saved. His play contained both exploration and a strong element of wish fulfilment. On some occasions, Louie made the clowns watch while he played on the real computer game, thus he was empowered. On other occasions, he engaged in using the clowns as toys that he could control, sending the clowns smashing into the walls. Once more in Louie's play, elements of control and aggression are combined. He needed to see someone else being a victim, just as he is a victim of his illness. Children find release in seeing the clowns suffer, safe in the knowledge that what they are witnessing is performed, rather than true, suffering. In this way they are able, for a short time, to forget their own suffering.

Medical staff can also request that the clowns are present while a child is undergoing an invasive or painful procedure. The intention is, in line with Mahoney's distraction research outlined above, that the children will not be so aware of their pain and discomfort if they are distracted from giving it their full attention. Sometimes, nothing can distract the child from the pain of the procedure (broviac cleaning, blood tests, lumbar punctures, bone marrow transplants), but, at others, the tactic is successful. Clown-doctors can also be helpful in persuading child patients to take their medication. In one incident recounted in *The Clown Doctor Chronicles,* one clown is victimized by the other in order to persuade a child to take her pre-lunch medication. The first tablet is swallowed when the clown is shut in a cupboard and the second when cold water is poured over the same clown's head. Such an example also demonstrates the freedom the clowns have to behave in unexpected and usually unacceptable ways for the good of the patients. The clowns also allow the sick child to express his or her naughtiness, which would find ready outlets in a normal child but which may have been repressed in the sick child. In this way, the clowns are contributing to furthering the child's normal development.

Some children benefit from helping the clowns during their visits to the ward. Martin, aged five, was a regular visitor to the haematology ward. During one stay, the clowns enlisted him to make announcements as they moved from room to room and bed to bed. As with the earlier examples, this experience allows Martin to be perceived differently by the staff on the ward 'because his status has changed, going from patient to performer' (Simonds and Warren 2004: 63). He is also able to make contact with other patients who may, in turn, be given hope by seeing another patient performing with the clowns.

Clown-doctor costumes are designed by the individual clown-doctors but commonalities do exist. Clown-doctors tend to wear a red nose together with a white coat, which can be decorated to suit their clown personality. Beneath the white coats, the clown-doctors tend to wear brightly coloured garments, often with baggy trousers or plenty of pockets in which puppets, props and squeakers can be hidden. Many clown-doctors also wear hats, as can be seen in the pictures in *The Clown Doctor Chronicles.* The visual similarity to clowns in both circus and theatrical settings is clear, but the use of the white coat also connects the clowns to their frame in the world of medicine. Clown-doctors working with Clown Doctors UK began working in white coats, which were sometimes tie-dyed or trimmed with brightly coloured fabric, but as their work has progressed, their costumes have become more subtle, as the illustration below demonstrates. As Clare Andrews explains:

> Our approach has become much gentler than we could have anticipated in the planning stages, and both costume and delivery has now been 'toned down' to make the Clown Doctors more accessible to all patients and families. (personal correspondence with the author 2008)

Here, the only addition to the white coat is a red nose and a hat or scarf. The clown-doctors working with this organization do not wear make-up, although they do sometimes use wigs.

John Quinn, clown-doctor, at work.

This more subtle approach is less threatening for the patients and allows the clown-doctors to provide opportunities for play based on character rather than costume.

A basic principle for clown-doctors, whether they are working with adults or children, is that the patient has the right to refuse a visit even if medical staff feel that it would be beneficial. Some children are scared of clowns and in this situation clown-doctors might work very gradually to reach a point where the child is no longer scared and can enjoy clown interaction. The Clown Doctor Chronicles contain accounts of Dr Giraffe and La Mouche working with children from as young as two through to teenagers of seventeen and eighteen. The nature of the clown-doctor intervention varies according to the age, character, physical and emotional state of the patient. Clown-doctors, therefore, tailor their activities to whatever the child either expresses a desire for or appears to need, and this can range from simple silent activities like blowing bubbles, through singing and dancing to noisy, raucous improvisations. Experienced clown-doctors judge by the mood and physical state of the child what kind of intervention they might enjoy. Witnessing their child enjoying clown-doctor performances, seeing them smile and laugh, can remind parents that, despite their illness, the child is still capable of that most fundamental of childhood activities, play. Similarly medical staff are encouraged to see that the children are individuals rather than diseases. Clown-doctors have to observe hospital rules about confidentiality, safety and hygiene, but they are also at liberty to do things that no one else would think of doing in a hospital ward. This can be seen as doing 'what is needed, not simply what is allowed' (Simonds and Warren 2004: 19).

Doing what is not allowed may mean breaking the ward's rules in the interests of the child, particularly if that child is dying. Clown-doctors can sometimes ask for exceptions to be permitted that a child's parent would not dream of requesting. One father wanted his little girl, who was dying of cancer, to be able to hold her cat one more time, but he was concerned that this would break hospital rules. He would not have dared to ask the medical team but the clown-doctors were able to act as go-betweens. The clown-doctors were told that bringing a cat onto the ward is against hospital rules but the nurse granted the request with 'a glorious wink and a sigh' (Simonds and Warren 2004: 101), and so the little girl held her cat one more time before she died. Clown-doctors also take liberties in more everyday ways. Clown-doctor play may involve moving furniture around, throwing things, spilling water and, as mentioned above, being violent or facilitating children in playing out their aggression.

> We encourage [Martin] to throw imaginary punches at us that send our bodies splattering onto the walls like bugs on windshields. He really can't get enough of this game and keeps yelling: 'Encore, encore! I want to nail you to the walls!' It permits him, from a lying position, to play a hard-nosed macho boy, without really hurting a fly. (Simonds and Warren 2004: 114)

A child who is too ill to engage in the rough play that comes naturally to many little boys can express this side of his nature and have some fun, even when he is too ill to leave his bed, because the clown-doctors respond to his slightest move. The violence is imagined rather than real and, therefore, entirely ethical, but the exaggerated physical response of the clown-doctors as they splatter against the walls runs counter to the behaviour usually expected on a hospital ward. The clown-doctors are noisy and make huge physical gestures more in keeping with a school playground.

Clown-doctors are not, however, always noisy. At other times, a more gentle approach is required and the clowns might turn to techniques, such as song, music and bubbles. There are times when too much loud noise or physical movement would be more than a sick child could bear. 'When you tell a sick child to close their eyes, it can be a big relief for she does not feel like she has to talk or partake in the clown play' (Simonds and Warren 2004: 36). At times like this, singing gentle songs or playing classical music might help the child to relax and enable him or her to receive attention from the clown-doctors without being worn-out by it. Clown-doctors need to develop their sensitivity to recognize what a child might enjoy, or is capable of withstanding. Blowing elaborate bubbles is another gentle activity that is used as a non-threatening contact with very young children or as a visually pleasing game for a child who is exhausted.

The use of symbol and metaphor permeates clown-doctor practice at many levels. The clown-doctors develop linguistic codes to allow them to talk about death without having to use the word. So children who are close to death might be described as 'sprouting wings'. More importantly, clown-doctors have to be alert to the use made of metaphor by the child patients and the ways in which clown-doctors can use metaphor to help them. One patient describes himself as the wind, prompting the clown-doctors involved to ponder on the significance of his choice. The difficulty with the interpretation of subconscious choices is that the interpreter may misinterpret. In the example given, Dr Giraffe decides that there might be a variety of reasons for the boy choosing the wind. 'Does he mean to tell me that no one will ever catch the wind? That the wind has its own laws and that the wind can escape illness?' (Simonds and Warren 2004: 44). The same metaphor of the wind is also used by the clown-doctors themselves with another patient who is angry and disappointed when he discovers his leukaemia has recurred. Dr Giraffe shouts at the boy from a distance not to dare to blow on the clown-doctors. 'An impish smile appeared as the boy puffed up and both of us went flying down the hallway to splatter onto the walls...Once again, the power of a metaphor spoke volumes' (Simonds and Warren 2004: 44). This may be a particularly appropriate way of working with children who have readier access to a land of imaginative play than adults may do.

As the title suggests, *The Clown Doctor Chronicles* chart the clown-doctors' visits to a number of children in chronological order. It, therefore, provides example of the different kinds of intervention that can be used with the same child at different times and to different effects. Examples are drawn from the interactions between Dr Giraffe and her partner La Mouche and a girl called Rosa, some of which are more successful then others. The clowns use a range of play techniques, but it becomes clear that mock-violence and victimization of one of the clowns are most likely to elicit play and laughter from this patient. When the clowns first meet Rosa, she indicates her readiness to play by creating a creaky voice for one of her toys and using this as a way of communicating with the clowns. 'A hospitalized kid uses "play violence" as a tool to channel pent-up fear, frustration, anger, boredom even loss and sadness' (Simonds and Warren

2004: 43). Rosa's direction of the torture of one of her soft toys soon escalates into a repeated scenario where La Mouche tortures and beats up Dr Giraffe for Rosa's entertainment. When a child is suffering, physically and emotionally, it can be releasing for that child to control and witness someone else taking the victim role. In any clown-doctor marriage there is always the traditional pairing of the high-status Whiteface in opposition to the low-status Auguste. This is a fertile combination for the previously described games of mock-violence which have long been a technique of clown performance. The red noses and the clowns' costumes emphasize for the child that what is occurring is not real and they, therefore, do not need to feel any responsibility for anybody really being hurt. Rosa is empowered by the fact that the clown-doctors follow her instructions. In a situation where Rosa has little control over any other aspect of her life, the clowns become a tool for her to experience a sense of control once more.

There are also occasions where the clown-doctor interventions with Rosa do not include violence. On one occasion, after a painful procedure for Rosa, they host a party in her room and persuade a group of doctors to flap around like penguins. Such interventions are pure entertainment and serve to remind the patient that fun and laughter are still possible, even in the midst of treatment for a life-threatening condition. Another sequence of play revolves around the use of jars of hair gel as the clown-doctors attempt to persuade Rosa away from violence. The game involves tipping a whole jar of hair gel onto the head of one of the clowns and styling her hair bizarrely. This is a typical example of the clown being prepared to make a fool of him or herself for the amusement of others. There is also a resonance in the fact that the little girl they are performing for is bald from her treatment. The message seems to be that even people with hair can look ridiculous. Thus it can be seen that the clown-doctors are able to encourage patients towards a range of different kinds of play. They are also able to respond to changes in the children rather than confining them within premeditated play routines. When Rosa returns to hospital after a long period at home, her nature has changed and the clowns play gentle games with her that involve singing her toy monkey (the object of torture in her last hospital stay) to sleep.

Rosa was only six years old and it is therefore not surprising that she was able to enter into clown play relatively easily. The clown-doctors also worked with teenagers on the Haematology ward, including Diane and Momo, who were both seventeen. These two teenagers demonstrated different attitudes to the clown-doctors. Momo was resistant to the clowns, believing they were for little kids. However, Dr Giraffe, in particular, continued with what she describes as terrorist clown raids: 'you must work quickly and precisely with teenagers and you have to sincerely love them' (Simonds and Warren 2004: 54). Dr Giraffe introduced the notion of being attracted to Momo and a series of brief interactions followed around the theme of Dr Giraffe being desperate to see Momo and Momo rejecting her. Another ploy which the clown-doctors used with this teenager was to get one of the younger children to put on a show for Momo. What eventually developed was a relationship in which Momo could talk to the clown-doctors about his hopes and fears. There was less play involved here and more demonstration of the clown-doctors' ability to adapt to individuals, and to listen. The other teenager, Diane, was more open to the clown-doctors because she had experienced them when she was in hospital two years earlier. Their interactions with her often involved singing and music. On one occasion when Dr

Giraffe was working with Dr Bob, he became a rap machine for Diane and all Dr Giraffe had to do was keep feeding him imaginary coins. On another occasion, a more subtle variation of the victimization theme seen earlier with Rosa was played out. Dr Giraffe and Diane ganged up on Dr Pew-Pew, teasing him about his height. Even the teenagers could feel better by being nasty to someone else when they knew that no permanent harm would be done.

As well as interacting with the patients, clown-doctors can also interact with, and have a beneficial effect on, the patients' families and on the medical and nursing staff on the wards. Often they persuade the parents to join in with the clowning, perhaps even getting them to dress up. Children find it very funny to see their parents doing something ridiculous that they would not normally do. This also has the effect of showing the child that, despite their worry for the child's health, the parents can still laugh, and this in turn gives the child permission to laugh.

Rather than working with children in hospitals and hospices, the Elderflowers programme run by Hearts and Minds (Scotland) takes pairs of clowns into residential care homes for the elderly. The programme has a particular focus on working with the elderly suffering from dementia. The analysis of clown techniques and their impact in this section is based on a video called *Red Nose Coming*. According to the clowns, who in this setting are defined as arts-in-health practitioners rather than clown-doctors, the red nose is a symbol that is readily identified by the elderly, and signals that the clowns are not ordinary visitors but an opportunity for humour and play. Just as the earlier example of clown-doctors working in hospitals located their work in relation to humour and laughter therapy, so the Elderflowers locate themselves alongside research into the use of humour in dementia care. They believe that humour can be used to increase communication, break down barriers, facilitate relationship-building, and lift the spirits. The Elderflowers are prepared to look foolish, which may make the elderly dementia sufferers feel more comfortable with their own mistakes and confusions. Also the Elderflowers' performed inability to remember words, make decisions and complete tasks may lead to the elderly residents identifying with them. This, in turn, is likely to increase the communication between clown and resident and lead to more positive relationships being created. One of the sequences on the video involves Sweety-pie trying to choose a hat to wear on a date. She tries on one hat after another, asking an elderly lady to help her choose something suitable. The theoretical basis behind this activity is that it encourages the patient to participate in the decision-making process. In practice, the patient said no to each hat until she was persuaded to say yes to the final hat. The example given, therefore, was unconvincing as evidence that such activities necessarily result in any benefit to the patient. The most effective example on the video in terms of convincing the viewer of the value of the Elderflowers is the opening sequence. First, we are shown a shot of a residential home lounge in which a number of elderly residents are sitting. They appear bored and disengaged and no one is talking. As soon as the Elderflowers appear, the residents visibly brighten up and begin to make comments both to the Elderflowers and to each other.

In terms of practice, the Elderflowers work in pairs, as has been seen elsewhere. They keep notes on their interactions with individuals and try to build, week by week, on what they have discovered about the resident's sense of humour and personality. The Elderflowers use techniques which have much in common with the techniques used by clown-doctors in other settings but their interactions tend to be quieter and less physical in nature than is the case for clown-doctors working with children. The Elderflowers use scarves, hats, ribbons and a dog puppet, which all provide the opportunity for physical contact. They also use songs with individuals and as a way of encouraging the residents to participate in an activity together. There are two examples on the video of the Elderflowers encouraging the residents to sing. In one sequence a gentleman sings 'There's no business like show business' with the clowns and it is clear from his facial expression, body language and from the energy with which he sings the song that he is enjoying the experience. Another sequence shows the Elderflowers sitting with two residents and singing 'Daisy, Daisy' accompanied by actions. Some of the actions are instigated by Tiny, one of the Elderflowers, and some by the gentleman resident. This indicates a level of engagement. These activities give the residents a chance to express playfulness and creativity which might otherwise be lacking from their lives.

It is clear from the interactions shown on the video that Tiny and Sweetie-Pie (the two Elderflowers featured) are aware of the potential dangers of using humour with sufferers of dementia. There is always the possibility that humour will be misunderstood and that the dementia sufferer might be upset. These dangers are avoided by the sensitivity of the performers, who keep the tone of their voices gentle and who are gentle and non-threatening in their movements. One interaction involved the resident repeatedly touching the red nose of one of the clowns. It is not clear to what extent she understands the significance of the nose or of what she is doing. The only evaluation on the video is provided by the staff at the residential home who 'recognized the gentle teasing out of the withdrawn'. Another member of staff suggests that the Elderflowers 'are not laughing at or putting down people with dementia. They're opening up channels for them to be able to express themselves' (*Red Nose Coming*).

It is difficult to establish to what degree the Elderflowers' interactions are successful because they are clowns and how far the residents simply benefit from being given individual attention by visitors who are friendly and approachable. It may be that the Elderflowers' visits are welcomed because they represent a break from the usual monotonous routine. Perhaps a community sing-a-long would have a similarly beneficial effect. More evaluation of this programme needs to be carried out, probably by independent observers, as was the case at The Northern Hospital, Australia and at Clown Doctors UK, Newcastle, because of the obvious difficulty of getting evaluative feedback from elderly dementia sufferers.

All of these clown-doctor practitioners use techniques and modes of behaviour that have been demonstrated by other clowns in other periods of history and in other settings. The status pairing of Whiteface and Auguste, together with the use of the red nose and costume, has already been discussed. A variety of forms of transgression are at play in the work of the clown-doctors. The clown-doctors transgress one societal norm simply by being present in a hospital. Hospitals are traditionally quiet, serious places. Clown-doctors in hospitals appear to misbehave by making a noise and also, frequently, by making a mess. The clown-doctors push at the boundaries of what is acceptable in a hospital or residential care setting. The use of violence has already been discussed. The clown-doctors inflict mock pain on each other, on parents, on toys, and on medical staff. We have seen how clowns in the circus throw water around and the clown-doctors use a similar technique to persuade Rosa to take her medication. However, the most important technique used by the clown-doctors, both with children and with the elderly, is to play. Patients, whether they are old or young, need help to reconnect with their own ability to play because of the beneficial effects of play, both on a sense of well-being and, through laughter, on the physiological responses of the body.

Reconnecting with an ability to play is also important for the millions of children around the world who live in countries that have been affected by natural disasters (such as the 2005 Tsunami), by local health issues (Aids in Swaziland), or by war or political unrest (Darfur or Palestine).There are several organizations that are based on the principle of using clowning techniques and clown performances to help such children learn to play again. The most significant organization working in this way is Clowns Without Borders (CWB) (known in some countries as Payasos Sin Fronteras), which was founded in Barcelona in 1993, following visits to Croatia by the clown Tortell Poltrona, who was invited to perform in a refugee camp in Savudrija. The initial visit by the organization took place in February 1993, when Poltrona performed as a clown to seven hundred children. Later in the same year, Poltrona returned to Croatia to perform again; this time in Zagreb and Varazdin. In the dozen or so years since these initial visits, a number of Clowns Without Borders organizations have been created: in Canada (founded 1994), and France (founded 1993), where the organization is known as Clowns Sans Frontières. In Belgium, the organization includes clowns and magicians and is known as Clowns et Magiciens Sans Frontières. In 1996 the American branch of the organization was founded by Moshe Cohen.

Patch Adams and the Gesundheit Institute also operate regular clown projects with under-privileged children and adults. One such project, which ran in 2002, was known as Patchwork for Peace. Patchwork for Peace was the idea of Stefano Moser, an Italian documentary filmmaker. Moser's plan was to take Italian clown-doctors to work in Kabul. Moser mobilized support for his plan in Rome, where he raised money and persuaded organizations to make donations of medical supplies, food, equipment and clothing. When Patch Adams was persuaded to lead the Italian troupe for the first three days of its missions, he brought with him other clowns from around the world. The nature of the work done by Patchwork for Peace, and the techniques used by them, are analysed later. Serious Road Trip is another circus-based organization which worked originally as an aid organization taking food and supplies into the Balkans in the early 1990s. However, once the desperate need for basic supplies had passed, Serious Road Trip continued to visit the area with a focus on cultural and entertainment-based projects.

All of these organizations begin from the principle that children, no matter what the difficulties of the region in which they live, have the right to play and to laugh. It is often impossible for local adults whose lives are seriously disrupted by illness or political unrest to ensure that their children have the chance to play. When Clowns Without Borders arrives in an area, they have the ability to bring smiles to the faces of the children (and also the adults). In doing so, they seek to relieve suffering and 'bring levity, contemporary clown/circus oriented performances and workshops into communities so that they can celebrate together and forget for a moment the tensions that darken their daily lives' (www.clownswithoutborders.org).

Between them, the various Clowns Without Borders organizations have visited an impressive number of countries. The Spanish group regularly visits Guatemala, Salvador, Nicaragua, Mexico, Columbia, the Balkans, Israel, the Sahara, Mozambique, Namibia and Palestine. They also made trips to Sri Lanka after the Boxing Day Tsunami in 2005. In addition to this, they work within Spain as clown-doctors in hospitals. The Belgian group works within Belgium and further afield in Albania and Asia. The Swedish Clowner utan Gränser work in Nepal, Mexico, Algeria and Palestine. According to their website, Clowns Sans Frontières – France have, in the last twelve years, used four hundred and fifty artists on sixty six projects in around twenty countries (including Afghanistan, Gaza, Rwanda, Russia, Thailand and Mongolia). Clowns Without Borders – USA has the most comprehensive website, which is available in English and which provides journals written by the clown volunteers during their time abroad, and it is this resource which provides the basis for an analysis of the techniques used by CWB on their projects.

Two of CWB's projects will be analysed in order to establish the range and nature of their work, including an exploration of the ways in which clowning techniques and performances are used, sometimes in cultures where the audience do not have a ready familiarity with western clowns. In April 2005, CWB visited Louisiana and Mississippi to perform for adults and children who had lost their homes as a result of the destruction caused by Hurricane Katrina. Whereas hospital clowning relies on highly individual work between a pair of clowns and no more than one or two patients at a time, CWB often work through performance to large audiences (1450 adults and children across four shows in one day). The framing of these shows varies. Sometimes CWB perform outside in whatever open space is available. At other times they perform in makeshift performance spaces in large indoor spaces such as sports halls. The emphasis here is on reaching the masses rather than on high production values. The children participate as audience and one or two may act as volunteers and come up onto the stage, if there is one. It is likely, therefore, that these shows are less about empowering the children and more about freeing the children to laugh by providing the opportunity for fun. Clearly the focus of this project was to provide some light relief for people who had experienced a life-changing natural disaster.

The project for Swaziland in 2006 was educative in its intent. Three CWB clowns and a juggler went to Swaziland on a mission with a two-pronged objective: to entertain the children and to train a group of local people in clowning and performance. The sketches and performances combined clowning and circus skills with social messages and were performed in the open-air, near to the centre of the village, in order to attract the largest possible audience. The use of a central open-air performance space increases the accessibility of the performance but reduces the notion of a formal performance frame.

One sketch performed in such an informal performance frame is referred to as the 'Women's Empowerment Sketch' and two of the local female performers walked seven foot tall (on stilts) as a visual demonstration of the possibility of female empowerment in a country where women have few rights. Whilst the main thrust of the show was about providing entertainment and provoking laughter, the sketches were devised around themes of HIV/Aids prevention (crucial in a country where 42 per cent of the adult population is infected with the HIV virus).

Wherever they take a project, the CWB clowns follow a gruelling schedule, often performing three or four shows a day, with only an occasional day off. In many of the places they visit they also have to contend with adjusting to a different climate and a different cultural environment. Part of the success of CWB's Swaziland project seems to have arisen from the close collaboration between CWB clowns and local performers. In training and rehearsing together, the SiSwati performers learnt a great deal about clowning and performance and were able to teach the Americans about local issues and local cultural sensitivities. The project is clowning with a social purpose and, whilst the clowns look like clowns described in earlier chapters, there is an emphasis on circus skills rather than clown behaviour. In this setting the clowns are playful but not transgressive.

However, there can be difficulties in taking western clowns into non-western cultures, as Patchwork for Peace discovered in its work in Kabul. A transcript of an ABC radio programme, 'Clowning in Kabul 2002', about the project (www.abc.net.au) describes how the clowns were caught in a crushing throng which was lashing out and pushing. The aggression seems to have been provoked by a female clown slowly pursing her lips and blowing bubbles. To western eyes this seems an innocent invitation to play, but the clown doing this realized that 'for these men, who put their women in burqas, to see a woman's face, a blue-eyed woman's face pursing her lips and showing how to blow bubbles slowly, it was the most stupid thing I probably could have done' (www.abc.net.au). In this instance, the clown was transgressive without meaning to be. The transgression of cultural norms arose not from a desire to challenge but from a lack of anticipation of possible responses. The difficulty also arose out of a situation where the clowns had no clearly defined performance frame but were mingling with local people in a busy market area. It is one thing for an American or European clown to work in a western circus or theatre and break the usual audience/performer divide, but it is quite another for a western clown to work with a non-western audience who may not recognize the conventions of the performance they are witnessing. In the West, however transgressive or challenging the clown's behaviour, the audience understands it within the conventions of clowning that dictate that clowns may behave in unexpected ways. When the clown is removed from its usual cultural setting, its conventions are lost. Despite John-Paul Bell's claim in the same interview that 'clowns almost have diplomatic immunity from cultural taboos' (www.abc.net.au), it is clear that clowns can transgress cultural taboos inadvertently and if the transgression is not supported by a mutually understood performance convention, it can lead to violence.

Both CWB and Patchwork for Peace make use of circus skills. In Swaziland, in addition to three clowns, there was a fourth CWB volunteer who was a juggler and magician. The clowns taught people to walk on stilts. Both organizations use songs and music to help them connect with their audiences, and extensive use is made of mime in order to overcome any communication difficulties. However, Patchwork for Peace makes greater use of parody and transgression. For example, performing in a state-run orphanage in northern Kabul, the clowns opened their performance with a parody of a military parade. In the West this might not be very challenging, but in a country which has experienced war and Taliban rule, the parody is much more dangerous. The common clowning transgression of bodily functions was also made use of when the clowns performed at the end of their visit. The skit involved a glowing ball being seemingly swallowed then extracted from the clown's bottom. Then the procedure was reversed and the ball was inserted into the bottom and extracted from the mouth. 'You know, they had tears running down their face with this complete, crude clowning, which always works, no matter what culture you're in' (www.abc.net.au). In contrast with the earlier inadvertent transgression, this transgression was framed within a clearly defined performance area. Just as in circus clowning or theatre clowning, the framing of the performance here had a significant influence on how it was received by the audience.

As well as performing, the clown volunteers working for CWB also run workshops teaching both children and adults about clowning and circus skills. In this way, the children are encouraged to become more actively involved in play, which is one of CWB's primary aims. The children may also feel empowered by learning new skills. In many of the places visited by CWB the children have either not learnt to play or have stopped playing as a result of starvation, fear or illness. According to Cattanach 'Play is used as a medium of communication because it is the way children make sense of their world' (2003: 1). Without play, children struggle to assimilate new experiences and events. Children who have been traumatized are more likely to have difficulty playing. By reminding the children how to play and encouraging them to play, the clowns increase the children's chances of surviving with their psychological well-being intact.

It is important to recognize that there are potential difficulties with clowning in refugee camps and in war-torn countries and many of these dangers are dealt with in Wilding's *Don't Shoot the Clowns* (2006). Having initially visited Iraq to gain a first-hand understanding of the situation there, Jo Wilding returned with a small group of performers to take circus (including clowns) to the children of Iraq.

> Play, laughter, a sense of community with the outside world and a bit of psychological healing...were things Iraqis were barely able to give one another so that was what we tried to bring them. (Wilding 2006: 140)

The benefits to the Iraqis were real but were only a small part of the help they needed (and continue to need) in order to rebuild their lives in a war zone. Whilst the circus performers may have had a positive effect, the risks to themselves are significant. As has been highlighted above, there is a chance that the clown performance will inadvertently transgress cultural boundaries, drawing the clowns into undesired conflict with the very people they are seeking to help. Given the cost involved in sending clowns and equipment to disaster zones, it could also be argued that the money might be better spent sending food and medical aid: it is difficult to see how children can respond positively to clowning when they are starving. According to Maslow's hierarchy of needs, emotional and cultural needs are only considered once the basic needs necessary for survival have been met. One medical student who encountered the Patchwork for Peace clowns claimed that 'aid money is more important than a moment's laughter' (www. abc.net.au).

It is necessary to consider, therefore, what the value of clowns in such a setting might be. The implication of the medical student's words is (in line with Maslow) that the frivolity of clowns is out of place when such basic needs as food and security cannot readily be met. When the clown-doctors work in hospital settings, the patient's basic needs have been met. Within the boundaries dictated by his or her illness, the child is well looked after and whatever play the clowns create becomes a beneficial adjunct to the other treatment that is going on, offering the child distraction, fun, empowerment or some combination of these things. The individual nature of the clowning ensures that the child's needs are identified and met. However, in the locations in which Clowns Without Borders volunteer, clowns work with children who are often hungry, if not starving. 'I went into this room and it's filled with beds and every bed has two children, and a variety of ages and states of consciousness, and definitely the states of consciousness had as much to do with starvation as they had to do with disease' (www.abc. net.au). Under such conditions, it must be more important to secure hygiene standards and food than to encourage the children to smile at a clown and her puppet. Whilst the work that CWB do is often worthwhile, there is a danger that the value of clowning becomes over-stated. Clowning is an important therapeutic tool (as are art, dance, drama and music; each of which has recognized models of therapy) but it is not a panacea.

CONCLUSION: THE CENTRALITY OF PLAY IN CLOWNING

The notion of clown permeates our consciousness. The word has crept into our vocabulary to describe a range of behaviours and situations: class clown, clowning around, tears of a clown; politicians are described as clowns (enter the word 'clown' into Google and as many references to George Bush and other politicians are returned as to clown performers, clown-doctors or clown-ministers). While there are positive features to this ubiquity, in that it means the clown has achieved iconic status, there is also an inherent danger in such familiarity. When the clown becomes over-familiar, it becomes debased. Society loses its wonder at the clown. Instead, the clown becomes a children's entertainer, a figure of speech, and little consideration is given to the way in which a clown performer develops his or her clown, and the material for his or her show. In this situation, the skill of the clown is no longer recognized, nor is the potential benefit which the clown can bring to society. As this study has illustrated, each culture has the clown or clowns it needs and the particular frame in which it operates. Whereas the frames in earlier or non-western cultures tended to be ritualistic, and whilst the predominant frame for clowns in western society was the circus, during the twentieth and twenty first centuries both the frames and functions of the clowns have expanded. Thus some functions have been retained, but the frames in which they occur have been modified. The sacred clowns of the Pueblos and the shamanistic clown healers have been replaced by modern clown ministers and clown-doctors, who are carrying out their function in frames such as churches and hospitals, where clown performance has not previously occurred. I have demonstrated how one clown function, that of political commentator, has largely disappeared, perhaps because society has developed other modes of allowing humorous political comments through political cartoons, satirical television programmes and stand-up comedians. It appears that the ability of clowns to act as a commentator or critic of the society in which they operate has largely been lost. Just as political clowns have lost their impact, so the religious truth-telling of clowns has been diminished. Clown Ministers no longer parody or criticize either the church or individuals within the churches. Instead they have been reduced to providing what is almost a form of children's entertainment to make the church and Christianity more accessible.

There remain, however, a number of functions which the clown has retained or expanded. For example, the role of the clown as entertainer was once limited to the circus and to pantomimes in the theatre. Now, however, the number of frames in which entertainer clowns can be found has increased. Clowns can be found in both traditional and contemporary circuses as well as in a range of theatrical settings and forms. This demonstrates the appeal of clowns and physical comedy and also emphasizes the range of ways in which the clown can now communicate with an audience. The many types of theatrical clown performance and the increase in clown performance styles, their use of the theatrical performance frame and their interaction with their audience, demonstrate the potential the clown has for remaining a force within society. This study has demonstrated the importance of play, often established through the physical nature of the performance, in the way in which clowns impact on and engage with their audience, and has shown that play is the single most vital element of clown performance and activity in our society today.

Indeed, De Castro and the Performance Arts Lab have carried out research which introduces teachers at both primary and secondary level to clowning techniques which they can use in their classroom practice. The Lab that De Castro was involved with in 2005 was for 'Teachers and Artists who Work with Volatile and Challenging Young People'. De Castro used clowning and play to explore failure and risk with senior teachers. This Lab was part of a larger three-year Creative Science Teaching Lab programme. What it demonstrates is that the application of clowning and play to areas with which they are not normally associated is beginning to be valued. According to De Castro, '[t]aking risks is an essential part of learning and this implies the right to fail. Clowns enable us to embrace failing as part of learning' (www.contemporaryclowningprojects.com). The purpose of the project was to encourage teachers to explore their own creativity in relation to their work. PAL recognised 'extraordinary transformations in participants – the clowning awakening hidden aspects of all individuals involved' (www.contemporaryclowningprojects.com). Clowning here was being used in a non-performative frame, but the impact of play and the freedom to fail had an extraordinary effect on the teachers involved.

Just as clowning can be used in non-performance contexts to train individuals to approach their professional life differently, so Lecoq recognized the importance of play and clowning in actor training. The clown and the related notion of playful theatre with its ready recourse to the physicalization of emotions and humour have contributed to the emergence of a new kind of theatremaker, who aims to create theatre which encourages an active involvement between the performer and the audience. The clown is a particularly useful tool in establishing this connection, as is encouraging the audience to witness or engage in play. Using clown as part of actor training enhances the actor's readiness and aliveness on stage. It also encourages the use of self in a way which opens the actor to the audience. This forms a strong contrast with the way self is used, for example, in Stanislavski-based actor training where personal experiences are used to enhance the actor's emotional range but not his ability to connect to the audience.

Indeed it could be said that Stanislavski's concept of circles of attention actively discourages the actor from being fully aware of the audience. For Lecoq, clown is inextricably linked to *jeu* and *complicité* which highlight the relationship between clown and play. Ultimately, the clown's ability to play and to help the audience to play is central to modern clown performance in both theatrical and non-theatrical settings.

Indeed, the popularity of clowns stems from the fact that, wherever they appear, they have the potential to provide something vital for our society. They are necessary because they are able to help us reconnect to our inner child. Western society discourages adult play except within clearly defined societal areas such as computer gaming and the playing of sports. The fact that society discourages adult play does not mean, though, that this is the best way for humans to live. In this area, society has developed in a way that represses a natural human instinct and makes that instinct the preserve of children. Even children do not have unlimited access to play. Once they reach school age, their freedom to play is seriously curtailed, unless they attend a school which advocates learning through play. Theatre clowns, as has been demonstrated, reveal the fun to be had in playing for the sake of it, while the performance venues in which they appear are evidence that their shows are aimed at adults at least as much as children. The clowns, therefore, remind the adults in the audience of the importance of play, and the importance of remaining connected with the child within us.

There are various points in our lives when we need to be reminded of the existence of our inner child, when it is important for us to reconnect with our own ability to play. In order to adjust to life situations over which we have little or no control, we need to be able to respond spontaneously. This notion of the spontaneous response can be found in the writings of Moreno (e.g.1947), the founder of Psychodrama, but clowns create a short cut to play and, therefore, to increased spontaneity. This is why clowns are found in so many areas of life today.

There is an increasing interest in clowning as a means of personal development. Whilst long-term clown training is still lacking in the United Kingdom and Europe, short courses are proliferating that are not all aimed at performers. Many people use the discovery of the inner clown as a way of increasing self-awareness. Finding the inner clown can reveal both strengths and insecurities, and the blocks and resistances encountered in approaching clown training can be enlightening. The potential of the clown to bring about personal change is linked to the centrality of the self in much clown training. This emphasis on the self provides a link to post-Freudian psychoanalysis, psychotherapy and counselling. In common with active forms of therapy such as dramatherapy, the clown operates and exists in the land of imagination and metaphor, rather than in the mundane world of the everyday. For some individuals, simply working in this creative way can bring about catharsis. For example, at the end of the first week of the two week 'How to Be a Stupid' course, De Castro uses an exercise called 'spinning'. In this exercise, participants wear the clown costume they have developed over the previous two days, based on a picture drawn after a meditation and visualization to help them create their personal Land of Why Not. According to De Castro, the Land of Why Not is an imaginary place in which anything is possible, and it is there that the inner clown can be found. The spinning exercise requires the participants to work with a partner. The two people begin by facing away from each other. They turn slowly to face each other and look into each other's eyes. While this is happening, De Castro provides a positive monologue that represents the thoughts which the participants should be having about how beautiful the other person is, how lucky they are to have found them, how wonderful their outfit is. As the monologue continues, the pair maintains eye contact. At some point they feel an irresistible urge to move towards each other, then to hold hands, then to grasp each others wrists, then to spin. Throughout the exercise they maintain eye contact. De Castro describes them diving into each other's eyes. Eventually they stop spinning and gradually they let go of each other and back away from each other. By the end of the exercise, several people are in tears. Usually people's explanation of their tears relates to the powerful emotion stirred by being fully looked at and accepted. The level of trust required to spin is also a powerful provoker of tears. This example of the cathartic power of clowning is based on personal observation but there is also a very limited amount of literature which deals with the potential of clowning in the areas of personal development and psychotherapy.

Additionally there is some literature that details the ways in which clowning can lead to personal development, and even be used helpfully in psychotherapy. At the heart of this application of clowning is what Bob Berky identifies as 'a kind of freedom from personal and cultural limitations which may inhibit life; we can begin to make room for creative experiences' (Berky and Barbre 2000: 241). His language also has echoes of the ideas expressed by existential philosophers and clowns, tending as it does toward the notion of authenticity. In Berky's view, clowning is about empathy. Empathy in a theatrical frame relates to Lecoq's notion of complicité and Berky describes it as finding out where the audience is. For Berky, clowns are more than 'grotesques with goofy facepaint, but are also practitioners of thought processes, of trying to figure out what is it we are doing, why are we doing it, and wouldn't it be fun if...' (Berky and Barbre 2000: 243). The connection is once again to the existential emphasis on questioning the meaning of life. However, the mention of fun locates the questioning clearly within a clown frame. Through performance, the clown connects with the audience, and in that connection comes the opportunity for recognizing that 'the role that the clown plays in society is they allow us to see ourselves more clearly' (Berky and Barbre 2000: 244). Barner and Vermillion-Witt (1992) also believe in the ability of clown to facilitate self-awareness and, from this, they suggest that discovering your own clown becomes a voyage of self-discovery and self-development. The Center Ring (1992) describes how each of them came to discover their own clown and goes on to explain the way in which they help others to discover their clowns. 'The clown helps us take risks and try the fresh approaches which give us new experiences. Our clowns give us the opportunity to express ourselves differently' (Barner and Vermillion-Witt 1992: 31). There is a clear connection between their views and those of Berky and Barbre. The clown offers the opportunity to reveal new facets of the self and, therefore, to discover different ways of behaving. For Barner and Vermillion-Witt, discovering and working with one's inner clown increases the ability to take risks and to trust to instinct. Clown can help in this way because the clown is curious rather than rational. Often in everyday life, people cling to what makes sense; they reason things out. Clowns are not rational characters. They are inclined to be open-minded and to respond with curiosity to the world around them. Barner and Vermillion-Witt clown under the names Argus and Blue and, as this duo, they clown in schools and hospitals as well as running their own workshops in discovering the inner clown. They claim that the workshops can be extremely therapeutic, citing the example of a woman who was able to use 'her clown as a vehicle for reframing an unhappy childhood and transforming her fears' (Barner and Vermillion-Witt 1992: 63). Through her clown, in the workshop, the woman was able to vent her fear and anger at her unsatisfactory childhood. For Barner and Vermillion-Witt, the power of the clown lies in its universality, which in turn relates to the clown and fool's existence as archetypes.

This connection between clowning and the notion of Jungian archetypes provides the theoretical and psychotherapeutic basis for Carpman's article 'Clown Therapy: The Creation of a Clown Character as a Treatment Intervention' (1998). Carpman outlines the principles of clown therapy, together with its goals and objectives. She also describes various clowning techniques and exercises that could be used in a psychotherapeutic setting. Her approach to therapy is Jungian and she bases her ideas on the Jungian archetypes of the trickster, the fool and the clown. Earlier, in 1987, Ulanov and Ulanov analysed the significance of the Jungian clown archetype, suggesting that the qualities of the fool represent an expression of the internal self. For Carpman 'the trickster, fool and clown, as emissaries of the Self, help create relatedness between the conscious and unconscious aspects of the personality' (1998: 246). As well as the clown providing a link with the unconscious, Carpman also recognizes the importance of clown play in a therapeutic setting suggesting that it helps to 'counteract the power differential between client and therapist, enhancing the empathic relationship' (1998: 247). The implication is that the clown's ability to parody or be subversive may free the client to take a less submissive part in the therapeutic relationship. The importance of empathy in clowning is also noted again. For Carpman, a number of central features of the clown are helpful in therapy. These are what she identifies as the five principles of clown therapy:

1. Each of us has the capacity to internally experience the qualities embodied in the clown.
2. Play, spontaneity, lightheartedness, humor and creativity are primary ingredients in the healing process.
3. The clown provides a creative outlet through which to discover and work with unconscious contents.
4. The body is the medium through which the clown character expresses itself, giving symbolic voice to the unconscious.
5. The relationship between the therapist and the client is an essential component of clown therapy.

(Carpman, 1998 249)

These elements, identified by Carpman in relation to therapy, are the very elements which make the clown so vital to modern society. The clown provides a visceral and instinctive connection between elements of ourselves that normally go unacknowledged. By exploring these facets of ourselves we increase our creativity, spontaneity and potential for play. These elements are helpful not only to our psychological but also to our physical health.

In recent years, developments in medical science and in popular psychology have begun to shift society's focus so that, as well as an impetus towards material success, the notion of quality of life is becoming more prominent. As quality of life becomes more important, notions of personal development, self-fulfilment, the ability to laugh and to have fun, become increasingly central to the way many people live their lives. It is this emphasis on quality of life which has led to the introduction of clowns to areas of society where they have not previously existed. This was certainly the case for the clown-doctor movement. As awareness increased of the positive role of laughter and the endorphins created by laughter in enhancing the immune system and increasing tolerance to pain, clown doctors began to appear on wards. Initially, the connection, through play therapy and hospital play specialists, was with sick children, but a number of hospitals are now using clown doctors in adult wards and in accident and emergency units.

The perceived success of programmes such as Le Rire Médecin, Cliniclowns and Theodora Trust has led not only to an increase in the number of clown doctors but also to an increase in the number of other social and community settings in which clowns might appear. These new frames in which clowns can be found will require further research as they become more established. At present, many of these developments are too new to be fully evaluated. For example, in Amsterdam, following the success of Cliniclowns, a new programme is being launched which will introduce clown police officers. The proposal is that those police officers who are interested in using clowning as a way of diffusing difficult situation will train in clowning and clown techniques. Subsequently, those who wish to continue with clowning will work as clown police officers for one day of each working week. This indicates a level of integration within the mainstream police force which is impressive. Holland is also the location of another development in clown engagement with society in non-performative settings: there is one clown who, at the family's request, attends funerals.

That clowns are beginning to have a presence not only in the traditional frame of the circus but also in the newer frames of the theatre, churches and hospitals, and beyond those into experimental frames in the police force and at funerals, demonstrates the centrality of the clown to modern society. It is difficult to imagine a frame in which a clown could not now appear.

However, whilst the clown's ubiquity is important, as this study has illustrated, what is most significant is the close link between clowning and play. This link to play is one of the features of clowning which allows the clown to operate outside the usual cultural and societal norms. Certain techniques, such as the double-take, the clown's inner monologue, the clown's short memory and clown logic, enable the clown to deviate from usual patterns of behaviour without appearing to be insane. This clown behaviour can have a freeing effect on both the performer and the audience. The clown demonstrates ways of playing and the audience member observes and shares in the clown's pleasure in play. Individual audience members are, therefore, encouraged to acknowledge the value of play. In the case of shows like *Paperworld*, *Slava's Snowshow* and *Semianyki* the audience is encouraged to participate in play so that they experience its liberation at first hand.

The exploration of the ways in which clowns use play and the impact this may have on the audience have been facilitated by a consideration of Play Theory, which provides a language for analysing and evaluating the function of play in society. In this way, this study has demonstrated where the functions of the clown and the functions of play overlap.

Clown play may appear to be frivolous but in each frame in which it occurs, that play has a serious purpose: to communicate life truths to us, to help us access the healing power of laughter and to be reminded of the importance of play in a world where its value is too often diminished. As the value of play for adults is undermined in our society, its importance needs reasserting and, if society permits them to, clowns have the ability to do so. Play can just be frivolous, and that kind of play is important, but play can also be serious and serious play reconnects us with how to live our lives and reminds us what we should value. Play helps us to create the link between reality and imagination, and to bring more creativity and joy into everyday life. Clowns show us the way.

Clown Index

Adams, Patch (1945–)
Trained as a medical doctor and then realized the value of humour in healthcare. Credited with developing the concept of clown doctors; leads regular clowning trips to Russia and under-privileged parts of the world. Founded the Gesundheit Institute in Virginia. Was inspiration for Hollywood film starring Robin Williams.

Antonet (1872–1935)
Real name was Umberto Guillaume. Born in Italy in 1872. Credited with introducing the Whiteface clown's spangled costume. Worked in pairings with Little Walter, Grock and Beby. Influential in creating early circus clown entrees.

Armin, Robert (c.1568–1612)
Early stage clown who worked with William Shakespeare. Wrote two books about his performances *Foole upon Foole* and *Quips upon Questions, A Nest of Ninnies*.

Auriol, Jean Baptiste (1808–1881)
French clown of circus stock. Talented as an acrobatic clown and famous for an act in which he balanced on bottles.

Bain, Roly (1954–)
Son of Richard Findlater, biographer of Grimaldi. Christian clown minister who uses clowning and circus skills to spread a Christian message. Ordained as a priest in 1978. Co-Founded Holy Fools in 1982. Slackrope specialist.

Belling, Tom (Unknown–Unknown)
According to circus legend, Tom Belling was the first Auguste. He created the character in 1869 by accident when dressing up in mis-sized clothes.

Borge, Victor (1909–2000)
Born in Copenhagen and trained as a classical pianist and then developed a career which blended music and humour. His act also included his invention of 'inflationary language'.

Brick (Unknown–Unknown)
Early partner of Grock.

Brock (Unknown–Unknown)
Partner of Brick before Grock.

Byland, Pierre (living)
A Swiss clown who trained with Lecoq and returned to Lecoq's school to teach clown, introducing the red nose. He teaches a workshop called 'Homo Stupidens' which focuses on finding the inner clown.

Chaplin, Charlie (1889–1977)
Created the 'little tramp' character. Initially worked on stage with Karno's Troupe until a tour to the USA gave him the chance to join Sennett's Keystone Studio. A lengthy career with a variety of studios included such films as *The Kid*, *Limelight*, *The Great Dictator* and *Modern Times*.

Chocolat (Unknown–1917)
A Cuban whose real name was Raphael Padilla. Teamed up with Footit in 1889 and worked as Auguste to his Whiteface until 1910.

Christiansen, Michael (Living)
Co-founded Big Apple Circus, New York in 1977 and introduced their clown care programme in 1986.

Coco (1900–1974)
Real name was Nikolai Poliakoff. He was a Russian clown who joined Bertram Mills Circus in 1929. He performed in circuses until he retired in the 1960s. A famous Auguste.

Costello, Lou (1906–1959)
Teamed with Bud Abbott in 1936, played the lower status bumbling incompetent in the pairing. Worked with Abbott in burlesque theatre, radio, television and film.

Craeye, Thierry (see Les Witloof)

De Castro, Angela (living)
A Brazilian living and working in the United Kingdom. A theatre clown who also offers clown training through the Why Not Institute.

Doctor Fruit Loop (see Peter Spitzer)

Ducrow, John (Unknown–1834)
Early circus clown who performed at Astley's from 1826. Combined equestrian, acrobatic and comic skills and adopted costume and make-up similar to Grimaldi's, thus helping the transition of make-up into circus clowning.

Durang, John (1768–1822)
Often considered the first American-born clown. He was also a puppeteer, actor and dancer.

Fabri, Nino (Unknown–Unknown)
Real name was Jean-Antoine Arnault. A French Whiteface who performed with Mimile. Was performing in the 1940s.

Fo, Dario (1926–)
Italian playwright, director and clown. He creates satirical pieces which draw on the traditions of *commedia dell'arte*, storytelling and clowning to make social and political points.

Footit (1864–1921)
British equestrian, acrobat and clown. Teamed up with Chocolat in 1889. Played an abusive and controlling Whiteface. The pairing split in 1910.

Fratellini, Albert (1886–1961)
Redefined the role of the Auguste, working as part of a trio with his brothers. Together they created extended entrées, lasting up to 45 minutes.

Fratellini, Annie (1932–1997)
French clown, grand-daughter to Paul Fratellini. She founded the Fratellini Circus School in France in 1974. She performed as an androgynous Auguste, using her skills on a variety of musical instruments.

Fratellini, Francois (1879–1951)
The elegant Whiteface of the trio. With his brothers, he was part of a resurgence in the popularity of circus in France in the 1920s.

Fratellini, Paul (1877–1940)
Developed the role of the counter-auguste, working between the Whiteface and Auguste of his brothers.

Gaulier, Philippe (1943–)
Founded L'École Philippe Gaulier in 1980. Leading teacher of clown and buffoon who trained with Lecoq.

Gontard, Jean (Unknown–Unknown)
French clown who performed at Franconi's in the 1820's and at Astley's in 1838 as a grotesque and buffoon.

Griebling, Otto (1896–1972)

German born tramp clown who established his career in America. As a tramp clown, Griebling played on the audience's emotions rather than relying on slapstick.

Grimaldi, Joseph (1778–1837)

Grimaldi was the original pantomime clown, developing the previously buffoonish charcter into a mischievous rogue. Introduced clown face paint. Was a skilled acrobat and tumbler.

Grock (1880–1959)

Born Adrian Wettach in Switzerland. Began his career working in partnership with Brick and then Antonet. Developed a highly individual Auguste, performing entrees which lasted as long as 75 minutes.

Hardy, Oliver (1892–1957)

Began his career as a silent film actor, often playing the 'heavy'. Teamed up with Stan Laurel in 1927, establishing a silent clown double act in which Hardy was often the straight man. Made the transition to sound movies in 1929.

Hayden, Billy (Unknown–Unknown)

A leading English *clown parleur* who was also a capable acrobat. Developed entrées which involved his clown in conversation with the Ringmaster. Skits usually revolved around gender confusion. Performed in the second half of the nineteenth century.

Henri (living)

Clown performing with Billy Smart's Circus in 2005. An amalgamation of Whiteface and Auguste.

Hoyle, Geoff (living)

English clown who went to America. Worked with the Pickles Family Circus from 1975–1981. During his time with the Pickles Family Circus, Hoyle played a variety of clown styles. Has since worked with Cirque du Soleil and created solo shows.

Ingimarsson, Kristjan (1968–)

Born in Iceland. Physical theatre performer and clown. Collaborated with Paolo Nani from 2002–5 on *The Art of Dying* and *The Head*. Performs as clown using red nose and minimal makeup.

Irwin, Bill (1950–)

American clown, director and playwright. Trained at the Barnum and Bailey Clown College in 1974. In 1975 co-founded The Pickles Family Circus, which he left in 1979 to pursue a solo career.

Jackson, Joe (1873–1942)

Austrian-born clown who toured Europe and America. Began performing with a serious bike act but this developed into comedy routine. Performed as silent tramp clown. His character and his act were taken over by his son, Joe Jackson, Jr.

Jacobs, Lou (1903–1992)

German-born performer who emigrated to America in 1923. Began career as acrobat and contortionist. Developed into Auguste clown, performing a number of innovative production numbers.

Kaboodle

British clown theatre company founded in 1977 by Johnny Melville. Currently directed by Lee Beagley.

Kelly, Emmett (1898–1979)

American performer who created 'Weary Willie' tramp clown character, having begun as a Whiteface.

Keaton, Buster (1895–1966)

Began his career as a vaudeville performer. Best known as a silent film comic. His trademark was a deadpan face combined with physical comedy. Films include *Steamboat Bill Jr* (1928) and *The General* (1927).

Kempe, Will (c.1560–c.1603)

Principal clown in William Shakespeare's company in the 1590s.

Langdon, Harry (1884–1944)

American performer who began his career in vaudeville before moving on to circuses, minstrel shows and burlesque. Joined Sennett's Keystone Studios in 1924 and began career as silent film comedian. Developed an innocent Man Child character with strong similarities to a Pierrot.

Laurel, Stanley (1890–1965)

Born in Britain but spent much of his working life in America. Teamed up with Oliver Hardy in 1927 and played the bumbling, incompetent Auguste to Hardy's straight man.

Lecoq, Jacques (1921–1999)

French actor, mime and acting teacher. Founded L'École Internationale de Théâtre Jacques Lecoq in 1956. Influential on the development of physical theatre and clowning as part of actor training.

Les Witloof

A Belgian clown duo (Daniel Van Hassel and Thierry Craeye) who trained at L'Ecole du Cirque Bruxelles. Their original company, founded in 1989 was called Les Routlabi. In 1996, after a successful production, *Witloof Cabaret*, they changed their name to Les Witloof. They specialize in circus-influenced clown theatre.

Licedei

Russian clown theatre company. One of its founding members in 1968 was Slava Polunin.

Lulu (Unknown–Unknown)

Real name Lucien Senechal, a French Whiteface who performed with Tonio. Was performing in the 1940s and 1950s.

McBurney, Simon (1957–)

Trained with Lecoq. Founder member and artistic director of Complicite.

Mankin, Joan (living)

Worked for the Pickles Family Circus in 1975 with Ralph Deliberate as her partner. Returned to the Pickles Family Circus in 1988 and went on to form rare female clown duo with Diane Wasnak.

Marceau, Marcel (1923–2008)

Born in Strasbourg. Trained in mime under Decroux and created his famous alter-ego 'Bip' in 1947. Toured the world, giving mime performances. Was inspired by Charlie Chaplin.

Mason, Bim (living)

Trained with Lecoq and Desmond Jones. Was a member of Kaboodle Theatre and was a founder member of Mummerandada. Founded the circus training school, Circomedia.

Mimile (Unknown–Unknown)

Real name was Emile Coryn, an Auguste who perfromed with Fabri. Was performing in the 1940s.

Mimirichi

Ukrainian clown theatre company founded in 1989. The company tours internationally.

Mummerandada

Street theatre company, blending commedia, clowning and other circus skills. Formed in the mid-1980s by Bim Mason.

Nani, Paolo (1956–)

Italian physical theatre performer and clown. Collaborated with Kristján Ingimarsson from 2002–5 on *The Art of Dying* and *The Head*. Performs as clown, using red nose and minimal makeup.

Narr, Claus (Unknown–1515)

Court fool in Saxony, first mentioned in 1461.

Pino (see Diane Wasnak)

Pisoni, Larry (living)

Co-founded the Pickles Family Circus in 1974 and performed with them until 1987. Has since performed with Circus Flora and in a number of one-man shows. His clown, Lorenzo Pickle, was a counter-Auguste.

Poliakoff, Nikolai (see Coco)

Polunin, Slava (1950–)
Studied mime in St Petersburg. Founder member of Licedei. Founded the Theatre of the art of Modern Clowning in the early 1980s. *Slava's Snowshow* has been running since 1993 and demonstrates his largely silent form of existential clowning.

Popov, Oleg (1930–)
Clown, mime, slackrope artist, juggler. Trained at the Russian Circus School in Moscow. First appeared as a clown in 1952. Developed a realist Auguste clown.

Queenie Moon (see Joan Mankin)

Rae, Nola (living)
Emigrated to London from Sydney in 1963. Trained at the Royal School of Ballet, then with Marcel Marceau. Performs as a clown-mime in a range of self-devised shows. Original instigator of the London International Mime Festival.

Rice, Dan (1823–1901)
Known as President Lincoln's Court Jester. Developed a highly individual clown costume of red, white and blue stripes with a star-spangled cloak. His performance style was based on that of William Wallett.

Shaffer, Floyd (living)
American clown minister who is regarded by many as the father of clown ministry.

Snider, Peggy (living)
Co-founder of the Pickles Family Circus. Created a clown called Peggy Pickles. Also a skilled juggler.

Somers, Will (Unknown–1560)
Fool to Henry VIII. Had particular skill in improvising verse and riddles.

Spitzer, Peter (living)
An Australian GP who also works as a clown doctor, Doctor Fruit Loop, both in Australia and overseas. Founder of the Humour Foundation, Australia.

Tarlton, Richard (Unknown–1588)
Early professional fool. Began his career in the court of Elizabeth I and later performed on stage, in Shakespeare's plays.

Tonio (Unknown–Unknown)
Real name was Roberto Bellego. An Auguste who performed with Lulu. Was performing in the 1940s and 1950s.

El Tricicle
Catalan clown trio which was founded in 1979. They specialize in visual and physical humour.

Van Hassel, Daniel (see Les Witloof)

Walker, Whimsical (Unknown–Unknown)
Real name was Thomas Dawson Walker. Began performing in 1865 and was still performing in the mid 1930s. His visual style was very similar to that of Grimaldi.

Wasnak, Diane
Created a hyper-animated clown character, Pino, for the Pickles Family Circus. Influenced by silent comedy and cartoons, Pino is either silent or talks in gibberish.

Wettach, Adrian (see Grock)

Yengibarov, Leonid (1935–1972)
A clown-mime from Armenia who never performed outside Eastern Europe and the Soviet Union. Studied at the Moscow Circus School. His costume and character were similar to Marceau's Bip character.

REFERENCES

Adams, Patch, *Gesundheit! Bringing Good Health to You, the Medical System, and Society through Physican Service, Complementary Therapies, Humor and Joy*, Rochester, Vermont: Healing Arts Press, 1998a.

Albrecht, Ernest, *The New American Circus*, Florida: Florida University Press, 1995.

Babinski, T, *Cirque du Soleil: Twenty Years Under the Sun*, New York: Harry N. Abrams, 2004.

Bain, Roly, *Where Fools Rush In*, Michigan: Zondervan, 1993.

Bain, Roly, *Playing the Fool*, Norwich: Canterbury Press, 2001.

Bain, Roly and Forbes, Patrick, *Clowning Glory*, London: National Society/Church House Publishing, 1995.

Barner, Pat and Vermillion-Witt, Judy, *The Center Ring*, Norfolk, Virginia: Hampton Roads Publishing Company, 1992.

Bateson, Gregory, *Steps to an Ecology of Mind*, St Albans: Paladin Frogmore, 1973.

Beckett, Samuel, *Complete Dramatic Works*, London: Faber and Faber, 1990.

Bergson, Henri, *Laughter*, London: Macmillan, 1911.

Berky, Bob and Barbre, Claude 'The Clown's Use of Empathy: An Interview with Bob Berky', *Journal of Religion and Health*, 39: 3, (Fall 2000), pp. 239–246.

Billington, Sandra, *A Social History of the Fool*, Sussex: Harvester Press, 1984.

Billington, Michael, 'Review of A Minute Too Late', *The Guardian*, (January 28th 2005).

Bradby, David, *Waiting for Godot*, Cambridge: Cambridge University Press, 2001.

Brecht, Bertolt, *Life of Galileo*, London: Methuen, 1986.

Brecht, Bertolt, *Collected Plays. Vol.2, Part 1, Man equals Man and The Elephant Calf*, translated by Gerhard Nellhaus; edited by John Willett and Ralph Manheim. London: Eyre Methuen, 1979.

Buber, Martin, *Between Man and man*, London: Collins, 1961.

Carpman, Cheryl, E., 'Clown Therapy: The Creation of a Clown Character as a Treatment Intervention', *The Arts in Psychotherapy*, 25: 4, (1998), pp. 245–55.

Cattanach, Ann, *Play Therapy: Where the Sky Meets the Underworld*, London: Jessica Kingsley, 1996.

Chamberlain, Franc and Yarrow, Ralph, *Jacques Lecoq and the British Theatre*, London: Routledge, 2002.

Cole, R., 'Anglo-American Anti-fascist Film Propaganda in a Time of Neutrality: The Great Dictator, 1940', *Historical Journal of Film, Radio and Television,* 21:2, (2001), pp. 137–52.

Cousins, Norman, *Anatomy of an Illness* New York: W.W. Norton, 1979.

Cox, Harvey Gallagher, *The Feast of Fools: a theological essay on festivity and fantasy,* Cambridge, Mass: Harvard University Press, 1969.

Croft-Cooke, Rupert, *The Circus Book,* London: Sampson Low, Marston and Co. Ltd., 1945.

Csikszentmihalyi, Mihaly, *Flow: The Psychology of Optimal Experience,* NY: Harper and Row, 1980.

De Toro, Fernandez, *Theatre Semiotics: Text and Staging in Modern Theatre,* Toronto: Toronto University Press, 1995.

Esslin, Martin, *Theatre of the Absurd,* London: Eyre Methuen, 1974.

Farrell, J and Scuderi, A., *Dario Fo: Stage, Text and Tradition,* Carbondale and Edwardsville: Southern Illinois University Press, 2000.

Felner, Mira, *Apostles of Silence: The Modern French Mimes,* London: Associated University Presses, 1985.

Findlater, Richard, *Joe Grimaldi, His Life and Theatre,* London: CUP, 1978.

Fo, Dario, *Plays:1,* London: Methuen Drama, 1997.

Fratellini, Annie, *Destin de Clown,* Paris: La Manufacture, 1989.

Geertz, Clifford, *The Interpretation of Culture: Selected Essays,* London: Hutchison, 1993.

Godfrey, J.R , 'Conversation with the Experts "Towards Optimal Health"', *Journal of Women's Health,* 13: 5 (2004), pp. 474–9.

Gordon, Mel, *Lazzi,* New York: PAJ Publications, 1992.

Grock, *Life's A Lark,* London: Heineman, 1931.

Grock, *King of Clowns,* London: Methuen, 1957.

Hall, Felicity, *Strategy and Report on Circus,* Arts Council of England, 2001.

Harvie, David; Milburn, Keir; Trott, Ben and Watts, David (Eds.), *Shut Them Down!,* Leeds: Dissent! and Autonmedia, 2005.

Heidegger, Martin, *Basic Writings,* London: Routledge, 2003.

Hoare, Jo, 'The Best Medicine', *Nursing Standard,* 19: 14 (2004), pp. 18–19.

Hudak, D.A., Dale, J.A., Hudak, M.A. and DeGood, D.F., 'Effects of humorous stimuli and sense of humor on discomfort', *Psychological Reports,* 1991, 69, pp. 779–86.

Hugill, Beryl, *Bring on the Clowns,* London: David and Charles, 1980.

Huizinga, J., *Homo Ludens,* London: Routledge and Kegan Paul, 1944.

Jenkins, Ron, 'The Roar of the Clown' in *TDR,* 30:1 (Spring 1986), pp. 171–179.

Jenkins, Ron, *Subversive Laughter,* New York: Theatre Communications Group, 1994.

Lawson, Wendy, 'Taking Humour Seriously', *Positive Health* (June 2003), pp. 18–20.

Kelly, Emmett, with F. Beverly Kelly, *Clown – My Life in Tatters and Smiles,* London: Robert Hale Ltd, 1956.

Lecoq, Jacques, *The Moving Body,* London: Methuen, 2002.

Lecoq, Jaques, McCaw, D., Kernaghan, L. and Bradby, D., trans., *Theatre of Movement and Gesture,* London: Routledge, 2006.

Litherland, Janet, *The Clown Ministry Handbook,* 4th edition, Colorado Springs: Meriwether Publishing Ltd., 1989.

Litherland, Janet, *Everything New and Who's Who in Clown Ministry (with 75 Skits for Special Days),* Colorado Springs: Meriwether Publishing Ltd., 1993.

McDermot, Phelim, 'Programme note to *A Minute too Late*' National Theatre, (2005) n.pag.

Mahony, Diana L, 'The Effects of Laughter on discomfort thresholds: Does expectation become reality?' *Journal of General Psychology,* 128:2 (April 2001) pp. 217–26.

Marcon, Mary, 'Humour for Good Health in The Emergency Department and Child Adolescent Health unit (The Clown Doctor Programme) Final Report, The Northern Hospital, Australia, June 2005.

Mason, Bim, 'The Well of Possibilities: Theoretical and Practical Uses of Lecoq's Teaching' in Franc Chamberlain and Ralph Yarrow (eds.) *Jacques Lecoq and the British Theatre* London: Routledge Harwood, 2002, pp. 45–55.

Mayer, Hans, 'A Dog and Beckett's Godot' (trans. Jack Zipes) in S. Mews and H. Knust (Eds) *Essays on Brecht: theater and politics* New York : AMS Press, 1979.

Mitchell, Tony, *Dario Fo: the People's Court Jester,* London: Methuen, 1999.

Moreno, J.L., *Theatre of Spontaneity,* New York: Beacon House, 1947.

Murray, Simon, *Jacques Lecoq,* London: Routledge, 2003.

Murray, Simon, 'Tout Bouge: Jacques Lecoq, Modern Mime and the Zero Body. A Pedagogy for the Creative Actor', in Franc Chamberlain and Ralph Yarrow (eds.) *Jacques Lecoq and the British Theatre,* London: Routledge Harwood, 2002, pp. 17–44.

Nightingale, Benedict, 'Review of Slava's Snowshow', *The Times,* (30th January 2004).

Orenstein, Claudia, *Festive Revolutions: The Politics of Popular Theatre and the San Francisco Mime Troupe,* Jackson: University of Mississippi Press, 1998.

Otto, Katherine, *Fools are Everywhere,* Chicago: University of Chicago Press, 2001.

Pearce, J.M.S., 'Some Neurological Aspects of Humour', *European Neurology* (November 2004), pp. 169–71.

Plautus, Titus Maccius, *Menaechimi,* Cambridge, Mass: Harvard University Press, 1975.

Popov, Oleg, *Russian Clown,* London: McDonald, 1970.

Remy, Tristan, (Bernard Sahlins, trans.), *Clown Scenes,* Chicago: Ivan R Dee, 1997.

Robb, David (Ed.), *Clowns, Fools and Picaros,* Amsterdam and New York: Rodopi, 2007.

Salamon, Esther, *Clown Doctors in North East England: An Evaluation – Phase 1,* Cultural Partnerships & Developments, 2007.

Sartre, Jean-Paul, *On Being and Nothingness,* London: Routledge, 2003.

Saward, John, *Perfect Fools: Folly for Christ's Sake in Catholic and Orthodox Spirituality,* Oxford: Oxford University Press, 1980.

Schechner, Richard, *Performance Theory,* London: Routledge, 1988.

Schechner, Richard, *The Future of Ritual,* London: Routledge, 1993.

Schechter, Joel, *The Pickle Clowns: New American Circus Comedy,* Illinois: Southern Illinois University Press, 2001.

Schechter, Joel *Popular Theatre,* London: Routledge, 2002.

Shaffer, Floyd and Sewall, Penne, *Clown Ministry: A How-to Manual and Dozens of Skits for Service and Worship,* Loveland C.O.: Group Books, 1984.

Shakespeare, William, *As You Like It,* London: Methuen, 1975.

—— *King Lear,* London: Methuen, 1972.

—— *A Midsummer Night's Dream,* Cambridge: Cambridge University Press, 1984.

—— *Much Ado About Nothing,* Oxford: Clarendon Press, 1993.

—— *Romeo and Juliet,* Cambridge: Cambridge University Press, 1984.

—— *The Tempest,* Cambridge: Cambridge University Press, 2000.

—— Titus Andronicus, Oxford: Clarendon Press, 1984.

—— Twelfth Night, London: Methuen, 1975.

Simonds, C. and Warren, B., The Clown Doctor Chronicles, Amsterdam and New York: Rodophi, 2004.

Skidmore, James, 'Crossing Borders: The Multimodal Language of Cirque du Soleil', An International Conference and Virtual Symposium on the Multimodality of Human Communication: Theories, Problems and Application, University of Toronto (2002), (www.semiotcon.com/virtuals/talks/skidmore.html).

Slade, Peter, Child Play: Its Importance in Human Development, London: Jessica Kingsley Publishers, 1995.

Smith, Alistair, 'Review of Sous Pression', The Stage (2 February 2005) n.pag.

Sutton-Smith, Brian, The Ambiguity of Play, London: Harvard University Press, 1997.

Swortzell, Lowell, Here Come the Clowns: A Cavalcade of Comedy from Antiquity to the Present, New York: Viking Press, 1978.

Taylor, Paul, 'Review of Slava's Snowshow', The Independent (2 February 2004) n.pag.

Thomson, Peter and Sacks, Glendyr (Eds.) The Cambridge Companion to Brecht, Cambridge: Cambridge University Press, 1994.

Towsen, John, Clowns, New York: Hawthorn Books, 1976.

Turner, V., The ritual process: structure and anti-structure. Chicago: Aldine Publishing Co, 1969.

Turner, Victor, From Ritual to Theatre, New York: Performing Arts Journal Publications, 1982.

Ulanov, A. and Ulanov, B., The Witch and the Clown: Two Archetypes of Human Sexuality, Wilmette, Illinois: Chiron Publications, 1987.

Van Blerkom, Linda Miller, 'Clown Doctors: Shaman Healers of Western Medicine', Medical Anthropology Quarterly, 9:4, (1995), pp. 462–75.

Videbæk, Bente A., The Stage Clown in Shakespeare's Theatre, Westport, CT: Greenwood Press, 1996.

Welsford, Enid, The Fool: His Social and Literary History, London: Faber and Faber, [1935]1968.

Wilding, Jo, Don't Shoot the Clowns: Taking a Circus to the Children of Iraq, Oxford: New Internationalist Publications Ltd., 2006.

Willson Disher, M., Clowns and Pantomimes, London: Constable and Co., 1925.

Winnicott, D.W., Playing and Reality, London: Routledge, 1991.

Wright, John, Why is that so Funny?, London: Nick Hern Books, 2006.

Further suggested reading

Adams, Patch, House Calls: How we Can Heal the World One Visit at a Time, San Francisco, California: Robert D. Reed Publishers, 1998.

Adams, Patch, 'Humour and Love: the origination of clown therapy', Postgraduate Medical Journal, 78, (2002), pp. 447–8.

Axline, V., Play Therapy, Edinburgh: Churchill Livingstone, 1989.

Begley, S. 'The Science of Laughs', Newsweek, 136:15, (2000), pp. 75–6.

Bouissac, Paul, Circus and Culture: A Semiotic Approach, Indiana: Indiana University Press, 1977.

Brightman, Robert, 'Traditions of Subversion and the Subversion of Tradition: Cultural Criticism in Maidu Clown Performances', American Anthropologist, 101: 2, (1999), pp. 272–87.

Brown, Ismene, 'Review of Derevo', The Daily Telegraph, (26th January 1998).

Caillois, Roger, Man, Play and Games, Urbana and Chicago: University of Illinois Press, 2001.

Calandra, Dennis, 'Karl Valentin and Bertolt Brecht', *TDR*, 18:1, T61, (1974), pp. 86-98.

Cattanach, Ann, *An Introduction to Play Therapy*, Hove: Brunner-Routledge, 2003.

Clarke, John Smith, *Circus Parade*, London: Batsford, 1936.

Clay, Alan, *Angels Can Fly: Modern Clown Performance*, Newtown: NSW, Arts Media, 2005.

Davidson, Clifford (Ed.), *Fools and Folly*, Kalamazoo, Michigan: Medieval Institute Publications, 1996.

Double, Oliver and Wilson, Michael, 'Karl Valentin's Illogical Subversion: Stand-up comedy and the Alienation Effect', *New Theatre Quarterly*, 20:3, (August 2004) pp. 203-15.

Fo, Dario, 'Contra Jogulatores Obloquentes', *World Literature Today*, 72:1, (Winter 1998), pp. 4-8.

Fox, Charles Philip, *A Ticket to the Circus: a pictorial history of the incredible Ringlings*, New York: Bramhall House, 1959.

Frost, Thomas, *Circus Life and Circus Celebrities*, London: Tinsley, 1875.

Hammarstrom, David Lewis, *Fall of the Big Top*, McFarland and Co. Inc., 2008.

Highwater, Jamake, *Ritual of the Wind: North American Indian Ceremonies, Music and Dances*, New York: The Viking Press, 1977.

Hirst, David, *Dario Fo and Franca Rame*, London: Macmillan, 1989.

Jenkins, Ron, *Acrobats of the Soul*, New York, Theatre Communications Group, 1988.

Jennings, Sue, *Introduction to Dramatherapy: Theatre and Healing Ariadne's Ball of Thread*, London: Jessica Kingsley Publishers, 1998.

Kiernander, Adrian, *Ariane Mnouchkine*, Cambridge: Cambridge University Press, 1993.

Leabhart, Thomas, *Post Modern Mime*, London: Palgrave Macmillan, 1998.

Little, Kenneth 'Pitu's Doubt: Entrée clown self-fashioning in the circus tradition', *TDR*, 30: 4, (1986) pp. 51-64.

McCabe, John, *Charlie Chaplin*, London, Doubleday, 1979.

McManus, Donald, *No Kidding!: Clown as Protagonist in Twentieth Century Theater*, Cranbury, NJ: Associated University Presses, 2003.

McVicar, Wes., *Clown Act Omnibus: Everything you need to know about clowning plus over 200 clown stunts*, Colorado Springs: Meriwether Publishing Ltd., 1988.

Milling, Jane and Heddon, Deirdre, *Devising Performance: A Critical History*, Basingstoke: Palgrave Macmillan, 2006.

Mills, Cyril Bertram, *Bertram Mills Circus: Its Story*, Bath: Ashgrove Press, 1983.

Parsons, E.C. and Beals, R.L 'The Sacred Clowns of the Pueblos and Mayo-Yaqui Indians', *American Anthropologist*, 36 (1934), pp. 491-514.

Pearson, Jenny, (Ed.), *Discovering the Self through Drama and Movement*, London: Jessica Kingsley, 1996.

Poliakoff, Nikolai, *Coco the Clown by Himself*, London: J.M.Dent, 1940.

Poliakoff, Nikolai, *Behind My Greasepaint: Coco the Clown*, London: Hutchinson and Co., 1950.

Red Notes, *Dario Fo and Franca Rame Theatre Workshops at Riverside Studios*, London, 1983.

Rivel, Charlie, *Poor Clown*, London: Michael Joseph Ltd., 1973.

Seigel, Fred, 'Clown Politics: Report on the International Clown-Theatre Congress', *TDR*, 33: 2, (1992), pp. 182-6.

Spitzer, Peter, 'Hospital Clowns - Modern-day Court Jesters at work', *The Lancet*, 368: supp 1 (Dec 2006), S34-S35.

Schechter, Joel, *Congress of Clowns*, San Francisco: Kropotkin Club of San Francisco, 1998.

Speaight, George, (1980) *The Book of Clowns*, New York: Macmillan.

INDEX